This is the first full-length coverage of the various dimensions, types and in-depth experiences of reminiscence and life review in old age. Dr. Sherman has based this landmark in the literature on aging and adult development on three intensive research studies—as well as extensive use of reminiscence in both individual and group practice with the elderly.

The text includes new findings and ideas on the imagery and language of reminiscence, the role of memorabilia and cherished possessions, and expression of life themes and personal narrative in reminiscence. Coverage also features creative and esthetic elements of reminiscence—expressed in both written and oral forms.

Reminiscence and the Self in Old Age

Edmund Sherman is Professor of Social Welfare, State University of New York at Albany, where he teaches graduate courses in aging as well as clinical practice and theory. He is also Faculty Research Associate in the Ringel Institute of Gerontology of the University at Albany. He received his PhD from the Graduate School of Social Work and Social Research of Bryn Mawr College. Dr. Sherman has published several books and numerous articles on aging and practice with the elderly. His most recent books include *Counseling the Aging, Meaning in Mid-Life Transitions*, and *Working With Older Persons*.

Reminiscence and the Self in Old Age

Edmund Sherman

91-1409

Springer Publishing Company
New York

Springer Publishing Company, Inc.
536 Broadway
New York, NY 10012-3955

91 92 93 94 95 / 5 4 3 2 1

Library of Congress Cataloging-in-Publication Data

Sherman, Edmund A.
    Reminiscence and the self in old age / Edmund Sherman.
        p.   cm.
    Includes bibliographical references and index.
    ISBN 0-8261-7550-3 :
    1. Reminiscing in old age.   2. Self-perception in old age.
I. Title.
    [DNLM: 1. Aged—psychology.   2. Ego—in old age.   3. Memory—in
old age.   4. Self Concept—in old age.   BF 724.85.R45 S553r]
BF724.85.R45S54   1991
155.67—dc20
DNLM/DLC
for Library of Congress
                                                                    91-4699
                                                                    CIP

Printed in the United States of America

*To my son, Eric, in love and in hopes that you live
a long life enriched and fulfilled by the treasures
of reminiscence.*

Contents

Foreword

The subject matters of autobiography, biography, and reminiscence are entering the mainstream of several academic disciplines. The present book is timely, providing a perspective on the uses and functions of reminiscence by older persons. In addition to writing about a life as an autobiography, there is the personal experience of reminiscence, not as an idle, ritualized review of the past but rather as one of the most meaningful experiences of a lifetime.

Reviewing one's life can change the view of oneself. Who we are and how we evaluate our past can be a dynamic and positive experience. Edmund Sherman points out how, in a period of life transition, there can be an active search for the answer to the question "Who am I?" Reminiscence is a review of past experience either for oneself or for telling to others, orally or in a published form. Sherman's book is based upon a study of reminiscence developed by the author at the Ringel Institute of Gerontology in 1984. The author casts his work in the context of science, gathering empirical data that tell us something about the process we are studying.

The participants in Sherman's reminiscence groups were found to express what they thought about the past in ways that demonstrated that they were coming to terms with the experiences of life. This prompts the question "Does reminiscence in a group setting encourage the development of wisdom about the self and life's experiences?"

Our personal experiences and the literature convince us that lives can be interpreted in many ways. What has been missing is the theme that lives can be reinterpreted, that the experience of reminiscence can give us different and important new perspectives. As this book shows, feelings about life and the affect and emotion that we attach to events can shift to a more pleasant attitude as a result of reminiscence. This is not unlike changing one's attitude toward the old drill sergeant or the shrewish teacher one had as a child. There is also a recovering of the details of life. We refresh our experience with the content of life by going over it with other persons. Then, there is the outcome in terms of motivation, changing our views of ourselves, and releasing motivation to do new and different things.

In the above sense, reminiscence can be a delivering experience as we sift the grain of life and lighten our load by letting the chaff blow away with the wind. Sherman's is a book that will turn the afternoon of life into an unusual humanizing experience.

JAMES E. BIRREN

Acknowledgments

A number of people were highly instrumental in the evolution and completion of this book. At various times and in various ways over the past several years, the following individuals provided constructive criticism, insights, encouragement, support, and inspiration: James Birren, Mihalyi Csikszentmihalyi, Eugene Gendlin, Howard Goldstein, Ira Progoff, Max Siporin, and Sheldon Tobin. My thanks and gratitude to them all. Particular thanks go to the many older persons who participated in the studies and interviews reported here. They provided not only the flesh and bones but the very spirit of this book. Finally, I would like to thank the AARP Andrus Foundation for its generous funding of the research that initiated this extended study of reminiscence.

1
Introduction

This book represents something of a journey, a journey of exploration in greater and greater depth of a phenomenon that is usually taken for granted as a rather common and mundane feature of old age. In fact, reminiscence and old age seem to be taken as synonymous in the popular mind, so much so that a stereotype of the elderly person is that of one who thinks and talks continuously about the past. The sad result of this is that, rather than be stereotyped, the older person often tries to avoid thinking or talking about the past, thereby foreclosing on a rich resource for enhancing the personal quality of life and also by cutting off the very source and sense of self in late life. After all, are we not a youthful and forward-looking society that has little time for things past? Indeed, "The past is past" is an expression I have heard many times from older persons themselves, and it was not until this exploration into the subject of reminiscence proceeded beyond its rather practical and applied beginnings that I realized what an impoverished view of life and old age that expression represents.

This realization was totally unanticipated when I began my first empirical study of reminiscence in 1983. In fact, the subsequent exploration has been something that neither my training in empirical social science methods nor my training and experience in direct gerontological practice with elderly individuals and groups could have anticipated. That practice began 25 years earlier, when I was a caseworker in a public welfare agency and had a caseload made up predominantly of elderly recipients of federal Old Age Assistance. However, neither that experience nor my later graduate training and subsequent practice is social work, counseling, and psychotherapy with older adults could have provided the perspective, the findings, and the actual life experiences that make up the substance of this book.

There are several reasons for this. One is that the perspective or focus of applied gerontological research and practice is on problems, problem solving, and being able to demonstrate the efficacy of any problem-solving efforts in as tangible and even quantifiable terms as possible. This emphasis, or focus, on problems and predetermined objectives tends to overlook the more subtle cognitive and emotional processes and the emergent experi-

1

ence that take place in the recipients of our problem-oriented efforts. It can be said with justification that social science methods, whether used to demonstrate practice effectiveness or to discover new knowledge about aging, are so geared toward the external, objective, and measurable aspects of those phenomena that they miss the essence of what this book is largely about—the actual *experience* of reminiscence and its many ramifications in the quality of late life.

It is this experiential dimension of reminiscence that forms the core of this book. This is the more subjective dimension of reminiscence that represents not only the lived experience of the reminiscing person but also the actual process of reminiscing itself. What is it like? Is it a positive, negative, or indifferent sort of experience? How does it work? When and how do people find themselves engaging in it? What evokes it? What does it do for them? Are the memories or images in the process of reminiscing vivid, colorful, dull, eventful? Is the experience of recollecting and reminiscing about events from the past an event in itself worthy of future remembering?

Not only is the concern here with the experience and the effects of reminiscing on the reminiscers themselves, it is also about what it is like to experience others reminiscing and what it is like to share memories with others. Social reminiscing is a contagious phenomenon, as will be seen in the material to follow. The social context of reminiscing also calls forth and displays certain dimensions and aspects of the phenomenon that might not be the case in private reminiscing.

A great deal of attention has been paid, in the field of gerontology, to the subject of reminiscence. Dozens of articles have been published in gerontological journals about the nature, role, frequency, and particulary the effects of reminiscence on the morale, the self-esteem, and the psychological adjustment of the elderly. These writings, based largely on gerontological research and practice, have added a great deal to our objective knowledge about the more quantitative dimensions and effects of reminiscence in late life. The use of social science instruments and procedures involving observation, self-report questionnaires, and structured or semistructured interviews has given us a wealth of findings and data to ponder. The question here is "What is going on in the actual reminiscing process that helps us to understand these external, objective findings and figures?" Thus, in a major sense, this book will be an effort to put experiential flesh on the bare bones of our objectified and quantified knowledge of reminiscence and its correlates in old age.

The study that launched this whole exploration was, in fact, very much in the applied social science tradition. It was a funded project with empirical methods and gerontological practice implications that was entitled "Using Reminiscence to Enhance Social Supports among the Elderly." An experimental design was used to test alternative approaches to group reminiscence among community-dwelling elderly persons as a means of enhancing their social supports and, it was hoped, their morale, with a long-term view to preventing possible future institutionalization. It was these very practical purposes as well as the scientific design and procedures of the proposed study that led the AARP Andrus Foundation to fund it.

The results were quite remarkable and positive with respect to the purposes of the study, remarkable also in unanticipated ways, as shall be seen. Friendships, socialization, and resulting social supports were certainly enhanced in very demonstrable ways. The measured morale and self-concepts also appeared to be enhanced, although there were certain nonlinear patterns and relationships among these measures or variables that suggested greater complexity beneath the figures. There was an opaque quality to the statistical findings, and what was missing was the experiential dimension that connected the people engaged in reminiscing with the measures of that engagement and its effects.

Fortunately, one of the measures we used, called the Experiencing Scale, involved a perspective and methodology that greatly enhanced our understanding of some of this complexity. This was particularly true of our findings with respect to variations in self-concept when related to the experiential levels of reminiscing measured by the scale. It appeared that group reminiscing had either captured or triggered a process in a number of the participants that seemed to lead to changes in the quality and content of their reminiscing as well as in their morale and self-concepts. These changes were mostly positive, but sometimes they went in a negative direction with certain individuals. Yet in our follow-up interviews with these individuals several months later, there appeared to be a clear reversal in a positive direction.

These latter findings, together with a greatly increased desire to learn more about the experience of the process of reminiscence rather than its content, led to a follow-up study. This was called the Individual Reminiscence Survey because we conducted follow-up interviews with 88 individuals from the original 104 elderly persons in the initial group reminiscence study, which will be referred to as the Group Project hereafter. In some cases, two, three, and four private interviews were held with the same individuals over a series of months, especially if it looked as though some type of change process or late-life transition was going on.

The focus of this follow-up study with individuals was to get at the direct experience of reminiscence and any perceived changes it might have triggered in their lives. The study was undertaken in the spirit set forth by William James in his *Essays on Radical Empiricism*, in which he called for an approach to science that would insist upon the inclusion of direct experience in order for any empirical observations to be admissible as evidence (James, 1940). Although this called for the direct experience of the reminiscers themselves, it was anticipated that many of them might not be able to articulate that experience in just so many words because there are qualities to the reminiscing experience that are very difficult to describe in language. This called for methods of listening, observing, understanding, and interpretation that can best be described as phenomenological.

It is no accident that remarkable similarities have been found in the perspective and work of William James and the basic approach of modern phenomenology to such phenomena as human behavior, motivation (intentionality), and experience (Edie, 1978). Phenomenology, after all, has been called the "science of experience" and is noted for its "fidelity to experience (Edie, 1976). The fundamental methodological principle of phenomenology as set forth by its founder, Edmund Husserl, can be formulated as follows: "No opinion is to be accepted as philosophical knowledge unless it is seen to be adequately established by observation of what is seen as itself given 'in person'" (Cairns, 1973). The similarity to James is striking. Husserl's famous dictum, "To the things themselves," was carried even further by the French phenomenologist, Maurice Merleau-Ponty (1962), who gave priority and primacy to experience as the foundation of knowledge when he said: "To return to things themselves as experienced is to return to that world which precedes knowledge, of which knowledge always *speaks*." It should be noted at the start that the work of James, Merleau-Ponty, and certain other phenomenological thinkers very much influenced this "experiential study" of reminiscence. This will be seen as particularly true of the experiential approach to the language in which the reminiscing was expressed by our subjects. The method used in this approach was derived from Merleau-Ponty's original work on the phenomenology of language. James, on the other hand, was particularly important for the way in which the self was conceptualized in this study.

THE SELF IN REMINISCENCE

If someone were to ask you what the "direct experience" of reminiscence is like, you would probably have to reflect on what it is like for you your*self*. That is, after all, an experiential question that inevitably leads to an answer from the perspective of the self. However, even when participants in the Group Project reminisced about an event from the past that did not happen directly to them personally, those of us who conducted the groups could still tell what it was like for them to remember and recount the event. We could tell this by observing the way they expressed themselves about it verbally and nonverbally through gesture, posture, facial expression, and so on. We also found that we could tell this quite reliably from just the spoken reminiscences that were recorded on the audiotapes of the group sessions, without the advantage of direct observation of nonverbal cues. The methods we used in this will be spelled out and illustrated later, but the important point here is that the spoken references to the self and recollections from the perspective of the self were unmistakable and pervasive.

Later, when we analyzed our empirical data from that project we found that there were identifiable patterns of relationship between the kinds of reminiscing people did and their self-concepts, based upon the measures we used.[1] For example one group participant was preoccupied in her reminiscences about past negative interactions with a recently deceased sister. The self-esteem aspects of her self-concept were quite poor at the beginning of the project when she was engaging in this type of reminiscing, but they were considerably better when she was retested three months later. That was after ten sessions of group reminiscing in which she had worked through the earlier unresolved issues about her relationship with that sister. In general, those whose reminiscing seemed to be aimed at resolving issues and problems from the past showed lower self-concept scores.

Although these findings come from a rather practical empirical study of recent vintage, there is a long history of the intimate relationship between reminiscence and the self. Going all the way back to Socrates' famous imperative, "Know thyself," reminiscence has been the key ingredient in the "examined life," of knowing oneself. Socrates' method of dialogue and discourse was known as *anamnesis*, the argument from reminiscence or recollection (Flew, 1979). His dialectical method was always the same, to bring the questioner back to give an account of the conditions of his past and present life and then to examine and weigh the evidence arising from this autobiographic process. For Socrates, ontological issues about the nature of being and human existence, as well as ethical issues, had to be raised from sources deep in subjective experience. Any other method of learning and knowing was subordinate to this, in his mind.

Of course, this quest for knowing oneself and of leading the examined life was Socrates' daimon. Could we legitimately expect the same kind of quest from the majority of elderly persons in our modern American society? Probably not. His was, after all, a most consuming quest and a demanding method from a time and world that bears little resemblance to the present. Yet there are strong indications that a similar sort of autobiographic process does go on among the elderly in our modern society, a process called the "life review," and reminiscence appears to be an intrinsic part of that process. We will cover this phenomenon in greater depth shortly, but there are other even more obvious ways in which reminiscence and the self are inextricably related to one another if we think about it from an experiential perspective. One of the basic conclusions from Husserl's phenomenology is that the person never perceives an object (or memory, past event, etc.) except with reference to himself or herself. Our relation to the world is necessarily perspectival, that is, from the perspective of the self as engaged observer (Merleau-Ponty, 1963).

William James came to a similar conclusion, although he framed it in a somewhat different way. He noted metaphorically that there is a universal tendency in human experience to split the universe in two halves and that each of us attaches almost all personal interest to one of the halves. As he put it, we draw the line of division between them in a different place, that is, from a different perspective. He describes this as follows:

> When I say that we all call the two halves by the same names, and that those names are "me" and "not me" respectively, it will at once be seen what I mean. The altogether unique kind of interest which each human mind feels in those parts of creation which it can call *me* or *mine* may be a moral riddle, but it is a fundamental psychological fact. No mind can take the same interest in his neighbor's *me* as in his own. The neighbor's *me* falls together with all the rest of things in one foreign mass against which his own *me* stands out in startling relief. (James, 1961)

This general human tendency is particularly true of reminiscence. Edward Casey, in his fine phenomenological study, *Remembering*, observes that "reminiscing seems to involve a certain *ingrained egocentrism*, a tendency to recount only what concerns one's own being, one's own fate (even if this is a fate shared with others)?" (Casey, 1989) He goes on to say that, far from being a defect, this self-centeredness is essential to reliving the past through reminiscing about it.

The self-centeredness of reminiscence is obviously not unique to the elderly. There is probably no period in life in which the person is more acutely self-centered and self-conscious than in adolescence. This is reflected not only in the shared reminiscences on self in the conversations of teenagers but also in the proliferation of diaries at that stage of life. There is, in fact, empirical evidence to show that the frequency of reminiscence is no greater in the elderly than in teenagers (Cameron, 1972; Giambra, 1977).

It has been observed that this similarity between adolescents and the elderly with respect to reminiscence is that both periods of life represent transitions from a known past and self into an unknown future (Buhler, 1968). There is also a fear of loss of self in the two life-transitions; for the teenager it is fear of the loss of self as child, and for the older person it is apt to be fear of loss of self entirely to death or dementia. As a result of this, there may be a more active and conscious search for self in both age groups.

The most obvious difference in this search for self lies in the time dimension. All reminiscing takes place in the present, but for the young adolescent the question of "Who am I?" is much more related to the future, to "Who am I to become?" For the older person the question of "Who am I?"

is apt to be framed much more in terms of the past: "Who have I been all this time?"

In addition to this difference in the temporal dimension there is a difference in that reminiscence for the elderly is apt to be related to the self in more ways than at any time in the human life cycle. This is because there are more *functions for the self* in reminiscing in old age. When it is considered that in the aging process there are increased losses of loved ones, friends, relatives, and significant others and things, all of which are identified with the self, with who one is and has been in the world, then the impulse to remember and evoke the memories and images of these lost objects is understandable. In youth one is contemporaneously embedded in the social context of significant others and objects, but in old age this context of self must be recaptured, retained, and sustained in the present through reminiscence.

There are numerous other functions for reminiscence, as will be seen shortly, but consider for the moment some other ways in which reminiscence serves vital functions for the self in old age; for example, when a particularly troublesome memory comes to mind in late life, say a memory of having made a cruel or unfeeling comment to a loved one that led to rancor and distance in the relationship. This is experienced as a painful intrusion and dissonant element in the preferred conception of self. Such memories may take on lives of their own, becoming obsessive; therefore, it becomes necessary to reminisce about and reexperience and work through these memories so that they can be accepted and reintegrated into a more viable current conception of self. This kind of experience is apt to be much more common in later life, when there is an increased desire to repair old wounds and old relationships. This is often complicated by the fact that the loved one who was hurt by a cruel comment could be dead and unavailable for working through and healing the wound in an actual personal encounter.

Such painful memories not only have to be worked through, but they may have to be reframed within a larger life context, through a life-review process, in order to avoid utter despair in old age. Examples of such life-review processes will be provided in the course of this book, but for the moment it is important to keep in mind that it is reminiscence that provides the material for such a life review.

Consider, also, the very elderly person who is experiencing greater and greater forgetfulness, perhaps even senile dementia such as Alzheimer's disease. The need to reminisce about the self becomes even greater, and memories of the self have to be amplified, made more vivid, and dramatized for fear of losing the self.

The foregoing have been somewhat negative and problematic instances in which reminiscence functions in the service of the self, but there are many ways, perhaps most ways, in which reminiscence is experienced as positive and pleasant. The telling of a joyous or interesting earlier event to others is a pleasurable experience in itself. Even if the events are remembered in private, they evoke pleasure in the present. There is also the sheer pleasure of discovery or rediscovery of some forgotten aspect of the self or history of the self that can now be recalled intentionally for support or pleasure in the present and the future. These and other positive features of reminiscence will be expanded upon, but it is best to be clear first about what the phenomenon is.

WHAT IS REMINISCENCE?

A most direct and useful definition of reminiscence is given by Webster's dictionary as "the process or practice of thinking or telling about past experiences." This allows for both the public and private dimensions of reminiscence, and it served well as a working definition for research purposes and for the elderly research participants in the series of reminiscence studies that will be described in this and later chapters.

Reminiscence is commonly conceived of as a largely introspective and personal process, and this seems consistent with the preceding comments about its self-oriented nature. Yet, paradoxically, there seems to be no other private mental activity that has such an inclination toward sharing and mutuality in human discourse. It is also difficult to imagine another form of discourse that allows one to resonate so empathically with someone else's "me" and "mine."

Edward Casey, who earlier remarked on the inherent self-centeredness of reminiscence, contends that it is in this social sense that reminiscing differs most from other forms of remembering such as reminding or recognizing: "The most immediate, as well as most telling clue we have as to the inherently communal-discursive aspect of reminiscing is the mere fact that it *flourishes in the company of others*" (Casey, 1989). He goes on to say that it not only often occurs in a specifically social context but that it is "actively solicited" by such a context. This can be seen in how reminiscence arises spontaneously in social situations among the elderly. It is ubiquitous and something that has been remarked upon frequently. It is what leads to the popular generalization that "old people like to live in the past."

This feature of reminiscence has led gerontological practitioners, including this author, to use it as a central ingredient in group work with the elderly for the purposes of socialization and treatment (Sherman, 1981, 1984). It is a natural ice-breaker, and its inherent tendency toward sharing of private experiences makes it an excellent vehicle for the development of gerontological programs and services with a mental health as well as a socialization purpose. The broader possibility of using reminiscence as a mental health resource in a preventive sense occurred to this author in 1983. The problem was that much of the prior practice application of reminiscence had been on an ad hoc and expedient basis. What was needed was a systematic and empirically grounded demonstration of its effectiveness in engaging community-dwelling elderly persons in a structured reminiscence process that would enhance their morale and possibly prevent premature institutionalization in psychiatric or nursing home settings.

Fortunately, an opportunity presented itself for just such a demonstration under the auspices of the Ringel Institute of Gerontology at the State University of New York at Albany. In the fall of 1983 a structured approach to group reminiscence was developed and pretested by this author in a congregate housing setting for the elderly in the community, the kind of setting in which numbers of unattached and somewhat demoralized elderly persons are apt to find themselves. On the basis of this pretest, a proposal for a full-scale community-based project was developed and funded in 1984, as will be described shortly.

There had been numerous anecdotal reports by geriatric practitioners, usually social workers, about how well reminiscence groups worked in getting elderly residents of nursing homes and other old-age settings to interact and to enhance their sense of well-being (Ingersoll & Silverman, 1978; Lesser, Lazarus, Frankel, & Havasy, 1981; Liton & Olstein, 1969). However, these reports were mostly based on practice in institutional rather than community settings. Also, the findings reported were not based on studies in which the effects of group reminiscence were compared to control groups of elderly who did not engage in reminiscence. Further, they did not carry out follow-up contacts and assessments to see whether any social and emotional gains were sustained. Nevertheless, their reports corresponded with findings of some gerontological researchers to the effect that willingness and frequency of reminiscence was associated with positive affect, enhanced self-esteem, adaptive coping, and increased life satisfaction (Havighurst & Glasser, 1972; Lewis, 1971; McMahon & Rhudick, 1964).

One highly influential view of reminiscence in the field of gerontology is that it facilitates an introspective and integrative life review process in elderly individuals. Robert Butler (1963), a noted geropsychiatrist, proposed that increased reminiscence in old age occurs within the life review, which he described as "a naturally occurring, universal mental process characterized by the progressive return to consciousness of past experience and, particulary, the resurgence of unresolved conflicts." He believed that this introspective process is brought on by the realization of approaching death and the need for the older person to come to terms with his or her one and only life. He saw the process as beneficial when the result is the reintegration of past, present, and future, so that there could be ultimate acceptance of life experiences as they were actually lived. Thus, reminiscence has a key place in the lives of the elderly for the purposes of life review.

Butler's position was based primarily upon his extensive observations and experience as a geropsychiatrist, but he was also heavily influenced by Erik Erikson's (1963) thinking. Erikson's theory posits the final developmental task of the human life cycle as that of achieving ego integrity over despair. Ego integrity is an assured sense of meaning and order in one's life and in the universe in contrast to despair and disgust, which expresses itself in a feeling that one has failed and that there is not enough time remaining to attempt another life or find an alternative road to integrity.

Some confirmation of Butler's positive conception of the role of reminiscence came in an important study of 639 elderly persons in Chicago who were undergoing the stresses and trauma of relocation from their own homes into nursing homes. (Lieberman & Tobin, 1983). That study showed the persons who coped best with the relocation process actively used reminiscence in the process. While there was no attempt to claim that those persons achieved ego integrity under such trying circumstances, it was clear that they had managed to avoid the depths of despair evidenced by a significant number of those who did *not* actively use reminiscence. These and other findings from the Chicago study were highly influential in the design of the group reminiscence demonstration that I developed with my colleagues at the Ringel Institute of Gerontology.

The director of the Ringel Institute at the time of the pretest and development of the group demonstration was Dr. Sheldon Tobin, who had been the co-director with Morton Lieberman of the Chicago project. Consequently, we were able to pursue some of the questions raised by that project and to utilize some of the procedures that were found to be fruitful in it. The use of one particular procedure from that project proved to have profound and unanticipated consequences for my own perspective on and understanding of the nature of reminiscence in the elderly, a perspective and understanding that can only be called experiential, as will become abundantly clear as the book progresses.

WHAT IS "OLD" AGE?

Up to this point we have covered the question of what an experiential study is, what reminiscence is, and how the self is an integral aspect of reminiscence. Thus, we have covered all but one of the main terms in the title of this book. That term, "old age," is perhaps the most difficult of all to define. When does old age begin? Or to put the question in its most difficult form, when are we old? Gerontologists, who are presumably the experts in this area, show very little agreement on these questions. For one thing, they tend to come from different disciplines: sociology, psychology, medicine, economics, anthropology, theology, and so on. Thus, for example, a gerontologist whose discipline is economics might define the beginning of old age as 65, because of the importance of Social Security and related transfer payments in the lives of our senior citizens and in our national economy.

A psychologist, on the other hand, might choose an earlier age because retirement can be looked at as a "state of mind" as much as a vocational or economic state. After all, many people are now retiring at age 55 or even 50, rather than 65, and this frequently has to do with the wish to find a "new path" in life rather than simply to retire from work (Sheehy, 1981). In fact, one of the most influential distinctions by chronological age in the gerontological literature came from the psychological research of Bernice Neugarten (1975), who defined *two* categories of old age, the "young-old" (ages 55–75) and the "old-old" (over 75). On the basis of a series of studies done by her and her colleagues on the Committee on Human Development at the University of Chicago, it was determined that factors such as better health care and early retirement have made for a category of older adults who are vigorous, actively engaged, and significantly better off physically and economically than the category aged 75 and over. Those in the old-old category are apt to appear much more like our former image of the elderly: frail, vulnerable, dependent physically and economically, and so on. This is not at all descriptive of most 55- to 75-year-olds in our society, so the distinction has some descriptive power.

Yet we have to be extremely cautious about this distinction, just as Neugarten herself later became. Even from the more obvious criteria of physical appearance and capacity, we can go terribly wrong. Just a moment's thought makes it evident that two people of the same chronological age — say 75 — can vary immensely in such things as stooped posture, baldness, skin changes, and physical strength or frailty. This says nothing about how old the person *feels*. Most older people will tell you they feel much, much younger than they look. Actually, the person's subjective perception of his or her age is often a strong indicator of the person's morale and emotional well-being in old age (Edwards & Klemmack, 1973; Linn & Hunter, 1979; Phillips, 1957). The more "old" the person feels, particularly if the person feels "very old" when chronologically young-old (e.g., 65), the more likely that person is to have low morale.

Subjective perception of age not only varies greatly among individuals but also varies by social class position and other socioeconomic factors. Thus, blue-collar workers tend to define "old" as age 65, when they are entitled to Social Security and retirement, often after a life of hard physical labor; whereas people in white-collar occupations, who expend more mental than physical effort in their work, are apt to define "old" as age 75. All of this should give us pause in taking a categorical stand on what constitutes "old age." The best policy, and the one that seems to be followed by most gerontologists, is to choose a definition of old age that makes functional sense for the particular subject area being studied. You can go through the literature and find old age defined as beginning at 55, 60, 65, 70, and even 75, depending on the area and purposes of the study.

There are several reasons for choosing 60 as the beginning of old age for the purposes of this study. Primarily, it is because at around age 60 reminiscence begins to serve somewhat different functions, or a different balance of functions, in the person's life. This might have something to do with the location of individuals entering their sixties relative to the larger social and historical context of most Western societies. The Spanish philosopher José Ortega y Gasset (1958) developed a conception of generations in the history of society that views the generations in terms of their relative influence, power, and impact within societies. He identified the following five generations: (1) childhood, ages 0 to 15; (2) youth, ages 15 to 30; (3) initiation, ages 30 to 45; (4) dominance, ages 45 to 60; and (5) old age, age 60 +. He saw the dominance (in power) and initiation (entering positions of power) generations as having the greatest impact and influence on the functioning and direction of our societies. Granted that we might have individual septuagenarian leaders like President Reagan or octogenarian Supreme Court justices, it is the domination and initiation generations as whole *cohorts* that are most prominent.

Daniel Levinson and his colleagues used Ortega's conception in their study *The Seasons of a Man's Life* because they felt it gave a valid depiction of the career trajectories of the men they studied (Levinson, Darrow, Klein, Levinson, & McKee, 1978). Ortega's conception is quite consistent with another one that has had a much more profound and direct influence in gerontology and in this study in particular. That is Erik Erikson's eight ego stages of the life cycle (1963). His last stage, integrity versus despair, begins at about age 60; and the prior stage, generativity versus stagnation, has a central issue or theme that is quite consistent with Ortega's dominance generation. Since Erikson's conception of ego integrity versus despair is so central to much of the material that follows in this book, it makes sense to accept age 60 as the beginning of "old age" for the purposes of the book.

The three major studies reported in this book all had the requirement of a minimum age of 60 for participation. The first study, the Group Project, had an age 60 + requirement. Then, since the participants in the Individual Reminiscence Survey consisted of 88 of the original Group Project participants, they automatically met the 60 + requirement. The third, the Integrity Survey, required the same age minimum in order to maintain comparability in addressing questions raised by the two earlier studies. It might be added parenthetically that between the start of the Group Project in 1984 and the completion of the Integrity Survey at the end of 1989, I, as director of each of them, moved from age 56 to age 62. So it can be said that I got caught in a self-imposed designation of "old age" along the way.

PUBLIC BEGINNINGS

The Group Reminiscence Project was undertaken in July 1984 and completed at the end of June 1985 as an applied research and practice demonstration. It was funded by the AARP Andrus Foundation because of its clear implications for elderly persons who live in the community but who might at some time be at risk of institutionalization in either a psychiatric or nursing home setting. There had been a great deal of concern about getting isolated elderly persons into social settings such as senior citizen centers so that they could develop friendships that in turn could become part of an informal social support network. The federal government's Nutrition Program under the Older Americans Act of 1965, for example, had strong social purposes in that it was hoped that the subsidized and inexpensive "hot meals" program provided at the centers would attract isolated or just lonely older persons so that friendships, and possibly social support networks, could be developed.

One particularly influential study in the San Francisco area had earlier shown that there was a significantly higher rate of institutionalization due to emotional breakdown among community elderly who did not have at least one confidant, a person in whom to confide one's problems and concerns (Lowenthal & Haven, 1968). One of our purposes, therefore, was to develop, through the use of group reminiscence, friendships that could lead to confidant relationships and prevent unnecessary institutionalization. This was the primary *public* purpose of the project. Another purpose, of course, was to provide the opportunity for older persons to engage in the pleasurable activity of sharing memories of similar events and happenings in their lives. This had more of a purely social purpose as an end in itself. But we were also aware of the potential for a positive life-review experience for a number of the group participants, so that too was built into our design of the project and the group procedures.

When the group demonstration project began in 1984, three of the four settings in which it was conducted were member agencies of the Jewish Federation of Albany (JFA). This was because there was a mutual commitment and ongoing formal arrangement between the Ringel Institute and JFA for the testing of new and innovative services and programs for the elderly in the Albany community. Therefore, two senior citizen apartment dwellings and the largest Jewish community center affiliated with JFA participated in the study.

A sizable minority, about one-fifth of the residents in the two apartment dwellings, were non-Jewish, just as a number of the participants in the senior service program at the community center were. However, in order to obtain somewhat more ethnic diversity, a fourth setting was added. It was the newest senior apartment complex in the Albany area and therefore would benefit from a program designed to help develop social relationships and supports among elderly residents who did not yet know one another. Although it was sponsored by the Greek Orthodox Church, its residents represented a mixture of Protestant, Roman Catholic, Greek Orthodox, and Jewish backgrounds in that order of magnitude.

Even with this addition, two-thirds of the final 104 participants in the project were Jewish, a sizable number of whom had come to this country from Eastern and Central Europe — Poland, Russia, Rumania, Austria, and so on. This made for a rich historical and cultural tapestry of shared memories and associations of immigrant beginnings, which enhanced the interest of the native-born Americans whose own parents frequently came from similar backgrounds. The age range was from 60 to 91, so there was opportunity for some cross-generational sharing and comparisons in the group reminiscing.

The participants were all volunteers and in line with the experimental design of the study, and they were randomly assigned to one of three different types of groups: two reminiscence types with differing procedures and a control group that met only for the purposes of testing, not reminiscing. These three types of groups were constituted in each of the four settings of the study for a total of 12 groups in all. The size of the groups in each setting was determined largely by the size of the sample pool of volunteers available and ranged from a minimum of six to a maximum of ten members per group.

The testing of the participants consisted mostly of self-report questionnaires that provided measures of general morale or happiness, life satisfaction, and self-concept, as well as frequency and relative enjoyment of reminiscence (Sherman, 1987b). Data also were collected on numbers of new friends made and maintained and numbers of new confidants. Two other measures — type of reminiscence and experiential level of reminiscence — were assessed using three- to five-minute audiotaped time samples of reminiscence of each person in all of the 12 groups.

There were three testing periods: one when the groups began (pretest), one at the end of the ten group sessions (posttest), and a follow-up test approximately three months after the last group session, to see if any significant changes were maintained beyond the end of the group experience. Thus, the four control groups (one in each setting) met only three times for the testing, whereas the eight reminiscence groups met ten time for reminiscence sessions, including pre- and posttesting, plus the follow-up testing session. All 104 participants were paid for their time and willingness to

complete the testing forms and procedures. No money was paid for reminiscence sessions.

The group reminiscing sessions lasted one and a half hours each and
were conducted by a professional social work practitioner with an MSW degree. This worker led all eight reminiscence groups (two types in each of
the four settings) so that group leadership would be held constant and any
different effects could not be attributed to different leaders.

As noted earlier, there were two different types of reminiscence groups.
There were some essential contrasts between them, but both types followed
a life-span developmental perspective in that group participants shared
memories beginning with the earliest remembered ones from childhood
through adolescence and adulthood into the present. This procedure was
based on Butler's life-review concept, which was central to our thinking in
designing the project. Since this was not a new concept in the gerontological literature, the four experimental groups that were carried on entirely
under this format were called "conventional" reminiscence groups (Lewis &
Butler, 1974). We used this term purely to distinguish this type of group
from the other. In fact, it was not conventional in the sense that it was being
used all the time in gerontological practice. Actually, this was the only study
known to us that systematically used the life-span, life-review procedure in
an experimentally designed project.

At the beginning of each of the ten sessions, the practitioner introduced a
reminiscence topic that reflected a developmental stage of the life cycle,
such as the first day at school, the first pet, and so forth. Participants were
encouraged to share their memories with the group, but they were specifically reassured that this was entirely voluntary and no one person should
feel pressured to discuss topics that made him or her uncomfortable. An
open and flexible conversational approach was also used to encourage spontaneity in the sharing and discussion of memories.

The planned format for the ten reminiscing sessions was to spend two
sessions each on the following life stages: childhood (birth to 12 years of
age), adolescence (12–19 years), adulthood (20–40 years), middle-age
(40–60 years), and senior adulthood (60 years to the present). The childhood sessions began with recalling the earliest memory and went on to describing playmates, best friends, relationships with family members, typical
activities on weekdays and weekends, favorite toys, pets, and other possessions. Adolescence began with describing their first date, which brought on
the most titillation and the most amazement at the amount they could recall of the circumstances and details of that event. Other topics of adolescence included the first job, entering the service, going steady, and so on.

Topics for the two sessions on adulthood included courtship, engagement, marriage, occupations, and the good and bad points of their careers.
The middle-age sessions had them recall some of the things they were most

proud of during that period, any mid-life issues or problems, becoming a grandparent, and remembrances of family and school reunions or anniversaries. Some representative topics for the last two sessions on senior adulthood included discussion of pros and cons of being over 60, any slights or prejudice they might have experienced due to their age, how satisfied they were with the way their lives had turned out, and any ways in which they might have preferred their lives to be different. Although these and other topics were to be introduced by the practitioner, the natural flow of the reminiscing and conversation usually led into them without specific leads or prompts.

The second type or reminiscence group was called "experiential" because it incorporated a procedure called experiential focusing. It is a method developed by Eugene Gendlin of the University of Chicago for instructing a person on how to focus on a bodily felt inner referent or meaning of an experience (Gendlin, 1981). This procedure had been used in the Chicago study conducted by Lieberman and Tobin on the experience of relocation into nursing homes. However, it had been used entirely for research purposes rather than as a practice method. In other words, the investigators in that study used the procedure to get the elderly subjects into a relaxed and introspective frame of mind so that they could recall, attend to, and relate their memories and reminiscences on audiotapes and to the investigators. These tapes enabled the investigators to categorize and classify different content and type of reminiscence in their later analysis.

The focusing technique was not only effective in evoking memories and reminiscences from the subjects, but they found the procedure to be relaxing, pleasant, and helpful to them personally. Although the procedure was not used further in the Chicago study, many of the subjects said they would like to go through the focusing experience again because of its positive effects. This incidental and serendipitous finding led this author to conclude that the focusing method could be a valuable addition to group reminiscence practice, rather than simply a research device. Consequently, the method was implemented in the group demonstration project in the ways about to be described.

The experiential groups conducted in the four settings of the study used the same life-span format and selection of topics as the conventional groups. However, in the third session, participants were told that their group would begin the remaining seven sessions with a new and different way of focusing on experiences. They were informed that they would spend the first third of each session doing this, and the remainder of each session would be devoted to the life-stage topics according to the regular group format.

The practitioner described the focusing method as a set of steps or procedures for reminiscing that had been found to be relaxing, pleasant, and helpful in a study of older persons in Chicago. She said, "We will begin each meeting with a relaxing way of focusing on past life experiences. It is an individual and quiet process that I will guide you through and that will take only a few minutes. After we finish, we will the discuss life experiences and memories."

At the introduction of the focusing exercise in the third session and in all sessions that followed, the practitioner first led the group members through guided relaxation. She instructed all of them to get in as comfortable and relaxed a position as possible and to breathe deeply, just focusing on the way their bodies felt. They were asked to continue relaxing and breathing deeply, allowing their chairs to support their weight fully, and to keep focusing on the way their bodies felt as they relaxed. After a few moments of this guided relaxation, they were asked to sense the inside of the right knee, either through physical sensation, imagery, or bodily awareness. This latter step was not chosen because of any particular significance about the right knee or about that particular location. It was to keep the focus and orientation on their bodies, and indeed it seemed quite natural to them. Elderly persons are generally sensitive to, if not preoccupied with, the functioning of their bodies. So they found this procedure to be quite easy and syntonic, according to their descriptions of the whole experience afterward.

They were instructed throughout the relaxation process to pay special attention to their body sensations. After 30 seconds of this relaxation, the practitioner guided them through the initial silent focusing process by asking them to think of something they feel or felt good about and liked a lot. It could be a favorite place, a possession, an event, or anything else that came to mind, except for a person or a pet. These exceptions were explicitly made so that possible painful memories of recent deaths or losses could be avoided.

The participants were asked to focus on bodily sensations experienced in thinking about the pleasant thing and to try to find "feeling words" to describe the sensations or bodily felt sense of the pleasant thing. After about five minutes of this silent focusing, the practitioner opened discussion for sharing of individual experiences of guided focusing on memories.

In the second focusing session (the fourth group session), the practitioner guided the participants through the prefocusing relaxation steps but added that this time they could focus on pleasant (and only pleasant) memories of some person or pet. Then, after about five minutes of silent focusing, the practitioner opened up discussion for sharing of individual experiences as before. These first two focusing sessions were developed in this way so that the groups' introduction to the process was positive. It was presumed that this focus on pleasant and positive experiences would make participants more receptive to all types of experiences, negative as well as positive, and problematic as well as enjoyable. Thereafter, from the fifth to the tenth and last reminiscence session, the practitioner took the participants through the full sequence of steps in the focusing process, which included focusing on problematic and sometimes unresolved past issues and experiences. These steps will be fully described and illustrated in conjunction with an actual case at a later point.

By contrast to the two types of reminiscence groups, the control groups were intended to represent the no-treatment (nonreminiscence) condition in the experimental design. If the experimental condition of group reminiscence could be shown to lead to significant increases in numbers of confidants, new friends, self-concept, life satisfaction, and so on over the three testing periods of the study, and if the control groups could be shown to have no increase or significantly less increase over the three periods, then the experimental demonstration would be showing the desired and hypothesized effect. The control groups were paid in the same way as the experimental groups for the three testing sessions in which they met as a group for administration of the test forms and procedures, but they did not meet for guided reminiscence sessions. However, when all was done, the actual outcomes of this experimentally designed field study looked quite different from those of a highly controlled laboratory study.

PUBLIC OUTCOMES

One outcome that matched the intent of the project was that the participants in the two types of reminiscence groups reported a significant increase in the number of their friendships and further that they maintained these friendships into the follow-up or third testing period. However, there was no significant change in the number of confidants (i.e., a person to tell your personal troubles to). This was because over 90% of the participants already had confidants (mostly relatives but also friends) when the project started. This was particularly true in two older senior apartment settings, where quite a few participants were already friends. So there was really no numerical way to demonstrate any significant *statistical* changes in this.

However, there were more confounding findings on some of the other measures. For one, there was no significant difference between the reminiscence and control groups on measures of life satisfaction and self-concept. There were positive increases in both of these measures for the reminiscence groups, but this was also true of the control groups. Consequently, there was no significant difference between the experimental and the controls in the amount of *change* over time. Even more confounding, however, was the fact that the control group showed significant increases in frequency and enjoyment of reminiscence from pretest to posttest! How could that be?

Follow-up interviews with a number of the control group members gave us some indication of what had happened. For one thing, the controls had met as a group for the first testing, and by the time of the second testing they were actually referring to themselves as "a group." They had been questioning and discussing with their apartment-house neighbors who were in the reminiscence groups what was going on in those groups. This resulted in some informal discussion and demonstrations of and engagement in reminiscence. "Not to be left out of something good," as one control group person put it, the controls too identified themselves as belonging to a group. Not only that, they also felt they were engaging in something of a communal undertaking or process because reminiscing was "in the air" at those settings.

These are some of the vagaries and realities of doing social research in congregate settings. Ours were not true or "pure" control groups in terms of rigorous experimental methodology because they had been "contaminated" by the proximity and extracurricular interaction with experimental group members. This is certainly a drawback from a methodological point of view, but it dramatically illustrates the contagion of reminiscence, which Casey (1989) describes as the communal-discussive dimension of reminiscence from a phenomenological point of view.

There are some additional possible explanations of this "aberration" in the control groups. One is a phenomenon that has been found in other studies of group work and group therapy, especially where the participants who have gone through the group experience are tested together in the group at the end of the experience. The feelings at such ending sessions are generally marked by warmth and camaraderie and sense of having gone through something meaningful together. This has been called a "group high," which is reflected in the self-report testing instruments in the form of inflated positive scores.

There was certainly some evidence for this in all three types of groups but particularly so for the control groups. They showed evidence of a group high, and their posttest scores appeared to be inflated. This apparent inflation would help to explain the marked drop in their positive life satisfaction and self-concept scores from the posttest to the follow-up testing three months later. The participants in the two types of reminiscence groups also showed a decrease on those two measures at follow-up, but it was slight by comparison. The control group participants went back to their pretest levels of life satisfaction and self-concept as a group, whereas the scores of participants in reminiscence groups on those two measures were above the pretest level on average. However, their gains from pretest to follow-up were not great enough for statistical significance. Unlike the controls, who showed a linear increase and then decrease as a group on those measures from pretest to posttest and then to follow-up, reminiscence group participants showed a more mixed pattern across time. A number showed clear increases in the second testing and then somewhat of a drop in the third and last test. Others showed the same increases in life satisfaction and self-concept from first to second testing and then maintenance or even increases in these scores by the third testing. There also were some who showed a decrease at second testing but an increase at third. These differences in pattern of increase and decrease turned out to have important implications for our understanding of the role of reminiscence in the life-review process.

It appeared that the somewhat more homogeneous pattern of test results over time in the control groups was related to the type of reminiscence they engaged in and to the fact that the functions it served for the participants were substantially different. Based on follow-up interviews with most of these participants, it is clear that they tended to engage in a more sociable, enjoyable, and superficial type of reminiscing. However, the positive effects of this on the mood of those participants did not last into the follow-up period. It was a transient change in mood rather than in morale.

The difference between control group and reminiscence group participants was quite clear in terms of type of reminiscence engaged in as measured subsequent to the group experiences. The difference was a statistically significant one, as it showed up in the analysis of the audiotaped reminiscence samples. Type of reminiscence was measured by a classification of the taped reminiscence sample into a fourfold typology reflecting a continuum or scale of inclusiveness of engagement in reminiscence from (1) nonengagement/avoidance; (2) selective avoidance, in which the person explicitly avoids negative or unpleasant content; (3) selective engagement, in which there is no explicit avoidance but no negative content is discerned; to (4) full engagement/nonavoidance, in which negative as well as positive and neutral content are manifestly included.

Almost without exception, if there was any change in the control group participants, it was from a Type 1 (nonengagement) to Type 2 (selective avoidance) or Type 3 (selective engagement), or from a Type 2 to a Type 3. The majority of the participants in the reminiscence groups, however, moved to a Type 4 at posttesting and follow-up from a Type 1, 2, or 3 at pretesting. In other words, by the end of the project the reminiscence participants were significantly more likely to say that when they think about the past there are some unpleasant or negative memories, but in general these were more than made up by the good, positive memories. They were also more likely to say something like "You have to take the bad with the good; it's all part of living, and it's worth it." They would also share actual negative memories more readily than the controls did.

Our lead question for the three-to-five-minute taped sample of reminiscence was to ask, "When you think of the past, what do you think about?" This tended to elicit who or what they thought about (e.g., "my family," "my children," "my husband/wife," "my childhood," etc.) and would then be followed by specific memories about these people or things. If not, the research interviewer would ask for specific related memories or events. On the basis of these taped samples we were able to get very high (over 90%) interjudge agreement by project staff members who listened to the tapes and gave independent ratings of reminiscence type.

This was also true of the ratings on the experiential level of the reminiscences, which was evaluated by independent judges using a measure called the Experiencing Scale. It has a manual and a set of training procedures for evaluating the manifest content of audiotapes and transcripts (Klein, Mathieu, Kiesler, & Gendlin, 1970). This scale yields ratings on a seven-point scale (hereafter referred to as EXP scores) with which we were able to measure the extent to which participants experienced their memories as impersonal, unwanted, or unintegrated outside events that just "happened" to them (lowest, point 1 on the scale) or internally as highly integrated and accessible aspects of themselves in the present (highest, point 7 on the scale). As the EXP scores move up the scale, it means the memories are reported and articulated as more personal, internally felt experiences in the present and less impersonal and externally felt as dim or distant memories of the past. There is a more immediate feeling quality to the memories as one progresses up the scale; by the fourth level or midpoint on the scale, the person is moving toward dealing with, or at least looking at, some of the negative, unintegrated aspects of the past. Consequently, higher EXP scores were highly associated with Type 4 in the aforementioned reminiscence typology. In fact, there was a significant increase in EXP scores for the reminiscence group participants from pretest to both posttest and follow-up. There was no appreciable change in the control group participants, which meant the group reminiscence had a significant impact on this measure, in accordance with the experimental design. Also, the experiential group participants showed higher EXP scores at follow-up than did the conventional reminiscence group members. This latter finding is to be expected to some extent because the experiential group members had been using experiential focusing in their group sessions. However, the pattern of relationships between EXP level and the measures of self-concept and life satisfaction took on a significance that went beyond the statistical results of the analysis, as will be seen.

Much of the flux and change within groups and between groups could not be picked up in statistics, yet a number of observable (though nonquantitative) developments and changes occurred, which led to an unanticipated outcome that was very much in line with the purposes of the project. This outcome was that in three of the four settings of the project, various members of the reminiscence groups requested and were able to develop ongoing groups in their respective settings. They claimed to have gotten a great deal out of their group experience, and they wished to continue it, but with certain variations based upon the setting and makeup of the groups.

In the community center the initiative came from both the experiential and the conventional reminiscence groups. About half of the members of each of the two groups (a total of 12) asked the practitioner to assist them in reconstituting themselves into a single group so that they might continue on as a peer group without a professional leader. They wished to continue the friendships and mutual interests they had developed during the project, and they did indeed become an ongoing group that obtained formal recognition as a regular programmed activity within the center.

In one of the senior apartment dwellings, which had been in existence for 15 years and already had a network of friendships, some of the newer residents requested an ongoing group. These consisted of participants from the two reminiscence groups and even two who had been controls. They asked that they be reconstituted as a reminiscence and "socialization" group. They preferred to have a professional practitioner as leader rather than a peer group. This was begun by a practitioner from our research project staff, and the leadership was later turned over to the professional social worker who was a staff member at the apartment setting.

Participants from the two types of reminiscence groups in the third setting showed a similar strong interest in maintaining and strengthening the relationships for the purposes of friendship and social support, but they had a much different agenda. That setting was the new apartment dwelling under the auspices of the Greek Orthodox Church, and, as we came to find out, many of the new residents had experienced recent losses. Just about all of them had lost their own homes, which they had to sell because they were no longer able physically or financially to maintain the houses or because they felt too isolated in them. Then there were related losses of possessions, friends and neighbors, pets, and so on. Most of them were widowed, some of them fairly recently, Therefore, there was a strong recognition and articulation of their need to work on and grieve these losses.

They did not just want someone to facilitate their development into a peer group; they wanted a professional leader to help them become a "coping group," a term they chose. They were very clear that they wanted help to cope with recent losses of homes and spouses, as well as help with their transition into this new housing situation. In the course of the project they did not as freely engage in reminiscence as those in the other three settings because they found their memories to be sad and the process of reminiscence to be painful.

Although the practitioner who had worked with them in the reminiscence groups had left at the end of the demonstration project when its funding ended, we were able to assign an empathic practitioner from the Ringel Institute of Gerontology, a middle-aged woman with many years of experience in health-related geriatric settings, to take over the group. She worked with them for four months in coping with their losses, after which they decided to become a "social action group." Since this was a new housing setting with no well-established policies and procedures, the members of this coping group came to realize that they had certain common complaints, dissatisfactions, and ideas for change, which they could more effectively bring about as a kind of advocacy or "pressure group." Here, again, was an outcome we would not have anticipated in our design of the demonstration.

After all of the evaluative reports of the participants, including these of the controls, of how much they got out of the project and how much they enjoyed the group reminiscing experience, the fact that stands out most clearly is that in three of the four settings project participants chose on their own to continue as groups. This certainly met the avowed project purpose of enhancing social supports and friendships, even if it came out somewhat differently than anticipated.

These were the public outcomes. There were many, many private outcomes, not all of them positive, that came to light as we were winding down the project between the last of the group sessions and the follow-up testing. Several individuals, such as those in the "coping group," indicated privately to the group leader that they were experiencing some negative and unresolved feelings and issues that were evoked in the process of reminiscing. They did not wish to share these in the group but did want to discuss them with her or some other responsible person.

One 68-year-old widow from one of the experiential groups, for example, approached the group leader after the eighth group session and said she wished to share something she could not mention in the group. It was that her husband had physically abused her for the last six years of their life together (he had died two years earlier). She said that he had become verbally abusive to her during his fifties, but when he was forced to retire at age 62, when his company went out of business, he became physically abusive. She said she took it from him at first because she felt sorry for him, but then she became frightened and cowed. She admitted that she was "glad" when he died of a heart attack. Now she felt enraged that she had been subjected to his abuse for those last years. At the same time she felt guilty for all the rage she felt. She said, "You know, I come from a different generation [the practitioner was 25 years old], and we don't admit or talk about these kinds of things like you young women do." The practitioner saw her privately after the ninth and tenth group sessions so that her feelings of rage could be vented and validated as legitimate and understandable and so that the guilt could be dissipated. Afterward she said, "You know, if there are any women's groups, especially younger ones, I would be glad to talk to them and tell them what happened to me. I'd tell them they should not put up with the abuse the way I did, and I'd tell them to get out the minute it started."

We had anticipated that there might be some individuals for whom the reminiscing would conceivably raise some unresolved issues. With the exception of the woman discussed above and the "coping group," these were handled directly by me after the project. They usually involved just one or two private interviews with me of an hour or an hour and a half. Only three individuals asked to talk privately about problems, not counting the members of the coping group, but there was a more general interest among the project participants to discuss their experience in the project. This interest was not about specific unresolved problems or about evaluating how well the project went and what needed to be improved. They had already done that in the follow-up testing.

In all four settings they asked for feedback on our findings from the analysis of our project data when we had finished. But beyond this it was evident that they would welcome the opportunity to talk individually and privately about their experience. Many of them came into the project believing that it was wrong to reminisce because that meant they were "living in the past." Or they were conscious of the popular stereotype that "old people always talk about the past," and they did not want to be stereotyped. Once they were given permission and encouragement to do so, most of them went at it enthusiastically. Consequently, when we asked them at the time of the follow-up testing whether they would be willing to be interviewed individually about their reminiscing experience, almost without exception they answered in the affirmative.

This interest on their part coincided very well with my growing interest in the actual experience of reminiscence, not just its objective and external manifestations in our research instruments and procedures. As we listened to tapes and observed the group sessions, questions came to mind that could be answered only in an individual interview—questions like "What was it like personally for you?" "How does it feel as you remember that?" "Do you have an image of it?" "What seems to trigger it off?" "What does it do for you?" These and a multitude more came to mind, and since there appeared to be no prior systematic study of the *experience* of reminiscence among the elderly, this was a most opportune time for one.

This second study, the Individual Reminiscence Survey, began early in June 1985, immediately after we submitted the final report of the Group Reminiscence Project to the AARP Andrus Foundation, Basically, it was an interview survey using an open-ended method of asking questions that would be reflective and would follow the flow of the respondents' descriptions of their experience of reminiscence. There were also some general questions concerning possible life themes in their reminiscing or in their discussion and description of it. Eighty-eight of the original 104 participants in the group reminiscence demonstration project were interviewed in the survey. This author interviewed all 88 at least once, some as many as four times periodically for the next two years. Thus, there was an opportunity to obtain some perspective on the nature and effects of reminiscence over a more extended period of time for a few selected individuals. A number of the findings and impressions from this survey will be reflected in the next two chapters. These will represent, in a way, the more personal or private experience of reminiscence that began as a public demonstration of its efficacy in groups.

PLAN OF THE BOOK

Having covered the main features of the Group Project in this introductory chapter, in Chapter 2 I set forth some of the forms of reminiscence identified in that project and those reported in the private interviews of the following Individual Reminiscence Survey. Chapter 2 also explores the role reminiscence seems to play in the experiential quality of late adult life. This is followed by a description of various functions of reminiscence, including self and mood enhancement, coping and adaptation, reparation, retention of the past, self-narrative, and life review with its relationship to ego integrity status in old age.

Chapter 3 describes the experience of reminiscence from the perspective of the person reminiscing as well as that of the person observing or listening to such reminiscing directly or from audiotapes. A method for determining different levels of experiencing in reminiscence, the Experiencing Scale, is presented, along with examples. This is followed by a discussion of experiential phenomenology, which provides the theoretical and philosophical basis for the experiential methods and approach to this study of reminiscence and to the related phenomena of life reviews and life narratives covered in this book. A description of life-review therapy using a method called experiential focusing is illustrated in considerable detail with a case presentation. Chapter 3 ends with an explication of the concept of embodied reminiscence, based on the preceding discussion and illustrations.

Chapter 4 deals with the language of reminiscence and describes how language expresses and reveals the level of experience in the course of reminiscing. It also deals with imagery in reminiscence as well as imagery's role in the language in which reminiscence is expressed. This is followed by a discussion of metaphor in reminiscence and the pull toward self-narrative in the reminiscing process.

Chapter 5 addresses itself to the topic of "the aging self" and deals with the subjective experience of self across the life cycle, with particular emphasis on late adulthood. It begins with the conception of an embodied self and moves on to the development of a socialized self. Recent conceptions of the self in the gerontological literature, which draw heavily on the earlier work of William James, are set forth. This is followed by discussion of "the older self" and processes of maintenance and change of identity in old age. A dialectical process conception of the self is set forth to address questions about integration and disintegration of self in old age.

Chapter 6 deals with the role of time in the interactive relationship between self and objects. Objects are discussed as symbols, cherished possessions, and memorabilia for reminiscence in old age. The effects of time on the changing relationship between self and objects in late life is then discussed, and this is followed by a discussion of the difference between historical and narrative time and truth.

Chapter 7 is devoted to a consideration of life themes as these emerged in the Individual Reminiscence Survey. The concept of life theme is delineated, and its application in the survey is described. This is followed by two cases presented in depth, with verbatim discourse from the interviews, to illustrate two basic types of life theme: (1) a "discovered" theme and (2) an "accepted" theme. A discussion of the descriptive and explanatory value of the life-theme concept for this experiential study concludes the chapter.

Chapter 8 is entitled "Variations on a Theme," and that theme is the self. The content of this chapter is based on findings from the third and last survey in this series of studies on reminiscence, the Integrity Survey, and on the dialectical/process model of the self from Chapter 5. Variations in the depiction and experience of self and themes are illustrated in self-narratives with verbatim excerpts by three elderly individuals who participated in the survey and who represent distinctly different life narratives. These narratives are analyzed in terms of Erikson's concepts of identity and ego integrity as well as our measures of integrity status and morale.

Chapter 9 is entitled "The Art of Reminiscence" and is devoted to the creative and aesthetic aspects of reminiscence in its spontaneous, life-review, and self-narrative forms. Self-creativity through identity reformulation and then creation of new meanings through reminiscence are discussed and illustrated via the self-narrative of a woman from the Integrity Survey. This is followed by a discussion of written reminiscence in the form of autobiographies, diaries, and journals. Considerable attention is given to the intensive journal method of Ira Progoff and its relevance for the elderly and for gerontological practice. The chapter ends with the section called "The Poetry of Reminiscence," which illustrates reminiscence in that form from known writers and from certain participants in the Integrity Survey who were willing to share their poetry for the purposes of this study. Chapter 10, "Private Endings," represents the end of the journey that began with the public uses of reminiscence in the initial Group Project. It starts with a recapitulation of certain key points and findings from the experiential study of reminiscence and discusses their implications for gerontological practice and then for the experience of aging in general. The correspondence between these findings and prior gerontological research is explored next, particularly with respect to the impact of attitudes and values on the aged and their experience of old age in our society. These implications are pursued in greater depth in the following two sections. The first addresses the otological implications of these findings for the existential experience of aging, or simply "being" in old age, while the second addresses the implications for change and "becoming" in old age. The next section is entitled "Personal Reflections" because it represents my personal reflections on major competing views of aging in America. The last section consists of intimations about qualitative differences in the natures of experience in old age as related to self, world, objects, and others. Since this last chapter represents more subjective and personal speculations than objective and empirical findings, the chapter title "Private Endings" seemed most apt.

NOTE

1. The instrument we used involved the presentation of seven-point semantic differential scales on which the subjects were asked to rate the concept "My Characteristic Self" on 21 polar adjective pairs, such as Strong–Weak, Confident–Unsure, Bad–Good, Worthless–Valuable, and so on. The instrument was developed by Rolfe H. Monge of Syracuse University and was used to compare the connotative self-structure of five life-stage groups ranging in age from 9 to 89 years in a sample of 4,540 subjects. For the results of the comparative study and the scoring of the test see R. H. Monge (1975).

2

Forms and Functions of Reminiscence

Reminiscence is a remarkably rich and complex phenomenon, so varied and textured in its forms, functions, and dimensions that any attempt to classify it or break it down seems a disservice. Yet in order to begin to appreciate its variability and manifold forms, some attempt has to be made.

The more one studies the phenomenon, the more evident it becomes that reminiscence serves a number of purposes or functions in the lives of older persons. Even when it occurs spontaneously and without conscious intent or purpose, as it so often does, upon later reflection there is little difficulty in seeing that it has contributed something or served some purpose for the person in the context of his or her current life situation. Furthermore, it is evident that the form the reminiscence takes varies according to its purpose or function. Therefore, the different forms will be presented in terms of their functions in the following discussion.

One of the first things that becomes apparent when you observe older persons reminiscing with one another is that the process usually is an enjoyable one; it gives pleasure. It can certainly be entertaining, especially when the reminiscence is vivid and lively in the telling of past events and experiences. When that happens, it is also clear that the telling lifts the spirits of the reminiscer just as the hearing does for the listeners. On the basis of these quite common findings about the process of reminiscence there can be little doubt that it does serve to enhance the quality of life in the here-and-now of the elderly participants.

Then there are forms of reminiscence that clearly serve to enhance the self-image or sense of self-worth of the older persons who are telling of their past accomplishments, positions, performances, exploits, and so on. There are numerous other, less obvious ways in which reminiscence serves to enhance the self, and these will be explored in considerable detail. There are also ways in which it serves other adaptive functions, frequently by enabling the older person to cope with some problem in the present or anticipated future. Then there are forms of reminiscence that appear in various ways to be serving the function of the live-review process, enabling the older person to reintegrate past issues and experiences in the present for the purpose of achieving a sense of meaning and ego integrity in Eriksonian terms.

DIMENSIONS OF REMINISCENCE

The functional forms of reminiscence will be covered in greater depth and detail in this chapter, but at this point it would be helpful to identify several dimensions of reminiscence that tend to show varying patterns in the different forms and functions. The first of these is time. The temporal dimension has to do with the salience and direction of the current reminiscence experience rather than the specific location in time of the remembered event or occurrence. The origin in time of all memory and reminiscence is, of course, the past. However, the salience or experiential meaning of the reminiscence may be very much in and for the present or even in anticipation of and projection into the future. What is being discussed here is the *functional locus* of the reminiscence. That is, the reminiscence may be functional for living in the past, the present, or the future.

For example, when reminiscing, the older person may be living back in the past in order to be there, to live there at least for the moment, in preference to being in the here and now. This is the kind of reminiscing that younger persons are apt to refer to when they stereotype the elderly as "living in the past." This form of reminiscence does, of course, exist and is not at all uncommon, but it tends to have an experiential quality and meaning that is markedly different from other forms of reminiscence.

The spatial dimension goes hand in hand with the temporal. When a person locates a memory in time, it usually has an identifiable location in space, a place where the past experience occurred and was situated. In some forms of reminiscence this spatial dimension predominates; the place is the central and most salient feature of the experience. In other forms, place is practically unidentifiable and insignificant.

Another important dimension is the public–private one. Does the reminiscence occur in the absolute privacy of oneself in a totally intrapersonal sense? Or does it occur in the presence of others, or even conjointly in a mutual reminiscing? Does it occur in a small intimate group or in a larger aggregate? It can be seen that there are combinations and degrees of public and private. Or, from a somewhat different perspective, is the reminiscence for public/interpersonal or private/intrapersonal consumption? What is thought or talked about in reminiscing about the past is very much determined by who the consumer will be.

A third dimension of reminiscence might best be described as an active–

passive one. Sometimes a remembrance occurs with no prior warning or forethought; it just comes upon the person. This may set off a train of reminiscence that seems to unfold and flow of its own accord, and the person experiences it as a rather passive recipient. On the other hand, that same train of reminiscence may set off a very active search to recapture a specific memory that has been lost or forgotten and now seems important to retrieve. There is now a more purposeful aspect to the reminiscence, and the person assumes a more active stance in the process. In this instance there is a conscious intentionality to the reminiscence that had not been there earlier. At other times, the person might begin with an active stance in the reminiscing process. This is frequently the case in structured group reminiscence where the participants might feel socially impelled or obligated to share memories. However, it is also the case when the person is actively trying to cope with something problematic in the present, for example, in grieving the recent loss of a loved one and invoking memories of the lost one in the process.

Another dimension of major significance is the affective one. It has to do with the emotions attached to the memories experienced in the reminiscing process. Are the feelings associated with the memory experienced as pleasant or unpleasant, happy or sad, positive or negative? It is possible, of course, to experience some memories as rather neutral or bland, which suggests that this dimension is on a continuum from highly positive to highly negative. However, this is too simple and linear a conception of a complex process, for it can have mixed positive and negative elements. In his phenomenological study of remembering Edward Casey (1989) comments on the frequently wistful or bittersweet nature of the process:

> Bittersweetness pervades reminiscing of many kinds and lends body to its wistfulness. It is evident that the sweetness stems ultimately from the basic pleasure we take in recollecting things situated in the remote past—a past we can now afford to savor, thanks to its very distance from the present—while the bitterness bears on the fact of transience, on the past's immutable closedness. It is also evident that in reminiscing wistfully, we combine the bitter with the sweet, cherishing or honoring a past we might otherwise regret or vilify.

This wistfulness and the bittersweet quality of reminiscence became more evident in our group project as the groups were coming to an end, after the participants had gotten to know one another better and when their reminiscing had become more inclusive and less avoidant of negative content. For some, however, the reminiscing remained predominantly negative and painful, particularly for those who requested a coping group to work through their losses. This is indicative of how the different dimensions of reminiscence tend to vary in relation to its function, which in the latter instance was to cope with losses in a grieving process.

Fortunately, this negatively experienced form of reminiscence is not the most frequent type, and when experienced, it is generally transient. Our studies and those of others have indicated that most elderly persons find reminiscence to be an enjoyable and pleasant experience. Since it is such a frequent source of pleasure, there is good reason for asserting that one function of reminiscence is the positive contribution to the experiential quality of life in late adulthood. The objective physical and material quality might not be the best, but reminiscing can help to enhance the subjective quality.

EXPERIENTIAL QUALITY OF LIFE

One of the most remarkable features of our initial group reminiscence project was the extent to which the participants appeared to enjoy the process of reminiscence. Almost from the very beginning, once they realized that they would not be judged as living in the past by reminiscing, the majority engaged in and enjoyed the process. They were also surprisingly clear about the fact that its enjoyment was in the present. A number of people said, "I enjoy reminiscing because of what it does for me *now*," or "It gives me a good feeling," or other such statements which indicated that it served to enhance their current mood.

Casey (1989) refers to this as the "revivifying" function of reminiscence. It serves to revivify a previous experience, and it does so in several ways. First, the person enters into it in the expectation of being refreshed or re-energized by the experience. Second, the remembered content comes back "to life," not just to mind, in a particularly vivid way; and when this process is successful, there is a momentary merging of the person's consciousness with what is remembered. This gives a sense of becoming at one with what is remembered, as implied in the descriptions of a number of the participants.

This type of revivifying reminiscence was very clearly illustrated by a 73-year-old man in one of the conventional reminiscence groups. His highly vivid engagement in reminiscence while sharing his memories in the group was plainly contagious. Others in the group would listen with rapt attention and then appear to emulate or strive to capture the same quality in their own reminiscences. The content of his memories was not unusual or exceptional; in fact, it was quite mundane and unexceptional—but not in the telling. He was alive, vivid, and wondrous at the pleasure the recollecting provided.

He was interviewed in some depth after the project because he seemed to exemplify the contagious quality of reminiscence that we found so re-markable. When asked what reminiscing was like for him, he thought care-fully and said, "It brings this to mind . . . I love to read, and . . . ah . . . this reminiscing is just like reading my life all over again. That's why I like this reminiscing class [*sic*]. I hear all these tales, and they fascinate me . . . be-cause I enjoy reading . . . and I enjoy listening." This speaks to the narrative and communal-discursive elements of reminiscence as well as its revivifying capacity. Although he said it is "like *reading* my life all over again," he could have as easily said it is like *living* my past all over again. Casey (1989) refers to this as reliving the past and says that reminiscence is an "especially pow-erful way of getting back inside our own past more intimately, of reliving it from within." Apropos, this same man said later in the interview that remi-niscing is "just like a treasure chest, and any time I want to dig down into it, I can." It was clear that when he did he came up enriched.

Although he exemplified it more than most, what came through in his form of reminiscing was the sensory, almost gustatory quality of it. In effect, he was able to relive and actually *savor* the past experience in the present. On one occasion he reminisced about the day he was inducted into the army, and he talked about how his father took him to a very fancy and ex-pensive restaurant in Albany, the kind he had never been to before in his life. The most vivid part of this recollection was of the pumpkin chiffon pie he had for dessert. He was immersed in the experience of that pie in almost childlike glee as he described it: "Pumpkin *chiffon* pie . . . with whipped cream! Oh . . . I can still see it, and what a taste! Pumpkin pie . . . that's al-ways been one of my favorites, but pumpkin *chiffon*? Oh no, I never had that . . . was *that* something!"

This form of reminiscing has led one observer to describe reminiscence as "quintessentially a sensory, especially a visual, experience (Castelnuovo-Tedesco, 1980). The sensory nature of the experience is quite evident, but the visual is not the only or preeminent sense in many reminiscences. For example, a 79-year-old woman in one of our experiential groups made the following animated observation: "I can remember my mother . . . as clear as day. I can see her in the kitchen . . . baking bread . . . and it's not just the bread I can smell. I can smell the starch in her apron. She always wore fresh starched aprons in the kitchen."

This excerpt captures the olfactory quality of the reminiscing experience as vividly as the visual. It also indicates how place and person can be more prominent than time in the reminiscence experience. If asked to try to place the time of the memory, this woman would probably have to recon-struct the time on the basis of her mother's appearance and other features of the memory. However, this would be a more intentional and deliberate kind of recollecting than the spontaneous and sensory form of the initial reminiscence. On the other hand, the memory of the pumpkin chiffon pie was immediately and specifically located in time as well as place. So the possibilities and variability of reminiscence by person, time, place, activity, and affect can be seen in the rather "uncomplicated," everyday reminiscence described above.

When experienced in this sensory form, reminiscence not only contributes to the quality of life, but many older persons consciously use it for this purpose in their lives. Well over three-quarters of the participants at the start of our group study reported that recalling positive or happy memories was pleasurable, enhanced their mood, and put them in a positive frame of mind. These findings are very congruent with the findings of gerontologists who have studied community-based elderly persons (Romaniuk & Romaniuk, 1981). However, the qualifier that should be made here is that they think about *pleasant* events and memories. The willingness to include negative or unpleasant memories was much less common in the beginning of the study. Unpleasant and negative memories tended to be associated with other forms and functions of reminiscence, as will become evident later in this presentation.

ENHANCEMENT, EDIFICATION, AND PRESERVATION OF SELF

Reminiscence is frequently used to serve the function of enhancing self-esteem and self-image. One investigator found that the need for reminiscence as a means of maintaining self-esteem and morale is increased in the face of threats or assaults on the person's self-image (Lewis, 1971). To the extent that a person's self-image or concept is identified with the social roles and functions the person has filled in life, the greater these threats and assaults become with advancing age. The losses of parental, marital, and vocational roles and functions bring with them a diminution of the person's sense of self unless some countervailing processes and stratagems take place. One of these is reminiscence. This explains in large part the findings of increased incidence of reminiscence among the elderly, who as a group have experienced more of the kinds of losses that threaten maintenance of self-esteem.

Reminiscence to enhance self-esteem does not, of course, occur only in the face of losses. Self-enhancement is a common human motivation, and there are several ways this can be done through reminiscence. By reminiscing with others it is possible to inform them of one's former status and accomplishments. The need to do this might be greater in a group of older retired persons who can no longer identify themselves by their current jobs or positions. Whatever the reasons for it, this form of reminiscing was a frequent one among most of the participants in the group project.

Another way in which the self is enhanced in reminiscence is by entertaining others with the telling of one's past experiences. Some older persons are accomplished storytellers, particularly about themselves. Observing group reminiscence among the elderly, it is not difficult to see that some persons give the impression of being "on stage" as they share memories. However, this should not be taken as a special form of reminiscence reserved for the more egotistical or "star" performers in the group. Most older people get satisfaction from entertaining others in the process of oral reminiscing. Indeed, one study showed that over 70% of its elderly subjects claimed that they sometimes reminisced to entertain others (Romaniuk & Romaniuk, 1981). It might be added that by entertaining others one can also be reciprocally entertained by their reminiscences, as described earlier by the elderly gentleman whose reminiscing was so contagious.

Reminiscence can also serve to inform and teach about the past, and it can thereby become deifying for the self and others in its communal-discursive form. This was, of course, one of the most important functions of reminiscence in preliterate societies, where the elders were the guardians and oral historians of the past. Their experience and knowledge was highly valued and essential for the preservation of the past, but as we all know, this valued societal function has been denied the elderly in modern industrial and postindustrial societies. However, it does still go on between generations within families to some extent. It certainly went on between the participants in our group project. As suggested earlier, some of the younger (sixties and early seventies) participants would encourage the older (80 and over) participants to tell them about their immigrant experiences, since their own parents had come from similar places and heritage. But it was not just age differences that led to this edifying form of reminiscence. Different life experiences in different cultures and locations, even among people of the same age, led to a great deal of interest and engagement in such reminiscing.

Moving from enhancement and edification of the self, we come to a more profound function of reminiscence—the preservation of self. This has been observed in the very old, who are threatened with the dissolution of self or the sense of self because of severe decrements in their physical, sensory, and cognitive (especially memory) capacities. It is found particularly in nursing homes and other long-term-care facilities. In order to compensate for this diminished sense of self, the older person will reminisce about self and significant others in a highly dramatized and grossly simplified way (Tobin, 1988). The self and others are made to appear larger than life and of heroic or mythic proportions.

Lieberman and Tobin (1983) found in their Chicago study that the very old, particularly those who were near death, depicted their parents and spouses as exaggerated, larger-than-life figures. They were significantly more likely to make statements such as the following in their reminiscences: "Mother was one of the most wonderful women in the world. Every-one loved her." Or "I had a mother, the most selfish creature on earth. . . . I gave the love to my sisters which my mother did not."

An example of a mythical conception of self in reminiscence was given in a report about an 81-year-old man recently placed in a nursing home. He boasted to everyone around him that he had beaten up his top sergeant in the army 60 years earlier, exclaiming, "And I could do it again if I wanted to, by God!" (Wacker, 1985). This man would not bathe regularly and had such a strong smell of urine about him that other patients would shrink from him when he came too close He attributed their behavior to a fear of his physi-cal strength. The authors noted that this form of reminiscence served to buttress his identity with the myth of his prowess so that he was certain he could handle any situation.

It can easily be seen how such dramatizing can preserve a sense of self. However, it would be easy to dismiss such grandiose conceptions of self as late-life paranoia or senile dementia. Even if one did make such an attribu-tion or diagnosis, this would not gainsay that it functions to preserve a sense of self. Given the physical insults and losses in the lives of the very old and the dissolution of one's personal sense of self, "it is not surprising that many individuals will forego commitment to the reality principle in order to serve a higher purpose—the maintenance of selfhood" (Lieberman & Tobin, 1983).

ADAPTIVE AND COPING FUNCTIONS

The view of reminiscence taken in this chapter speaks to its general adapta-tional value in old age. However, there are some forms of reminiscence that seem particularly associated with the need to adapt to current problems and sources of stress. Certain gerontologists who have studied the relation-ship between reminiscence and memory have emphasized the salience of the current person–environment transaction in reminiscence (Kvale, 1977; Meacham, 1972). Memory is so interwoven with present needs, fears, and interests that the content of reminiscence should not be divorced from present adaptive concerns, according to their view.

One study reported that about a third of its community-based sample claimed to use reminiscence to deal with current problems (Romaniuk & Romaniuk, 1981). A number of our Group Project participants displayed a tendency to recall earlier life experiences with certain kinds of issues and problems they happened to be experiencing in the present. In individual in-terviews after the group project, some of them acknowledged that this was the case even though they were not aware of the connection between past and present at the time. These memories seemed to be related to changes that were going on in their lives during the group project, and these issues generally had to do with separation and relocation. In fact, one study found that aged persons under the severe stress of relocating from their own to nursing homes demonstrated significantly more memories of personal loss, injury, and death of significant others in their "earliest memory reminiscence" than did elderly persons not undergoing relocation (Tobin & Etigson, 1968).

This study suggests that there may be a certain unconscious type of adaptation to the new institutional setting through a process of recall and working through of prior "loss thema" in their reminiscences. Some of our Group Project participants reported spontaneous (forgotten, if not unconscious) memories of earlier stresses or problems that were similar to the current one. Then they found themselves engaging in a more conscious and purposeful recollecting of those memories in attempting to deal behaviorally and emotionally with the current problem. More commonly, however, participants reported using reminiscence to enhance their mood, spirits, and sense of self-esteem in the course of coping.

Reminiscence has a major function in coping with the loss of significant others and in grief resolution. Gerontological practitioners have been aware of the need for recently widowed persons to reminisce about their spouses (Sherman, 1981, 1984). At first a benign reminiscence process focusing on pleasant memories of the deceased is fostered, but eventually there will be a need to recall some of the bad times with the good, and there will be a need to repeat this reminiscing until the memories lose the oppressive kind of painfulness. This process of repetition and working through would have to be done in order for complete mourning and grief resolution to take place, regardless of whether it is facilitated by a professional practitioner or by the widowed persons themselves. The retention of highly idealized and unrealistic representations and memories of the deceased spouse would be indicative of unresolved grief. Such a person could experience a delayed grief reaction in the more complicated form of a reactive depression later on. Or if that unresolved loss is added to others, it could eventuate in a total demoralization and sense of despair in line with Erikson's theory.

It will be recalled that in the newest senior apartment setting of the Group Reminiscence Project, a number of the participants requested a "coping group" to deal with just such losses. They were having a delayed reaction to their multiple losses, perhaps promoted in part by the reminiscence group experience, and they recognized their need to work through these losses. The experience of one woman from this group will be described later in this chapter, but that begins to bear on the subject of the role of reminiscence in the life-review process. So it would be best to hold that subject in abeyance until we have looked at some other forms of reminiscence.

REPARATIVE AND RETENTIVE FUNCTIONS

These two new functional types of reminiscence are not unrelated to the issues of loss and resolution raised in the preceding section on coping. In some respects they represent unsuccessful strategies or outcomes regarding those issues.

The word *reparative* is used to describe this first type of reminiscence because it appears to be directed at making amends or reparations. There is a good deal of guilt associated with it and an evident need for some kind of expiation. It is also an obsessive kind of reminiscence, usually about a particular situation associated with a negative affect. Despite the painful feelings associated with the memory or the situation, people who exhibit this type of reminiscing are unsuccessful in suppressing their memories, and they reminisce a lot. Robert Butler (1963, 1980–81), who generally viewed reminiscence as a positive force and an untapped resource in old age, warned that morbid and obsessional rumination about the same issue, if not handled by an experienced practitioner, could lead to a panic state or an outright clinical depression.

Fortunately, this is a relatively infrequent form of reminiscence. There were only a few participants in our Group Project who clearly engaged in this reparative type of reminiscence, but it presented problems for the other group participants as well. For example, one 75-year-old widower kept insisting that he had been a bad husband and father. The other group participants and residents of the senior apartment dwelling knew him to be a kind and gentle man who was well liked. So they would protest that he could not have been such a bad husband and father, based upon what they knew of him. The other group members repeatedly tried to raise his self-esteem and to be emotionally supportive, but he would insist upon his own evaluation of himself and his past.

He kept coming back to the fact that he had not spent enough time with his family when he was younger. He ran a used-furniture business and claimed he spent most of his time, from morning till night six days a week, running it. He felt guilty about all this time spent away from his family. He claimed that since the death of his wife three years earlier his only son, who lived out of state, rarely wrote or called him, and he would add, "I don't blame him; I was never much of a father to him."

From a temporal perspective reparative reminiscence represents an unwanted intrusion of the past into the present. Such reminiscers often say they do not want to think about the past, they dislike it, it does not do them any good, and so on, but they cannot help it—the past just keeps coming back.

This is quite a different phenomenon from the retention form of reminiscence in which the person actively wants to reenter and relive the past in distinct preference to the present. There is a definite holding-on quality to their reminiscing; hence, the term *retention* to describe it functionally.

These reminiscers tend to glorify the past and denigrate the present, so much of their reminiscing consists of recalling what was better about the past. They tend to fit the stereotype of old people who live in the past.

They do not generally demonstrate high morale in empirical studies. This is because most measures of morale include questions about current mood and satisfaction, and these reminiscers are quite dissatisfied with the present state of affairs in the world and in their personal lives. The most widely used measure of morale in gerontology is the Life Satisfaction Index, which includes several questions about the present and the future. Needless to say, the retentive type of reminiscer is quite pessimistic about the future and sees the world going to wrack and ruin.

Any discussion of the kind of reminiscing that serves the purpose of retention has to include the subject of nostalgia. Nostalgia is most frequently described as a longing for something long ago and far away, a yearning for an idealized past that cannot return. Pietro Castelnuovo-Tedesco (1980) has written about reminiscence and nostalgia from a psychoanalytic perspective, and he distinguishes between the two. He claims that nostalgia is an affect that accompanies some reminiscences, whereas reminiscence is an active process rather than an affect. He appears to be making a questionable distinction here, perhaps for analytic purposes. Whatever the reason for the distinction, he views reminiscence as essentially pleasurable and nostalgia as mostly painful. However, when he goes on to say that nostalgic people are past-oriented, have a dislike of the present and a dread of the future, he appears to be describing the retentive type of reminiscers described above. Perhaps he has equated the memories that are part of the reminiscence process with the whole process; but given the definition of reminiscence adopted in this book, the affects that accompany those memories would have to be seen as an integral part of the reminiscence process. Certainly, from an experiential point of view, feelings are an inseparable part of the reminiscence experience.

Edward Casey (1989), writing from a phenomenological perspective, sees nostalgia as a mixed or ambivalent sentiment: "the pain (*algos*) of being absent merging with the pleasure of returning home (*nostos*)." Thus, he identifies nostalgia with a place (i.e., home). Indeed, the first dictionary usage of nostalgia is "homesickness," in line with its Greek root. So place becomes quite prominent and salient in this form of reminiscence. However, it is the temporal dimension and the salience of the past with the dimming of the present that stands out in the general retentive form of reminiscence.

NARRATIVE FUNCTION

Cognitive, social, and clinical psychologists have become increasingly aware of how central and pervasive a role narrative plays in the intrapersonal and interpersonal lives of humans. The term *narrative* is used here as synonymous with *story*. So for reminiscence to have a narrative function it must somehow be able to fit into a "storied" form. Actually, it is hard to imagine reminiscence escaping the powerful human tendency toward making sense of life and experience in the narrative form. One of the giants of contemporary cognitive psychology, Jerome Bruner (1986), has proposed that narrative understanding is one of two basic modes of cognitive functioning, each of which provides distinctive ways of ordering experience and constructing reality. The other he calls the "paradigmatic" mode, which is the mode of cognitive functioning in formal science and logical reasoning.

There has been a growing recognition of the limitations of "paradigmatic" thinking and science for a truly comprehensive psychology, and Bruner's recent book is just one example of this recognition. Even social psychologists have proposed a "narrative psychology," which they see as enhancing their understanding of social psychological phenomena. In fact, one prominent social psychologist has proposed that the narrative is a root metaphor for all of psychology (Sarbin, 1986). Donald Polkinghorne (1988), a clinical and research psychologist, has gone even further by describing narrative as "the primary form by which human experience is made meaningful." He defines meaning as the drawing of connections between the contents of awareness, and in this narrative functions to organize elements of awareness into meaningful episodes.

It is the episodic nature of narrative that becomes apparent in reminiscence. When asked what they think of when they think of the past, quite a few of the participants came up with events that were presented as episodes in their lives told in the form of brief vignettes. The episodes were sometimes prototypical and contained a core idea or theme that the person would come back to at later points in the same session or a later one. It was common to hear something like the following: "Do you remember what I told you before about the time when my mother said to me that I had to be responsible for my younger brother and sister? Well, I just happened to think about a time when I had to take my brother and sister on the street car to visit our grandmother . . ." Then the participant would go on to relate how her brother teasingly ran away from her at the trolley stop and hid, which would then lead to vivid descriptions of her own and her siblings' actions, reactions, and emotions in the process.

The initial and prototypical episode related by this woman turned out to be thematic of a sense of premature and undue responsibility that pervaded most of her subsequent reminiscing. She never did identify or articulate this theme in the course of group reminiscing, although she did so later in a follow-up interview. In fact, one of the primary purposes of the Individual Interview Survey was to determine whether life themes were present in the reminiscences and narratives of the elderly participants.

There were often several such episodes or composite types of past experiences related by the participants in the course of the 10 group sessions. However, there was no evident attempt to pull these episodic clusters together into a story line or plot. It could be said that the format and time limitations of the groups did not allow for it, and that would be true. However, it has to be added that reminiscence and narrative are simply not the same thing.

Edward Casey (1989) observes that anyone can reminisce without telling stories, and anyone can tell stories without reminiscing. However, he also notes the deep affinities between narrative and reminiscence when he says, "The very telling of one's reminiscences to others induces or encourages a storylike form, and few can resist the temptation to embroider upon otherwise banal reminiscences." This speaks directly to an integral and essential component of the reminiscing experience as defined in this study: "the process or practice of thinking or *telling* about past experiences." It is this "telling," as in a story, rather than "talking about," in an expository sense, that is of greater importance here. One dictionary definition of *tell* is "to relate in detail: narrate," whereas *talk* is simply "the act or instance of talking: speech."

This narrative impulse to tell became very evident in the follow-up interviews with the same participants who had reminisced in the form of these episodic clusters in the groups. When interviewed alone in their own homes or another private setting, they actually began to engage in narration about these episodes and began to tie them together into some kind of coherent story line. This was done without direct request or reference by the interviewer concerning the specific episodes reminisced about earlier in the group sessions.

Interviews, whether for research or clinical practice, are much more conducive to the narrative function than groups are, even though groups are very effective in eliciting reminiscences. Mishler (1986) reports that "stories are a recurrent and prominent feature of respondents' accounts in all types of interviews." He adds that as long as we allow respondents to continue in their own manner until they indicate they have finished their answer, we are likely to find stories. Furthermore, it was our experience in the follow-up interviews that there was much more conscious effort and opportunity for our respondents to give a more coherent narrative or story line and to connect the stories or episodes with one another into some coherent pattern of time and meaning.

The narrative form is extremely important, not only in relationship to the general phenomenon of reminiscences but also for the central role it plays in the lives of older persons. For the elderly, perhaps more than for any other age group, narrative *is* "the primary form by which human experience is made meaningful." For example, recent research has shown empirically that elderly persons recall narrative text much better than expository text (Tun, 1989). They are every bit as able as younger persons to recall the narrative but significantly less able to recall the expository text. This led the researchers to conclude that narrative as a sequence of events unfolding in time appears to be the way the elderly best organize memory.

Given this, it is largely through narrative knowing that the elderly continue to learn and retain new facts and knowledge about others, about themselves, and about their lives. Because it is so important and ubiquitous in the lives of the elderly, the narrative function needs to be examined in relationship to one of the most widely discussed subjects in the field of aging, the life review. It became evident in the series of studies reported here that narrative is an integral part of the life-review process, just as reminiscence is. Reminiscence can initiate, stimulate, enrich, and facilitate the narrative process in the life review, while narrative gives form and meaning to the discrete and discontinuous contents of reminiscence in the review. We will return to the subject of narrative in life review at a later point, but we need to look first in greater detail at the form and function of reminiscence in the life-review process.

LIFE-REVIEW REMINISCING

It will be recalled from Chapter 1 that Robert Butler viewed the increased reminiscence of old age as part of a "naturally occurring, universal mental process" that he called the life review. He claimed that the progressive return to consciousness of past experience, especially the resurgence of unresolved conflicts, was brought on by awareness of approaching death and the need to come to terms with the past in its relationship to the present and future. The life review, if successful, would lead to an acceptance of life experiences as they were lived (good, bad, and indifferent) and attainment of what Erik Erikson called ego integrity.

Erikson's theory posits eight psychosocial stages or crises throughout the human life cycle, and the crisis of ego integrity versus despair represents the final one It can be called a crisis in the sense that the approaching end of life precipitates a period of intense reflection in which reminiscence, recollection of dreams, memories, and thoughts occur in conjunction with an attempt to reconstruct and reconstrue one's life and its meaning while coming to terms with death. While attempting to resolve this crisis the older person engages in evaluation of accomplishments and failures over the life-span and of changes in physical and psychological attributes and capacities, and in this evaluative process an integrated sense of self begins to emerge. It is compared with earlier images of what one's self was like in the past, and in the process the person lets go of earlier unrealistic images of an idealized self. There is an acceptance of this emerging sense of self that is more integrated and consistent with the realities of the past, present, and future. This has to occur in conjunction with a working through of the losses, illnesses, death, and relocations of significant others and how these have altered the structure of one's life. Briefly, in Eriksonian terms, ego integrity is a sense of identity which requires that a person be able to define himself or herself in terms of the entire personal life-span.

Now, that is quite a large order, and as we shall see, there have been questions raised in gerontology about how feasible and common an achievement ego integrity really is. However, the question here is "What would reminiscence look like in this process, and how would it differ from the other forms of reminiscence?" Perhaps the best way to answer this would be to provide an actual case illustration of a person who went through such a process.

Mrs. A. was a 78-year-old widow of two years who was living in a newly opened senior apartment dwelling under the auspices of the Greek Orthodox Church at the time of the Group Project. Despite its auspices, the dwelling was nondenominational, and there was a fairly even mix of Greek Catholic, Roman Catholic, Protestants, and a few Jewish residents. Mrs. A. was a practicing Roman Catholic and experienced no difficulty with the religious diversity in the setting. However, since the apartments had been open for only about two months, there were no well-established friendships or informal social networks within the setting. Consequently, there was some initial wariness and reticence among the participants in the experiential reminiscence group to which Mrs. A. had been randomly assigned.

It will be recalled that most of the residents in this new setting had experienced recent and frequently multiple losses. Almost all had recently lost their homes of long standing, usually because of being widowed, alone, or physically unable to maintain the homes. Because of these losses and the associated painful memories, there was more defensiveness and less willingness to engage in memory-sharing about their personal pasts. Mrs. A. was no exception to this at the start of the study.

Mrs. A.'s husband had died almost two years earlier but only after a prolonged illness and disability due to a series of strokes. Mrs. A. had to care for him at home for four years prior to his death. Shortly after his death she developed breast cancer and had to undergo a radical mastectomy. Although she was reassured that no signs of any cancer remained after the operation, she found it increasingly difficult physically and emotionally to keep up the house she had lived in for over 30 years. So she was pleased to be among the first of the residents admitted to this new setting.

Her scores on the morale and self-concept measures at the time of the pretest in the beginning of the project showed that she was very close to the mean or average for the total study sample of over 100 people. She was not exceptionally high or low on either of the two measures—very much in the middle. She was also very much like the others in her group in claiming that she did not reminisce much, saying, "I try not to think about it." This changed after the first few group sessions to a point where she (like most of the others in her group) would reminisce about pleasant and positive events and memories but would explicitly avoid sad and negative memories.

However, at the end of the ten group sessions she was very actively reminiscing, and much of it was negative in affect. She said that she often thought of her youth and that she would like to "skip over" her marriage and her children, but she was not able to. She said, "Since I've been ill [the mastectomy], I think about death and I know it could happen—I'm in my seventies. I get a sad, sort of fatalistic feeling . . . well, it's going to happen." Consistent with this, her test scores at the end of ten sessions had dropped to among the lowest quarter of the total sample on morale and self-concept. However, she appeared to be working on some of the issues concerning her husband and health despite the painful affect associated with them.

At the time of the follow-up testing three months later, Mrs. A.'s morale measure had gone up to near its pretest score, as had her self-concept score. She and seven other project participants in her setting were the ones who indicated a strong interest in developing a "coping group" at the end of the group demonstration project. She was one of the key actors in both the coping and the social action phases of the group as it evolved over time. She was also one of the participants who was very interested in being interviewed individually after the demonstration to share her thoughts about the reminiscence group experience and what it meant to her.

In that interview she admitted to being quite reluctant to share her memories when the group started "for fear of stirring them up." Then, when the group first engaged in experiential focusing on pleasant memories, she was able to do that and to share some of these positive memories with others, but she was not able to discuss the negative ones. She kept trying to suppress those thoughts and memories, but that was not working in private. Finally, by the seventh session, when she got to know some of the other group members better, she began to talk about the negative memories, and this seemed to give her some relief. This also started some of the other members sharing some of their painful memories and thoughts.

She reported that some of the feelings that arose in the negative reminiscences that she could not suppress were guilt over the anger she felt and was still feeling toward her husband for his prolonged illness and dependency on her. There was also deep frustration and resentment over her own illness after caring for him so long and further guilt for not really mourning for him after he finally did die. She also admitted to considerable anxiety about her own death, anxiety brought on by the radical mastectomy she had to undergo.

About these various issues she later said, "I remember how much I hated

him [her husband] for becoming so disabled, and so dependent, and so use-
less to me . . . but I loved him for all the good years we had together. Then I
began focusing on the feelings about those good memories, and there was
some meaning in that. I also remembered how hard I tried to make him
comfortable and help him live with his disabilities. Finally, I found I could
accept my moments of hatred toward him and see them as a normal thing
under the circumstances." She also related how she felt that she was "only
part of a person" after the mastectomy. Her self-image had been so impaired that she felt she would "never look whole again." This too changed in
the life-review process. Paradoxically, it was just that physical insult to her
body that made her aware of and accept her body as older: "It made me realize my body was not the same . . . not young . . . and I'd better admit it to
myself."

By the time the coping group had ended and was moving into its social
action phase, Mrs. A. appeared to have attained a more accepting and cohesive sense of self and a degree of ego integrity. The professional leader of
the coping group reported that Mrs. A. had become a role model for some
of the other women in the group. She was seen as someone who had "put it
all together and had come out on top." This could be rephrased to say that
she had put it together in terms of past, present, and future. She saw a future in her new setting, new friendships, and the contribution she was making there. In many respects, the coping group and Mrs. A.'s experience in it
fit the description by Robert Butler and his colleague, Myrna Lewis, of what
one can get out of an effective life-review therapy group: "a personal sense
of life's flow from birth to death, personal solutions for encountering grief
and loss regarding old age and death, and models for growing older and for
creating meaningful lives" (Lewis & Butler, 1974).

Now, what is the difference in the form of reminiscing Mrs. A. did in her
life review as compared to the other forms of reminiscence described earlier? Actually, much of her reminiscing looked like the other forms. For example, she displayed a lot of the reparative type of reminiscing for awhile
when she experienced guilty thoughts and memories of an obsessive nature
about her husband. There was also some retentive reminiscing in her attempts to reach back only for the positive memories at one stage in the
group process. There were also obvious attempts at *coping* by using some of
these positive memories to offset the mood-depleting effect of the negative
ones. However, the difference here was that she was evoking, working
through, and coping with negative unresolved issues and conflicts from the
past so as to reintegrate them into a more viable and realistic present. This
is quite different from reminiscence about earlier experiences of personal
happiness and effectiveness in order to cope with some problem that
presents itself in the *present*.

Another major difference in the life-review form of reminiscence is that there is a conscious attempt to pull together the discrete reminiscences, positive and negative, into some cohesive pattern or portrayal. In short, there is a narrative form to it. There were others in the very same experiential group as Mrs. A. who did not really change as she did. There was a willingness to recognize some negative aspects of the past in their reminiscing as the group progressed, but these remained discrete and unconnected. There was no attempt to pull them together in any narrative sense. Also, their self-concept and morale scores did not show the same drop and then continuing upward trajectory that Mrs. A.'s showed. This suggests that they did not go through the same painful but fruitful life-review process Mrs. A. did.

The ego integrity versus despair formulation seems to infer a dichotomy of outcome or ego integrity status in old age—either you have ego integrity or you are in a state of despair. Our studies did not show this kind of picture. Rather, there seemed to be several different outcomes or statuses, depending upon the pattern of relationship between reminiscence, life review, morale, and self-concept. Our findings corresponded rather closely to those of several other investigators in this area of study, so it would be well to turn to these findings now.

EGO INTEGRITY STATUS AND REMINISCENCE

Our group project data and follow-up interview findings corresponded most closely to four ego-integrity statuses identified by Walaskay, Whitbourne, and Nehrke (1983–84). The four statuses in their scheme are integrity-achieving, dissonant (in crisis), foreclosed (avoiding crisis), and despairing. A person in the integrity-achieving status would have examined and accepted his or her one and only life as it had been lived, in accordance with Erikson's formulation of ego integrity. The person in foreclosed status would defend against self-exploration and avoid the reflective processes of crisis and life review. This person would retain a relatively positive sense of well-being and morale but at the expense of an integrated sense of past, present, and future with any depth of insight and meaning.

The older person in dissonant status is undergoing a shift from the precrisis to crisis phase of integrity resolution and is in a state of dissonance, which impacts negatively on the sense of well-being and self. The person in the despairing status is unhappy with his or her past and present life, pessimistic about the future, and sees life as too short to make up for past mistakes and regrets. This latter status is seen as a chronic one in which the integrity versus despair crisis has been resolved in an unfavorable direction.

Mrs. A. was actually in three of these statuses in the course of our study. She was foreclosed at the time of pretest, when she was avoiding reminiscing about unresolved issues from the past, but she still retained an accept-able level of morale and self-concept. Then she moved into the dissonant status as she began to grapple with the past issues and to experience corres-ponding drops in morale and self-concept. Finally, as the coping group neared its end, she had worked through those issues and was integrating past, present, and future, which indicated she was then in an integrity-achieving status.

Lieberman and Tobin (1983) also found strikingly similar patterns among the elderly subjects in their Chicago study, even though they used some-what different terminology and methods in their classification scheme. For example, they identified a pattern of reminiscence in 15% of the elderly people in their study whom they called "conflicted" and who were almost identical in description to the "dissonant" status. These people were in an active life-review process such as that experienced by Mrs. A. They engaged in a great deal of reminiscence, much of it negative, with the most intense affect. They were quite ambivalent in their self attitudes, which fluctuated from positive to negative and back as they engaged in the process of self-evaluation in the life review. They also demonstrated a high degree of intro-spection and relatively low morale.

There was another group in the Chicago study, comprising about one-third of the sample, which was called "resolved"; they were very similar to the integrity-achieving status. They did not reminisce as frequently as the "conflicted" elderly, but they were found to have previously engaged in rem-iniscence quite actively as part of a life review that ended in adequate reso-lution of past issues and in successful integration. They were high in mental health and morale; they evaluated their lives positively but with only mod-erate affective intensity. They were relatively low in introspection and dem-onstrated a high degree of self-acceptance. They also tended to be older than those in the other categories, generally in their eighties and nineties. This seemed to lend more credence to the idea that they had gone through a life review earlier and were "resolved." By contrast, the conflicted who were in an active life review tended to be in their seventies or sixties.

Interestingly, a category equivalent to the status of despairing did not emerge from the Chicago data analysis. It is hard to know what to make of this, other than that it is an infrequent state or status in old age. There were only 4 individuals in our initial sample of 104 who appeared to fit the de-scription of that status. They reminisced relatively frequently, but the flavor of the memories was more negative, with more evidence of the reparative or obsessive form. Their morale as well as self-concept measures were the low-est in the sample. Given this pattern, it is indeed fortunate that there were not more who fit that category.

There was another category in the Chicago study that did not resolve the ego integrity crisis. In fact, this group seemed to have managed to avoid it and to avoid a genuine life review. They were categorized as avoiding the past or "in flight" from the past, very much like the foreclosed status. They were low in frequency of reminiscence, generally claiming they did not care to think about the past. There was not only no evidence of an earlier life review but nothing to indicate any likelihood of one in the future. Thus, the term *foreclosed* might be more descriptive. They were rather bland or neutral in affect, and they seemed unpracticed in reflecting on their own emotional responses. They tended to avoid looking inward and tended to define themselves primarily in terms of their instrumental roles, as worker or homemaker, or of their external family responsibilities. Consequently, they recited the narrative of their lives with minimal affective involvement, frequently glossing over negative events.

On the other hand, this group had moderately high morale and self-concept measures. So they appear to have worked out a modus vivendi that they found acceptable and comfortable. However, they had rather poorly articulated expectations for the future and, in fact, were quite negative about the future. This is in sharp contrast to the resolved group, who had highly articulated expectations for the future. Still, if the primary criterion of adjustment in old age is strictly in terms of the present, the foreclosed or "in flight" were not doing badly. The most remarkable thing about them was their numbers. The Chicago investigators found that 51% of their sample fell into this category!

It also appears that this was the largest category, if not the majority, of our initial sample. That makes this a most interesting and perplexing group of older persons. They appear to have survived into old age without having contemplated the meaning of their past and future, even though they have experienced the loss of loved ones, valued roles, and physical capacities. It is a group that has not been given much attention in the gerontological literature but one that will be explored in considerable depth as this book progresses. The last of our three studies, the Integrity Survey, was specifically designed to take a look at the whole issue of ego integrity and to what extent the four identity statuses correspond to the lived experience of older persons as described by themselves in questionnaires and life-history interviews.

3

The Experience of Reminiscence

One of the most remarkable features of the group reminiscence sessions from the very beginning of that project was the different ways some participants would get in touch with and share their memories. When they were asked to think and tell about the past, it was clear that this represented a qualitatively different experience for some as compared to others. It frequently showed in their expressions, their postures, or some other bodily indicators but above all in the way they talked about it.

For some it was obviously a chore, something they did not particularly care to do initially, and they said this in just so many words. They were also clear that this was generally the way they felt about thinking or talking about their own past experiences. For others there was no hesitation about sharing memories, but the memories would have a congealed, static quality to them — all wrapped up and ready to deliver in rote form. For others the memories were readily available, and they were told in colorful and entertaining storied form. For still others there was a clear willingness and interest in getting in touch with and telling about those memories. However, it was evident that when these persons did so they had gotten in touch with something new or problematic about that past experience, and this affected how they were currently experiencing it and telling about it.

In order to get at this experiential dimension of reminiscence we used the Experiencing (EXP) Scale, which was mentioned in Chapter 1 (Klein et al., 1970). It is designed to evaluate the manifest content of oral communications, in either audiotaped or transcribed form, in terms of the experiencing dimension. The phenomenon of "experiencing" that the scale measures is the centerpiece of a process conception of personality functioning that led to a new way of assessing change in counseling and psychotherapy (Gendlin, Beebe, Cassens, Klein, & Oberlander, 1967). It was found that successful change in counseling and psychotherapy occurred when the client or patient was able to attend to and hold onto the direct inner referent of their experiencing of the clinical problem and to make this the basic datum of their communications about the problem in therapy. This experiencing was a bodily felt sense, or "gut feeling," about the problem that was precognitive and not yet thought out, as well as preverbal or not yet in words. This brief description of the concept will be expanded later; but even though the felt sense or felt meaning is not initially in words, it can be described in words if attended to and drawn upon. Furthermore, this process of attending to and communicating about this inner referent can be reliably identified by outside observers, whether they be clinical practitioners or researchers trained in detecting it in recorded language.

We found that the EXP Scale was very appropriate for evaluating reminiscence on this experiential dimension, and we found that project staff who were trained in the methodology could do this very effectively. There were high levels of agreement among the trained project staff members about at what particular level or rating on the seven-point scale any particular taped segment of reminiscence would fall. The project staff in the Chicago study also had high percentages of agreement in applying the EXP Scale and in ascertaining its validity in relation to scores on an affect questionnaire (Lieberman & Tobin, 1983).

LEVELS OF EXPERIENCING IN REMINISCENCE

The EXP Scale defines seven stages or levels of experiencing that represent the degree to which a person manifests inward reference in his or her verbalizations.[1] The person is referring inwardly when trying to describe his or her inner feelings and reactions and when searching for the meaning of the personal events, feelings and ideas he or she is reporting. At the bottom of the scale the person's recorded discourse is markedly impersonal, resistant, or superficial. Going up the scale, there is a progression from meager, limited, or externalized self-references to inwardly elaborated descriptions of feelings and thoughts associated with the felt sense or inner referent. When applied to reminiscence, this requires the listener to attend carefully to the verbal descriptions of the feelings, images, and thoughts associated with the specific memory or past experience.

An EXP rating of 1 is given for the lowest stage of experiencing, in which there is a refusal to participate or in which an event it described but no personal referent is used. The person might be telling an episode or event with which he or she is connected in some way but does not use himself or herself as a reference point. The content of the reminiscence would be about external events, or if personal, the events would be expressed verbally as though they could be happening to someone else, and they would be described in an impersonal or detached manner.

In the beginning of the group project it was quite common to hear responses like "I don't think back too much" or "I don't get involved in memo-ries" when participants were asked what they thought of when thinking about the past. If asked what their earliest childhood memory was, they might say something like "What's to tell? It's all a blur anyway." Or if the person did come up with a memory, it had no personal referents and would be a narrative of events describing what amounted to a public picture. This is illustrated in the following response to the question of whether the group participants could remember their first day in school: "Well, the usual. You know, you go to school and you see all those other kids. . . . That's the way it is in a one-room schoolhouse. You never see so many kids in one place at one time when you live out on a farm." Note the lack of a first person pro-noun, the "I" that would have owned it as a personal experience.

At Stage 2 there are personal referents as well as ownership of a personal role in the narrative, but it is told about events external to the self; that is, it is about what "happened" to the person and is told in behavioral or intellec-tual self-descriptive terms. To expand upon this, the reminiscer would es-tablish the association between the experience told and the self by the use of personal referents, but he or she would be involved in telling only the story and would not go beyond it. Any comments about the story would not contain personal reference but function only to "get the story across." Any emotions mentioned are described as part of the story, not of the reminis-cer, and are not elaborated beyond the level of pure description. There is no ownership of a personal *reaction* to the story.

A 79-year-old man in one of our conventional reminiscence groups de-scribed himself as someone who "always liked to tell stories." When asked about the first day at school his response was, "Sure, I remember my first day at school. It was in the Brownsville section of Brooklyn. There were lots of tough kids in that school because it was in a tough section. It wasn't bad, though, because I got to see . . . and meet . . . some famous fighters over the years. You know, I met Dempsey and Jim Jeffries . . . and I even got to talk to Jim after his fight with Dempsey." It was clear that he enjoyed this kind of reminiscing, and his manner of expression was less mechanical and more spontaneous than someone reminiscing in Stage 1 of the scale. He also used the personal referent "I," but it was mainly to indicate he was there and could therefore talk about the events "firsthand." There was no personal "ownership" of a personal inner response to the events. For example, he did not say something like "Was I excited! There I was, this little kid looking up at this huge guy [Jim Jeffries], this famous fighter. That was some thrill, I want to tell you!" This latter example indicates a definite personal response to the event, and it contains self-description as well as an involvement that implies some personal ownership of the event. This would be more illustra-tive of Stage 3, which will be covered next. However, this particular gentle-man did not appear to go above Stage 2 in his reminiscing within the group.

If he had, he would probably have been a more popular storyteller in his group. Most of the time the other participants listened to him with a polite interest.

Another example of reminiscing at EXP Stage 2 is the following: "I remember the time we went to Washington when I was a kid, and I remember the gaslights there. You know, I was brought up on a farm, and I never saw gaslights before." Here again, there is an interested description of the event that includes self-participation and the personal referent, but it is about an external event with self-reference for informational purposes only.

Stage 2 reminiscing can also be about much more weighty emotional events, but the treatment of the content and the expressivity keep it at this second stage of experiencing. Consider the following: "I remember when I lost a brother in the war. It took me a long time to get over it," from a woman who appeared depressed throughout most of the project. She initially indicated that she preferred not to think about the past—"I can think about it, but there's not much to say." Although she indicated that it took her a long time to get over her brother's death, she did not indicate what her feelings were when she was reportedly getting over it or what her current feelings were in response to recalling or telling it. This is not to say she did not *have* such feelings or that she *should* have expressed them, but the fact that she did not do so has a direct bearing on the actual experiencing in the moment. This point will become much clearer later in this chapter in the discussion of the phenomenology of experiencing and in Chapter 4 in the discussion of the role of language in reminiscing.

The third level of experiencing, which is given a rating of 3 on the EXP Scale, consists of personal reactions to external events, with limited self-descriptions and behavioral descriptions of feelings. Events and experiences are described and expressed in a reactive, emotionally involved manner. In terms of reminiscing, expressions of personal and "owned" feelings are used as parenthetical comments in the narration of the memory. The feelings are still tied completely to the remembered situations in which they arose or remain unelaborated in terms of deeper personal meaning or significance. The affective involvement in the memory *does* go beyond specific content but bypasses deeper meanings.

The following anecdote was told by a widow who was born and raised on a farm in Massachusetts. In an early session of an experiential group she recalled having taken her husband and children to the farm. She said, "When I took my family there, it was a terrible disappointment. I'm sorry I ever went back to see it. I dig it out of my mind." Here she was being quite reactive and emotionally involved in the telling of it. She was giving her reaction to an external event (trip to the farm), and she indicated degrees of feeling in her behavioral description of her reactions as "terrible disappointment" and feeling "sorry." If she had elaborated on or explored these feelings beyond the behavioral labels of "disappointment" and "sorry" to express what the feelings were like then, or what they are like now in recalling the event, she would have moved from Stage 3 to another level of experiencing. But the content of the reminiscence was a group discussion on the topic of negative memories that get mixed in with positive ones. Therefore, she might have felt constrained by the group context not to elaborate on the feelings and to pass by any possible deeper meanings of the event within a life-span perspective.

The following example of Stage 3 was told by a woman who often reminisced about the pleasant times she had with her family as a child. They used to go for picnic lunches to various parks just about every Sunday. She told of remembering one particular park on one particular Sunday. She recalled that it was a beautiful park with a small zoo and some animals the children could feed, pet, or ride. She said, "I remember my father put me on a donkey, and I started to scream. But later on I was so thrilled to see a deer! I remember what a wonderful feeling it was to see such a lovely animal so close to me . . . and to feed it!" This experiencing of the memory of the deer was clearly at Level 3, because she elaborated on her feelings associated with the event in an expressive and reactive manner. The donkey episode, however, was at Level 2 because she simply gave the behavioral description, "I started to scream" without elaboration.

Stage 4 of the EXP Scale contains primarily descriptions of personal experiences and the feelings associated with them. This content is treated in a self-descriptive and associative manner. In terms of reminiscence, the person communicates what it is like to *be* him or her in the telling of the past event or experience. This could be done in several ways. There could be fluid expression of many feelings or expression of one feeling with time spent in elaborating on it in terms of significance for self-image. Or it could be specific expression of the fact that the feelings exist but that help is required to express them.

An example of Stage 4 experiencing was given by a retired businessman who was a participant in one of the reminiscence groups in the Jewish Community Center. He appeared to be grappling with a number of issues, and his affect and morale were quite negative. He seemed to fit the "dissonant" status in terms of the ego integrity types. He made the following summary comments about the past: "I don't look back with any nostalgia. I don't think the past was very wonderful. . . . There was disease, polio, and so on. The mothers struggled . . . the fathers struggled. . . ." Then he began to reminisce about a painful episode in his life:

> It was terrible when my daughter joined the Hari Krishnas. It was an awful time. . . . She didn't seem to know what she wanted. I'd talk to her; I'd plead with her with tears in my eyes. Trying to listen . . . trying to understand . . .

but it made me feel worse, because no matter what she explained to me I felt
. . . what? . . . I guess hopeless . . . because she sounded all mixed up. She finally married a black. It was a horrible experience because I thought I had
lost her. I used to read to try to figure out and understand the cult. . . . I'm
busy now. I only look back to understand the present.

There are several features that give this an EXP rating of 4. It is very descriptive of his feelings and it is an intensely personal experience. His han-
dling of the content was not only self-descriptive but it was associative in
the fluid expression of feelings in relation to happenings, beliefs, and relationships. He also gives some indication of difficulty or needing help to express some of these associated feelings and thoughts. Also, it is very clear
that the affective involvement goes beyond the specific episode in his life
and that this episode contains issues and meanings that remain unresolved
in the present.

It is also clear that there are life-review issues in this man's reminiscing,
particularly when he says, "I only look back to understand the present."
One can literally *hear* the association between the experiencing level in the
reminiscence with the life review, with his self-concept (as a troubled and
"unsuccessful" father), and his level of morale. The statistical association between EXP ratings, self-concept measures, and morale levels as well as their
changes over the testing periods of the project provided quantitative and
objective evidence of the importance of the experiencing concept and measure in understanding reminiscing and related late-life transitional issues.
This will be illustrated still further in the following sample of reminiscing
from Mrs. A., the woman described in Chapter 2 who went through a life-
review experience in the course of the group project and the subsequent
coping group in the new apartment setting. Much of the grief work described in Chapter 2 was at EXP Stage 4, which is true in general of much
of the experiencing of grief and mourning.

After having gone through that, Mrs. A. began reminiscing about experiences closer, temporally and spatially, to her current life situation. She recalled the experience of moving into her new apartment:

Moving in here was a tough thing. I can remember I really felt bad . . . really
down. I didn't like doing things in it all by myself. . . . But why did that bother
me so much? I had to take care of the house all by myself after my husband
died, but that didn't have the same bad feeling about doing things by myself.
Was it because that was *my* place? I know it didn't feel as bad as doing things
alone in a whole new place. It did feel strange. . . . It was a strange place, and
I think that made me feel more alone.

This description began at EXP Stage 4 as she was elaborating on the bad
feeling of doing things all alone in her new apartment. Then she saw that as

somewhat problematic and started raising questions about it in her description. At that point she had moved to Stage 5 on the EXP Scale. Such movement, by the way, was quite common within sessions but usually at lower EXP levels in the Group Project. That is why two EXP scores were given for each taped segment of reminiscing. One was the highest EXP level reached, called the *peak score*, while the most frequently occurring score within the segment was called the *mode*. This was consistent with use of the EXP Scale in psychotherapy research as well.

Stage 5 on the scale consists of problems or propositions about feelings and personal experiences, not just the description of the feelings and experiences themselves. This is done in an exploratory, elaborative, and hypothetical manner. This was true of Mrs. A.'s segment above, where she raised a question or problem about her feeling and then proceeded to offer hypotheses or propositions for why the feeling was the way it was.

This would be true of some reminiscing at this level, such as cases of exploration and elaboration of *one* feeling area and its personal significance. Another variation at Stage 5 would be where many situations are examined in terms of common feelings or the significance involved. A third variation would be exploration of one situation or aspect of self-image involving many feelings and their potential relationship. This latter variation was also experienced by Mrs. A. at another point when she was reminiscing about the aftermath of the mastectomy, when she felt like only "part of a person." In that she recalled thinking, "Now I'm not only a widow but not even an attractive widow." Needless to say, her self-concept measure had dropped at that time, as did her morale index when she began dealing with her losses in the group just prior to the end of the project and the beginning of the coping group. So the pattern we saw quantitatively in the statistical analysis of data and qualitatively in person as participant-observers in group life-review experiences like Mrs. A.'s was the following: At the beginning of the project reminiscing was at EXP Stage 1 or 2 concurrent with a relatively good self-concept measure and morale index, and participants appeared to fit the foreclosed status. Although there was some initial reluctance or concern about engaging in reminiscence, this dissipated somewhat in the camaraderie of the group process as the participants intentionally engaged only in positive reminiscence and memory-sharing. However, as they began to get in touch with negative and unresolved issues in going through the structured format of life stages in the group reminiscing, their EXP ratings began to have modes of 4 and sometimes peaks of 5, but their self-concept and morale measures dropped concomitantly. Later these latter two measures rose, indicating that the negative affect and mood associated with conflictual life-review reminiscing was transient.

It is interesting to compare this pattern with that of those who did not evidence a life-review experience. It began the same with EXP ratings of 1 or

2 and moderately positive self-concept and morale measures. The EXP ratings went up to 2 or 3 as participants selectively engaged in positive reminiscing and enjoyed the group process Their self-concept and morale measures went up somewhat and were higher (though not significantly) at the posttest. Unlike the participants who experienced a life review, however, their morale and self-concept measures later went back toward the old moderate pretest levels.

It might be instructive to make a brief comparison with another woman in Mrs. A.'s group, who did not evidence a life-review experience and who chose not to enter the coping group that was being formed. At the pretest she said, "I don't think much about the past. You try to block things. . . . I don't like those feelings." After the first session she did start to engage in selective positive reminiscing and enjoyed the group experience and the friendships she made. At the time of the follow-up test she said, "I concentrate only on the good things. I live for today." This pretty much sums up her strategy for coping in late life. She appears to be avoiding crisis and maintaining a foreclosed status. This seemed to be working for her, if we are to take her self-report measures of morale and self-concept at face value. It is an interesting and apparently common pattern of adjustment to late life and one that will be explored much more fully later in the book.

The fourth level of experiencing appeared to be the fulcrum around which life-review issues were handled, both in group and in individual sessions. Stage 5 was much rarer in groups, with only one person in the whole sample attaining that as a modal score. Five persons, including Mrs. A., achieved a peak EXP of 5 at least once in the course of the group project. Although one person had a peak rating of 6 at least once, not one person had a modal rating of 6 in the group project. This could have been because of the public nature of the group format. However, EXP ratings of 6 and 7 are quite rare, even in cases of extended psychotherapy (Klein, Mathieu-Coughlan, & Kiesler, 1986). Nevertheless, it is important that these upper levels of experiencing be described here so that the reader has a sense of the full potential range of this phenomenon in its operational form on the EXP Scale.

To describe these upper stages of experiencing adequately, it is necessary to go back to the fulcrum or pivotal point on this experiential continuum, which is Stage 4 on the EXP Scale. What happens at that point is a distinct move inward on the part of the person. It represents a shift from "self-as-object to self-as-subject (Rogers, 1958). When this happens, the *experiencing* of events is the subject of discourse rather than the events themselves. This requires the person to try to hold onto inner referents or the bodily feeling of the problem while trying to talk about it. By simultaneously attending to and presenting this experiencing the person communicates what it is like to be him or her. However, these inner views are just presented or described rather than being the focus for purposeful self-exploration or elaboration.

At Stage 5 there is a purposeful exploration of these feelings in which the person poses a question, problem, or proposition about the self in terms of those feelings. Further, the exploration must be focused on the inner felt referent as this is related to the initial question or proposition so as to expand the person's awareness of that experiencing.

At Stage 6 there is a new sense about the inner referent, and it begins to take on a life of its own. It is more than recognizable feelings such as fear, anger, sadness, or joy. There is a felt sense of potentially more than can be thought or named by those feelings. There is a sense of a larger whole or new perspective, of which those feelings are only part and which they only inadequately represent.

At Stage 7 the person demonstrates an expanding awareness of immediate feelings and internal processes, moving from one inner referent to another connecting them and integrating them in the here-and-now. Each new sensing and felt meaning leads to further exploration and elaboration.

It should be readily apparent why these upper levels did not occur in the group reminiscing. At Stage 5 the person is turned inward, speaking in a groping, halting way to get at the inner feelings and referent. This means there are moments of silence and halting efforts to describe the inner processes. This is hardly conducive to smooth discourse among people in a social situation. Even at Stage 6 there will be silent spots while the person attempts to read off or lift off the felt meanings in forming the words. Stage 7 represents the culmination of a transformative process marked by new insights and perspective. It is thus one of those relatively rare breakthroughs, even in extended psychotherapy, in knowing about one's self and one's existential state of being.

Perhaps the best way of making these upper EXP levels clear is by illustrating them through an example of someone who has experienced them. This will be done later in this chapter with a case illustration of a depressed elderly man in life-review therapy, but before going into specific applications it would be well at this point to present the philosophical and theoretical background of the experiential approach that underlies not only the specifics of the EXP Scale but also the concept and method of experiential focusing. This has particular relevance for the application of reminiscence in practice and for an understanding of the language of reminiscence as it is presented in Chapter 4.

THE PHENOMENOLOGY OF EXPERIENCE IN REMINISCENCE

The term *experiential phenomenology* refers to a phenomenological approach developed by Eugene Gendlin (1973), a philosopher, psychologist, and psychotherapist who currently teaches in the Department of Behavioral Sciences at the University of Chicago. His approach has been most heavily influenced by the French philosopher and phenomenologist Maurice Merleau-Ponty. Like William James and Edmund Husserl, Merleau-Ponty called for the study of phenomena as given in direct experience, stating that this should take precedence in any sustained scientific endeavor. He proposed that the body is at the center of our experience of the world and of our being-in-the-world. The body is not only at the center of our being-in-the-world, it is a reservoir of knowledge or "knowing." "The ontological world and body which we find at the core of the subject are not the world or body as idea, but . . . the body itself as a knowing-body" (Merleau-Ponty, 1962). Through the "lived body" there is an accumulation and sedimentation of experience at a tacit, nonconscious bodily level that invariably affects our perceptions of phenomena. It would therefore be necessary to get at this preconceptual "knowing" in order to begin with as open and unfettered a perception or experiencing of phenomena as possible. Merleau-Ponty also saw the need to reflect upon this type of perception. He proposed that the immediate perception or experiencing represents the spontaneous aspect of consciousness (the world os sensations, impressions, etc.) but that there is also a "world of thoughts" in our consciousness. This latter world is "a sediment left by our mental processes, which enables us to rely on our concepts and acquired judgments as we might on things there in front of us, presented globally, without there being any need for us to re-synthesize them. . . . The world-structure,, with its two stages of sedimentation and spontaneity, is at the core of consciousness" (Merleau-Ponty, 1962).

The question or dilemma in this formulation became one of how a person could both experience (spontaneously as subject) and yet reflect upon that same experience as object if this whole process is embodied. Eugene Gendlin's experiential phenomenology was aimed directly at this question.

Gendlin uses the term *experiencing* to describe what is commonly referred to among phenomenologists as "lived experience." This is a sense of what is going on at every moment that is felt but is not yet in words. The way to approach this lived experience phenomenologically is to allow a return to it in an open way, by what Merleau-Ponty called "inhabiting" it or through an "indwelling," as Polanyi (1966) described it. However, because of the nature of lived experience any return to it is momentary and elusive. It is difficult to grasp and hold onto because its presence is subjectively sensed or felt rather than being objectively and consciously present in our thought, so in order to describe it we must leave it to reflect on it cognitively. The point here is that we *do* want to describe it because it is only tacit or implicit knowing until it is made explicit.

Most of us pay no attention to it, and it remains tacit because there is usually no compelling reason to make it explicit. There may be a need for it when one is experiencing a state of affective distress that has not been connected in consciousness with some event or situation, or if the affect seems inexplicable in its intensity. What is missing here is a conscious meaning for what one is experiencing. In his seminal work on the phenomenology of experience, *Experiencing and the Creation of Meaning*, Gendlin (1962) made the point that it is necessary for people to go beyond the experiencing of gross, undifferentiated emotions if there is to be any meaningful change or movement in their intrapersonal lives. He notes that "meaning is *formed* in the interaction of experiencing and something that functions symbolically. Feeling without symbolization is blind; symbolization without feeling is empty."

Beneath the emotion, and larger than it, is a felt meaning that is sensed on a "concrete bodily level" but is experienced only in a bodily way, as preconceptual undifferentiated felt-mass of many aspects. An example of how this could occur in the context of a discussion should help to make this clearer. After listening to others for awhile we may feel the impulse to speak, and we "know" we have a point to make, but we do not yet have it in words. It is tacit, and our sense of it is already lodged in a concrete, bodily felt way. Then when we do talk, usually tentatively at first (some indwelling here), it becomes clear that we did indeed have a point that we "knew" all along. This happened quite frequently, in fact, with some participants in the reminiscence groups. They would be listening intently to someone else reminiscing on, say, what it felt like and what it meant to go on your first date. When the opportunity came to speak, some would begin in a halting way, reaching for the words that would capture what they had experienced and what the *felt* meaning of it was.

This felt meaning or tacit knowing can go far beyond these relatively common or mundane experiences to include such phenomena as the creative "hunches" that lead to scientific discoveries. Michael Polanyi (1966), an eminent physical chemist, posits a structure of knowledge in which tacit knowing is more fundamental than explicit knowing. He says this is a knowing that is prior to and occasionally beyond our "telling" of it, and we know it by "dwelling" in it.

To get back to the original problem of making lived experience explicit through a description of it, Gendlin delineated what he saw as the process by which this can occur. At any given moment we can be having a felt meaning or tacit knowing, and when we focus our attention on it, words can come from it. When we focus on the bodily felt meaning, it can select symbols (usually words but also images) that express, formulate, and explicate it. As he describes it, "symbols present themselves" and "words come to us" (Gendlin, 1962). This process he calls explication, and it is a subtle transformational linguistic process that will be described in greater detail in Chapter 4 under "The Language of Reminiscence."

Gendlin delineated this process, as well as his general conceptualization of the experiencing construct, in a paper entitled "Experiential Phenomenology (1973)." Shortly thereafter he elaborated upon and operationalized this construct for application in counseling and psychotherapy under the designation "experiential focusing," which is distinctly phenomenological in its origins and procedures. Initially, the experiencing construct was operationalized and tested by Gendlin and others in the Psychotherapy Research Group at the University of Wisconsin, from which the EXP Scale emerged (Gendlin & Tomlinson, 1967). Gendlin worked in close collaboration with Carl Rogers in the research group, and Rogers later identified Gendlin's experiencing construct as essential to the development of his own process formulation of human personality and change in psychotherapy. In fact, the seven stages on the EXP Scale are isomorphic with Rogers's seven process stages of personality growth and therapeutic change (Rogers, 1980).

The investigators in the group studied various theoretical approaches to psychotherapy, including client-centered, psychodynamic, and behavioral, with psychiatric inpatients and outpatients. They found that, regardless of theoretical approach, the essential element in the successful cases they studied occurred when the patients were able to attend to and hold onto the direct inner referent, or felt meaning, of the problems they were experiencing. This element also included their being able to make this felt sense or meaning the basic datum of their verbal communications about the problems in their therapeutic sessions. Gendlin extracted this essential element and developed a procedure consisting of six steps, or movements, for teaching the patient how to focus on this direct inner referent, or body sense, of an experience. These steps represented the process of experiential focusing and became more widely known as the therapeutic method of "focusing" (Gendlin, 1981).

Some of these steps were presented in Chapter 1 as we adapted them for use in the experiential reminiscence groups. At this point, however, it might be helpful to present a case illustration. This is the case of a person who began in a reminiscence group but who soon opted for individual life-review therapy as well because of a personal crisis he was experiencing at that time. I have chosen to call this experiential life-review therapy because it incorporates the full six-step experiential focusing procedure developed by Gendlin.

EXPERIENTIAL LIFE-REVIEW THERAPY

The case that has been chosen for illustrative purposes came from the very first reminiscence group in which we had attempted to incorporate the focusing procedure (Sherman, 1985b). Although I had often used reminiscence as a major adjunct to group work with the elderly prior to this, the focusing procedure was incorporated here as a pilot effort to test its viability for the development of experiential reminiscence groups in preparation for the Group Project that was later funded and implemented. The group was co-led by me and a second-year graduate social work student who had prior experience in working with the elderly.

The setting for this pilot group was an adult home that had private rooms for elderly individuals and couples and that provided communal meals for its ambulatory and well-oriented residents. The gentleman in the case illustration was Mr. K., a 71-year-old divorced man of Irish-American ancestry who had gone directly to this home from an inpatient psychiatric facility where he had been treated for depression over a four-week period. His psychiatrist at that facility strongly recommended that he participate in the reminiscence group when she learned that one was getting started. Although depressed and not very optimistic about its potential helpfulness, Mr. K. had no hesitancy about volunteering for the group, and his psychiatrist continued to monitor his progress throughout the duration of his participation in both group and individual therapy.

Mr. K. had been divorced many years ago, and all three of his adult children and their families lived out of state, so he had no family in the immediate area. Although he had been born and had spent his childhood in the area, he had only just recently returned to it on his retirement after being away for all of his adult years. He found that several of his old friends had died or had left, and he had not been able to reestablish some of his old friendships before he was struck with illness and a set of misfortunes leading to his current depression and state of crisis. He was feeling quite isolated, and he saw the reminiscence group as at least a chance to socialize and get to know others.

The group was made up of six persons ranging in age from 64 to 78 years and consisting of four women and two men. One of the women had also been recently discharged from the psychiatric facility where Mr. K. had been a patient. All six participants volunteered for the group, and all had been identified by the professional staff at the home as persons who could benefit from a group experience. They were introduced to the focusing procedure as described in Chapter 1. That is, it began in the third session, and they were asked to focus first on a happy memory of a place, possession, or thing—anything that would give them a pleasurable feeling. They were then asked to describe where and how they experienced this feeling in their bodies. This is usually experienced as a pleasant feeling of warmth or fullness in the stomach or lower chest area, and this was true for these participants as well. They were, of course, asked not to think about persons or pets in those first two sessions so as not to evoke painful memories of loss and sadness.

A full description of the six steps of the focusing procedure will be given now, and then we will take a look at how these operated in Mr K.'s case.

These steps or structured tasks seem a bit mechanical at first, but they begin to flow into one another in a more natural way as one gains more experience, and it becomes a process rather than a procedure. This is how the steps are taught sequentially to groups or individuals.[2]

Step 1, "clearing a space." The person is asked to relax as completely as possible and to take a moment to be silent within herself or himself. A relaxation technique, such as taking three or four deep breaths to let the tension flow out, helps. It also helps to rest the full weight of arms, torsos, and legs on the chair and floor, respectively. Then the person is asked to pay attention inwardly and to focus on a spot in the body where he or she tends to "feel" things the most. This is usually the stomach, chest, or throat. This can be done with the eyes open or closed, whatever the person prefers. The person is then instructed to ask silently and inwardly, "How are things going with me?" or "What is between me and feeling fine?" They are asked not to answer immediately but to sense what comes in the body and to allow the answer to come from that sensing. Usually, a current concern, worry, or preoccupation comes in conjunction with a bodily discomfort—a palpitation in the chest, a gripping in the stomach, and so on. The person is asked not to go into the concern or problem but to put it off at a distance—perhaps on an imaginary shelf nearby, in the corner of the room, or an arm's length away—wherever the person will not feel overwhelmed by it but where it will be acknowledged. This is an inner imaging act of distancing oneself from the issue but keeping it within range for possible attention and work in the immediate or near future. Ordinarily the person will have several worries, and he or she will be asked to put each one of them aside until there are no more bodily sensed problems left.

Step 2, the "felt sense." The person selects one of the problems that came from the bodily sensing in the first step. The person is instructed not to go inside the problem but to try to feel the unclear sense of the "whole of it." Even though there may be many aspects to the problem, it is best to get a full sense of these as a whole, as a gestalt. Frequently, people will have automatic thoughts that come to mind immediately, such as "There's that old guilty feeling again" or "How could I be so stupid as to do that?" These are usually habitual self-criticisms, self-analyses, or self-talk that the person characteristically engages in. They usually make things worse rather than better, so the person is asked to ignore them and get back to the vague sense of the whole problem. The person might be asked to spend at least one full minute on this step so as not to mistake the automatic self-talk for the bodily felt sense of the problem.

In work with individuals it is often the case that one central problem emerges in the course of reminiscing, and it becomes a continuing issue from one session to another. In such cases it is best to begin each time with the second step, getting a "felt sense," because that problem preoccupies the person and preempts all others. However, in highly active life-review processes there are often many memories crowding in on one another in reminiscing, and they are usually all problematic. So it is best to start with the first step each time because the distancing technique of "clearing a space" acknowledges the problems but gives the person "breathing space" between them. It allows the person to hold in abeyance memories or past issues loaded with anxiety, rage, guilt, sadness, and other emotions, without undue distress, while working on the most pressing issue of the moment.

Step 3, "getting a handle." This step is aimed at identifying the *quality* of the unclear, bodily felt sense of the problem. This is done by asking the person to let a word, phrase, or image come from the felt sense, and usually this is a word with a sensory quality such as "wound-up," "tight," "heavy," "jumpy," "scary," and so on. The person may try several of these words to capture the right quality of the felt sense and should be asked which quality word or "handle" fits best. Usually, the person experiences a slight bodily shift or release that indicates to him or her that the handle is right.

Step 4, "resonating." The person is asked to go back and forth between the quality word, phrase, or image and the felt sense to see if they match and resonate with one another. The person does this by asking inwardly, "Is that right?" If it is, there should be slight feeling of release or relief. If the handle and the felt sense match, the person is asked to resonate, to have the sensation of matching several times. Should the felt sense change, the person is asked to follow it and to allow the quality word(s) or image to change with it until there is a good match or fit.

Step 5, "asking." In this step the person asks inwardly, "What is it about this whole problem that makes me feel this [quality word(s) or image]?" Sometimes the "whole" problem seems so large and overwhelming that the person cannot get a whole sense of it, in which case the person should ask inwardly, "What is the worst part of it?" If the bodily felt sense can respond to that question, the next one would be "What does it need?" or "What should happen next?" In this step and all others the quick and automatic thoughts should be ignored in favor of the felt sense, and that sense will usually be accompanied by a felt bodily shift, a sense of slight "give," or release.

Step 6, "receiving." The person is asked to receive or welcome what came from the prior steps. It should be accepted in an open and appreciative way for whatever change or movement it brought about, however slight. It should be seen as just one step in an ongoing process that can be returned to at any time for further focusing. It is important that the person be asked to protect whatever came, for the critical voices or automatic self-talk might impede the process. Then the person is asked to remain awhile with whatever came, in silence, and to come out of that state whenever it is comfortable. It is sometimes the case that a solution or a direction for dealing with a problem can be found in one sitting, which may take anywhere from 10 to 20 minutes in beginning personal or professional practice with focusing. However, as the process becomes more natural and less mechanical, it can be done in a couple of brief minutes in just about any setting that allows for some degree of privacy.

Mr. K. began this procedure in the reminiscence group but mastered it and used it to a far greater extent in conjunction with his individual therapy sessions. Also, the life-span format was handled in the group, and issues that arose with respect to different life stages were then handled in his individual sessions. It should be reiterated that all of the other group members also had acknowledged, and were identified by staff as, experiencing psychosocial adjustment problems in their lives and in their new environment of the adult home. Therefore, in order to explore the potential therapeutic value of incorporating experiential focusing in a reminiscence group format for such persons, several assessment instruments were used to measure for possible changes from pre- to posttreatment testings for all six group participants. These instruments included measures of depression, anxiety, and self-esteem, which were the primary self-identified problems of the participants (Zung, 1965; Spielberger, Gorsuch, & Lushene, 1970; Rosenberg, 1979).

Although Mr. K. was referred to the group primarily because of his depression, he showed an exceptionally high degree of anxiety in the pretest assessment. The assessment also showed that he was indeed clinically depressed and that his self-esteem was quite low, as would be expected in a state of depression. He seemed to have no difficulty participating in the first group session, which consisted of getting acquainted, some round-robin discussion, and some beginning sharing of positive memories. He was able to share some positive childhood memories, but they were strongly tinged with a depressed feeling of longing and loss.

It was in the second group session that he began experiencing difficulty, and his anxiety came to the fore. Although the participants were asked to reminisce about positive experiences, Mr. K. became very upset by a negative memory that intruded itself into his efforts at positive reminiscence. It was the memory of abdominal surgery he had undergone six months earlier. He winced and felt his stomach as he related the memory, and this was followed by his recollection of the fact that he had been diagnosed as having a heart murmur shortly after the abdominal surgery. Although he had difficulty articulating the distress he was feeling, he could not seem to stop trying. He would say, "I can't tell you the awful feelings I get whenever I think about that [the surgery]," but "I can't stop thinking about it." He kept returning to this subject during the second, third, and fourth group sessions, even though the group was memory-sharing mostly about childhood experiences. This represented an obsessive and morbid type of reminiscence that was not rational since Mr. K. had already been given a clean bill of health for both conditions on the basis of extensive subsequent medical tests.

It was clear that Mr. K. was stuck and could not attend to what was being shared in the group. It has been recommended that in such cases the practitioner should concentrate completely on the person's problematic experience wherein "the goal should not be to cut off the obsessive reminiscence completely, but rather to focus it so that it can be used in the healing process until it is no longer needed" (Lo Gerfo, 1980–81). The best way to do this so as not to detract from the group process was to work with Mr. K. individually. Consequently, he was seen individually after the fourth group session on a weekly basis, concurrent with the group, for the remaining 12 weeks of the pilot project. These individual sessions quickly evolved into intensive life-review therapy.

Since he had already been introduced to the first steps of the focusing procedure in the group, Mr. K. began the first individual therapy session by attempting to focus on his obsessive preoccupation by using the second step — that is, by trying to get the "felt sense" of the problem. When he tried to get a sense of the "whole thing," he found it too big and too overwhelming, so he was asked to focus on the part of it that caused him the greatest distress. He was then able to get a felt sense of part of it as a "burning and grinding" sensation in the back of his stomach. He was able to progress through the remaining steps of the procedure with guidance while, by his own choice, keeping his eyes closed and remaining silent except for nods of acknowledgment when he had completed each of the steps.

When he opened his eyes, he reported that he became aware through the bodily felt sense that the burning sensation was associated with the intense pain and anxiety he had experienced when his gall bladder burst and he had to undergo emergency surgery. After saying this he began to relate the whole story, or series of episodes, leading to his current state of emotional distress, something he had not been able to do in the group. As he noted later, he experienced the telling of this story as an "unwinding of all the tension" he was feeling in the back of his stomach.

He related a series of events in his narrative that were marked by demoralizing experiences with the medical profession in terms of misinformation and life-threatening misdiagnoses. It began when the severe abdominal pain he had been feeling was misdiagnosed by several doctors as a manifestation of a lower back problem he had suffered from for several years. It was in fact an infection of the gall bladder. Since the infection was overlooked, it proceeded to fester, and the gall bladder burst. When he underwent the emergency surgery it was necessary for the surgeons to remove large sections of his intestines because of the damage caused by the perforation of the gall bladder. He was so upset by the trauma of that experience that he became extremely suspicious of the doctors and came to believe that they had removed so much from his intestines because he really had cancer. He felt the doctors were lying to him when they gave the perforated gall bladder as the explanation for such extensive abdominal surgery. He felt that the grinding sensation he experienced in the upper back of his stomach during the focusing was associated with his fear of cancer. He added, though, that this felt sense was also associated with and compounded by the fear he experienced when, shortly after the gall bladder surgery, he was told that it looked as though he had a murmur of the heart, even though further tests were required to confirm it.

When he received that information, he "went crazy." He left the doctor's office in a thoroughly confused state of mind and walked aimlessly into a nearby park that had a deep gorge running through it. He found himself walking up to the edge of the gorge in a state of such distress and discouragement that he had every intention of committing suicide. He recalled trying to push himself off the edge of the gorge with his legs, but one of them slipped and he suddenly "got scared" and stopped himself from going off the edge at the last split-second. He thought it was crazy that he got scared since he wanted to die anyway. He was not sure even at the time of this narrative whether he really intended to commit suicide, but once he kept himself from going over the edge, he was sure he wanted to get help with his problems. He voluntarily signed himself into the psychiatric inpatient unit of a local general hospital as an acknowledged attempted suicide.

When he was through telling this story in the first individual session, he started to describe his experience in using the focusing steps. He called it "strange," but once he got the bodily felt sense, he really did "get a handle on the problem a kind of perspective." This helped him to gain some insight and deal with the irrational anxiety and ideas associated with the problem. However, it also seemed to activate a whole set of new issues that he felt needed to be dealt with. There were strong, unarticulated feelings about these issues as well as the unrelieved depression. Consequently, in each of the remaining individual sessions he would go through the first focusing step of "clearing a space" and would metaphorically put each of the remaining issues "on the shelf" until he could get to them.

When describing his feelings before "clearing a space," he used the expression "I feel like I'm in a whole bunch of little pieces." Then, smiling, he pointed to his stomach and said, "Even though not all the pieces are there anymore." This was the first touch of humor he had exhibited in either group or individual sessions, but he went on to say, "A lot of other pieces are not there any more—childhood gone, children gone, broken marriage, old friends . . . lots of pieces." Then he proceeded to tell how homesick he was for the town of his childhood (Troy, New York) in the period just preceding his retirement. He described thinking and looking back nostalgically to all of the friends, family, and places he knew and loved in the town. So when he retired he did come back, and that turned out to be one of the saddest experiences of his life: "When I came back here, it all seemed so different . . . the old friends mostly dead or gone . . . all the close relatives. It really tore me apart. . . . The old places just didn't seem the same without them."

Then in rapid succession he went through each of these "pieces" in the remaining individual work. Since he kept coming back to these remaining issues, or pieces, the first focusing step of clearing a space was becoming a more and more effective and reassuring practice for him, which he used on his own outside individual and group sessions. Almost all of the painful working through of his experienced losses was done in individual therapy, although his painful nostalgia was very evident in the early group sessions. In focusing on and talking about this nostalgia he came to realize he was already depressed before the gall bladder surgery and misdiagnosed heart murmur. They were just the events that almost pushed him "over the edge."

While in this depressed state he was feeling that he had been a failure as a husband and father. He saw the divorce as proof of his failure, and although he was no longer a practicing Catholic, he was experiencing a lot of guilt about it. He also had strong regrets concerning the fact that he was not as close to his children as he could have been. He was now feeling that time was too short to make up for these deficits, one of the features of Erikson's definition of despair in old age. He did indeed claim to be in despair at the time of his suicide attempt. However, each of these regrets was now coming up as a reactivated issue for work in a fully engaged life-review process. They were no longer dead weight from the past; they were acknowledged, being worked on, or put on the shelf until they could shortly be dealt with.

In the second-to-last session of his individual therapy his focusing work consisted of animated verbal reflections on the different "pieces" that had been covered, with brief periods of silent focusing in between. Then he began associating these pieces with one another very much in the manner of EXP Stage 7, as will be discussed shortly. At any rate, he felt that he was integrating these previously disparate pieces into a more balanced view of his life. He said:

> It's funny, but I can get a kind of distance from these things, and then they begin to fall in place and make some sense. Actually, it [his family situation] wasn't all that bad. I still exchange letters and phone calls with my wife from time to time; we're still friends—and my kids keep in touch. Each of them visits me or has me for a visit once or twice a year. They don't seem to resent me.

Within the group he was engaging in less nostalgia and in more positive and pleasurable reminiscing. Much of this consisted of memories from what he felt was a happy childhood and adolescence. Additionally, he shared many memories of the adventures, misadventures, and camaraderie he had experienced as a deputy sheriff in a northern New York county bordering on Canada. He was a colorful and witty storyteller who began to get, and give, a good deal of pleasure out of telling action-filled episodes of chases and confrontations to and fro between the U.S. and Canadian borders.

It is worth discussing this shift from nostalgia to positive reminiscing in light of what Castelnuovo-Tedesco (1980) has termed as the "pathological" nature of nostalgia:

> It is basically a regressive state and a form of depression. . . . Nostalgia contains, in addition to an acute longing and idealization of the past and the realization that the past [and the loved object] are gone forever and inexorably. The feeling tone, which is bittersweet, at times even laceratingly painful ["It tears the heart," etc.], is bathed in conflict.

This is certainly highly descriptive of Mr. K.'s earlier state, and the following is equally descriptive of his later state:

> By contrast, during reminiscence the mood may be neutral or even joyful, as one savors the finding that the past has not vanished but is still available and serviceable. . . . Moreover, there is pleasure and satisfaction in the spontaneous exercise of one's memory which, in these instances, is a resilient and conflict-free activity. (Castelnuovo-Tedesco, 1980)

It certainly appears that Castelnuovo-Tedesco's psychoanalytic interpretation of the difference between reminiscence and nostalgia holds in Mr. K.'s situation. The only qualification I would make is that, given the working definition of reminiscence in this study, these are two different kinds of reminiscence rather than two distinctly different phenomena. This is not to dispute the qualitative significance of the difference, which was certainly evident in this case.

At the same time that Mr. K. was reminiscing so positively in the group, he was experiencing what he called a "breakthrough" in allowing the various conflicts and issues to connect and "fall into place." As a matter of fact, his use of figurative language instead of concrete terms (sad, guilty, angry, etc.) was indication that he was experiencing the issues at a higher level on the EXP Scale. Prior to this, he said, "I was stuck in each of these things [issues, pieces]. No matter where I turned I was blocked off. I had the feeling that if I made the connections between them I would crash . . . completely. It was an awful feeling."

He used these figurative expressions, "stuck," "blocked off," "tore me apart," "whole bunch of little pieces," initially as words or phrases, not as full sentences or thoughts. They came first in the form of isolated words and images ("handles") in the focusing process. These expressions are very characteristic of EXP Stage 6. What was needed by Mr. K. was a way (or perspective) to experience all of these disjointed, dissonant pieces and to integrate them. This is the essence of EXP Stage 7, where there is a whole set of felt senses that provide the linkage between what is said and the next thing said. The thematic unity is provided by this mode of moving from one thing to another while attending to the felt sense.

The fact that Mr. K. reached Stage 7 does not mean he reached a state or status of ego integrity The experiencing of Stages 6 and 7 is quite infrequent, as noted before, even in extended psychotherapy, although it is more apt to occur toward the end of therapy However, the person usually goes back to a lower EXP level, say 3 or 4, by the end of each session as well as by the end of therapy itself.

By the time Mr. K. had completed his 12 sessions of individual life-review therapy, it could be said that he was much closer to the integrity-achieving status and out of the dissonant status. However, it could not be said that he had definitely achieved ego integrity. In fact, it is misleading to refer to ego integrity as a fait accompli. It is much more a state of equilibrium in which the balance has clearly tipped in the direction of ego integrity and away from despair. Inevitably, there are still elements or a minimal degree of despair remaining because it is a dynamic state rather than a static one, according to Erikson. There is always the possibility that the balance could be tipped toward despair if some devastating physical or emotional event occurred.

On the integrity side, Mr. K. had overcome his depression and excessive anxiety and had reached a rather positive and balanced view of his life. He was more accepting of his life as he had lived it, although it is not clear whether he accepted it as the one and only life that had to be and "permitted no substitutions." It is also not clear whether he had an assured sense of meaning and order in his life and in the universe, as Erikson would have it, as a second element of ego integrity. Mr. K. had put a number of past issues into perspective, which enabled him to engage in a more positive present. He had developed a workable modus vivendi of, as he put it, "living from day to day and enjoying it." However, it is not clear whether there was more "meaning" beyond this. He was in fact fearful of death, by his own admission, at the end of therapy. He claimed that he now knew he had something more to live for (i.e., his day-to-day enjoyment of life). Given this and his close call with suicide, he was now more fearful of death, whereas earlier he might have welcomed it. Persons in the integrity-achieving status would claim that they would rather not die but that they could accept it because they feel they have lived a full life. Mr. K. was not yet there because he was just enjoying life again for a change. He was connecting with old places in his hometown and with a few of his remaining "buddies."

There are several other things that need to be said about Mr. K.'s case. He seemed to have an exceptionally good capacity to use the focusing procedure quickly and effectively. There are some possible explanations for this capacity of his, which will be discussed in the very next section, but it certainly made the therapy that much more effective. However, it should be added that not all of Mr. K.'s gains were due to the focusing and reminiscing. He was highly motivated to help himself, as witnessed by his willingness to sign himself in for psychiatric help, to join the reminiscence group, and to undertake individual life-review therapy. He had been physically depleted after his surgery, and he worked hard at regaining his physical strength by walking a great deal and literally forcing himself to eat, as his doctor recommended. During the four-month period of his 16 group reminiscence sessions his weight went from 125 to 152 pounds. So it can be seen that he was a good candidate for therapy, who brought a number of strengths and capacities to it.

His focusing ability is worthy of some additional comments. He was one of the few persons in my experience who showed clear evidence of reaching the upper levels (6 and 7) of experiencing on the EXP Scale. Unfortunately, this had to be inferred because there were no verbatim transcripts of those individual therapy sessions, but the indications were clearly there. There was a great deal of silence during the indwelling, and certainly this paid dividends in terms of his therapeutic gains. However, this is not characteristic of the "normal" reminiscence one sees in old age. After all, Mr. K. did have serious psychosocial problems for which he required therapy. Since these upper levels (Stages 6 and 7) of experiencing are relatively rare even in therapy, questions have to be raised about the applicability of these levels to the role of reminiscence in the normal course of aging (i.e., outside of life-review therapy). These questions will be systematically explored as the book progresses.

EMBODIED AND DISEMBODIED REMINISCENCE

The term *embodied reminiscence* is used here to mean expressed memory that is experienced in a bodily way. The embodied features of reminiscence are probably much clearer in Mr. K.'s case, given the physical assaults on and psychological insults to his body, than they would be with many other elderly persons. This is indeed one reason his case was selected to illustrate reminiscence in a life-review process. This might also explain, in part at least, his ability to focus quickly on bodily sensed phenomena.

This feature of Mr. K.'s reminiscence suggests the centrality of what Edward Casey has called "body memory." This does not mean memory of the body: "Body memory alludes to memory that is intrinsic to the body, to its own ways of remembering: how we remember in and by and through the body" (Casey, 1989). More specifically, Mr. K.'s body memory was of the traumatic type identified by Casey. Ordinarily, such memories remain at the tacit or marginal dimension of our experience, part of the ground rather than an explicitly highlighted figure of our experience This is usually so because we probably defend against the full replay of such painful memories by relegating them to the most peripheral position possible in our conscious life. However, Mr. K.'s trauma was so recent and central to his current psychosocial and physical state that it was obsessively focal in his consciousness. He might have wanted it to be much more marginal or peripheral, but he could not help it. There is also good reason to believe that Mr. K. would be willing and able to focus on that region of his body, given his motivation and capacity, even if it had not been traumatized.

At any rate, since body memories do not ordinarily occur spontaneously or with any frequency in the normal course of reminiscence, they do not account for much of the phenomenon identified as "embodied" reminiscence. Yet there is something that can be identified as embodied in reminiscence. It is what led Aristotle to say that "recollection is a search in something bodily for an image" (Sorabji, 1972). Indeed, recent research in neurobiology has indicated that all recollection, including reminiscence, is far from a disembodied process: "In a sense all acts of recognition, all acts of recollection, require some kind of motor activity. We come to perceive and understand the physical world by exploring it with our hands, our eyes, and the movements of our bodies; our recollections of the world are intimately related to those very movements we use to explore it" (Rosenfield, 1988). This was most apparent among the more active and vivid reminiscers in the Group Project. It was apparent not only from their bodily movements and gestures but also from the language they used in recalling past experiences.

Disembodied reminiscence is also apparent from bodily manifestations and language. In its most extreme form the person would tell about events from the past almost entirely from the vocal cords and mouth. There would be an absence of any gestures, facial expressions, or other bodily manifestations to indicate the subjective state of the person recounting the past. It was as though the person were re*counting* or re*collecting* "things" from the past in a purely factual and objective way. The spoken recollections, then, had a mechanical rather than a feeling or pensive and thoughtful quality to them. The actual words were used as signs to point to things (events, happenings, etc.) in the past rather than as symbols that convey something beyond the mere factuality of the things. Tillich (1959a) has noted that "the difference between symbol and sign is the participation in the symbolized reality which characterizes the symbols, and the non-participation in the 'pointed to' reality which characterizes the sign." Tillich's observation is very apt here because there would be nonparticipation in the past pointed to by the words in the language of disembodied reminiscence.

Symbols and symbolizing, it should be added, are based on our organic and bodily functioning. As Whitehead (1959) observed, "Symbolism from sense-presentation to physical bodies is the most natural and widespread of all symbolic modes." Needless to say, thoroughly disembodied oral reminiscing would be at the lowest level of experiencing, an EXP Score of 1. Conversely, the more embodied the reminiscence becomes, the more the person is focusing on the bodily felt sense of the past experiences, and the higher the EXP score becomes.

Just to test the idea that there is such a thing as embodied reminiscence, let us take two grief pieces of reminiscence from a source totally different from this writer's own research or practice. They are about markedly different experiences from the past, but they have something very much in common that would qualify both as "embodied" forms of reminiscence.

1. After my husband died, I would go into his closet and hug his suits, because they smelled of his own body odor, slight cigarette smell, and aftershave. I'd stand there, hugging his clothes, making believe, close my eyes, and cry (Gilbert & Wysocki, 1987).

The reader will probably pick up immediately on the common feature in this next piece of reminiscence:

2. The smell of kerosene brings back for me the memories of reading by a kerosene light, the feeling of closeness and safety and the shadows cast on the walls, the laughter of a grandmother dead almost 30 years (Gilbert & Wysocki, 1987).

The reader has probably identified the fact that the sense of smell plays a central role in both of these brief remembrances. However, it is not only the olfactory feature that gives them an embodied sense. In fact, the first piece also has a strong tactile feature in the hugging of the dead husband's suit and clothes, whereas the second has a visual (shadows) and auditory (grandmother's laughter) features. The overriding common feature, of course, is that both instances of reminiscence contain strong sensory elements, regardless of type. So it is fair to say that embodied reminiscence is most clearly expressed in a sensory mode or modes. It is not uncommon in this form of reminiscence to hear the person say things like "It gets me right here" (pointing to the heart or stomach), or "I feel a tug every time I think about it," or "It pulls at me," and so on. When said with feeling, these kinds of expressions are indicative of embodied reminiscence.

There can be no doubt that the woman who went to her husband's closet and smelled his clothes experienced his death and its aftermath in a bodily way. We "know" this because the body sense was expressed in her spoken language. We could even say it was embodied in her language. That brief spoken excerpt tells us worlds about this woman and what she has been through. Her verbal description represents raw, authentic experiencing. The sensory, visceral, bodily, and affective dimensions of grief are all there, and there is no denial, no foreclosure.

Let us take another brief excerpt from a different widow: "When he [her husband] died, it was difficult. It's not something to think about—or talk about, either." Although this was taken out of context, it was an actual statement that occurred within the context of a small group discussion about the experience of missing loved ones due to death and separation. The statement taken by itself expresses no thinking, no feeling, not even personal ownership of the experience with an "I" or "my." This is truly disembodied, and there is foreclosure and suppression, if not denial. She may indeed feel the memory of her husband's death very deeply, and probably does, but recall that embodied reminiscence is *expressed* as well as felt. The issue here is how we as observers or listeners can identify embodied reminiscence when we hear it and see it.

In the case of the first widow there was not only an expression of feeling, she had gone deeper than that into the *felt sense* of the experience. She managed to communicate this in her spoken language and was in fact experiencing it (the felt sense) as she was saying it. Further, the way it was said leads us to recognize that she either was or is working through her husband's death and that she has the affective capacity to integrate this into a life-review process if necessary. In short, she is less likely to remain foreclosed than is the second widow. This obviously has significance for gerontological practice, for the identification of such experiential indicators can be quite valuable in the assessment process.

The example of the first widow's reminiscence was marked by the use of sensory language that enabled us to identify it as "expressed memory that is experienced in a bodily way." Although the sensory language makes it easier to identify as embodied reminiscence, there are other ways and words for expressing and identifying the experience of embodied reminiscence. These will be covered extensively in the next chapter.

NOTES

1. The scoring form of the Experiencing Scale is provided in Appendix A.
2. A short form of the focusing process is given in Appendix B.

4

The Language of Reminiscence

When I first sat in on reminiscence groups as a participant-observer and later when listening to the tapes, it was the differences in the spoken language of the reminiscencers that made me aware that there must be differences in the actual experience of reminiscing itself among them. There was no question that the language made a distinct difference in how I experienced the verbalized reminiscences. But what was it about the language that might explain these differences?

That is what this chapter is about. It is what led me to undertake a study of certain relevant literature on language, particularly literature having to do with the kind of "natural" language that is characteristic of most elderly reminiscers. That study became a prerequisite for the full exploration of the many facets and extensions of reminiscence in the lives of the elderly that I wished to undertake. After all, most of the reminiscing experience is mediated through in language, and certainly all of the public aspect of reminiscence is expressed in language. This excursion into language will not be exhaustive, since the purpose here is to extract only those key elements and ideas that will enable us to explore reminiscence as well as the related phenomena of life reviews and self-narratives of the elderly. Some of the concepts and vocabulary of this literature will allow for a more detailed and informative exploration of these phenomena in the actual illustrative cases provided in later chapters. Some of the questions that might thereby be pursued are as follows: What is the language of reminiscence in life review? What is the language of self-narratives or simple life stories? What is the language of resolution in life review? What is the language of foreclosure? The reader probably has some intimations and ideas about these already based on a reading of the earlier chapters, but here we will look at them more systematically and in greater depth.

LANGUAGE AND EXPERIENCE

Given the experiential nature of this study and given phenomenology's identification as "the science of experience," serious consideration has to be given to phenomenological approaches to language. However, we are also concerned here with natural language, the everyday kind of language that is spoken by most elderly persons who do not have advanced degrees, extensive vocabularies, or formal knowledge of grammar and syntax. This kind of language has been the particular concern of the "ordinary language philosophers" such as Wittgenstein (1953) and Austin (1962). Central to Wittgenstein's study of language was the "act of usage," the speech act itself as it is expressed by people in general in the course of ordinary usage in everyday life. So too is *la parole* (speech act) the center of Merleau-Ponty's phenomenological study of language. In fact, it has been said that ordinary-language philosophers today are very similar to phenomenologists such as Merleau-Ponty in their fundamental concern with the active agent (person) as the locus of meaning and in directing our attention to the context of actual use of language for an understanding of words and expressions (Mays & Brown, 1972).

There is, however, a fundamental difference in these two similar approaches to language. Whereas the ordinary-language philosophers study actual usage intensively and contextually, phenomenologists are *also* concerned with the preverbal realm of experience that precedes and conditions the reflexive thought that leads to expression in spoken language (Edie, 1976). As noted earlier, this realm of prereflective awareness, which is given in a bodily felt sense, was an essential feature of the experiencing construct developed by Gendlin in line with the thinking of Merleau-Ponty.

This preverbal realm of awareness and experiencing will become increasingly important for this study as it moves more into the private domain of reminiscence and away from the public (spoken) realm. Since our interest is in both realms of reminiscence, it would be well to go directly to the thinking of Merleau-Ponty, who most extensively addressed both of them.

Basic to his theory of language is his philosophy of the "lived-body," which, by virtue of its very motility and its most basic sensory motor behaviors, acts "to distinguish and objectify the realities around us and bestow a sense on the objects of our surrounding world" (Edie, 1976). From this perspective it is the body that creates meaning, as it did in evolving from primitive and prelinguistic forms of communication such as gestures and sounds. Ultimately, through culture these evolved into the bodily expressed phenomenon of speaking. Merleau-Ponty had a special interest in the sound of language relative to the body, its distinctive intonations, rhythms, and patterns in various languages, or what has been called the "sound-sensuous meanings of words" (Edie, 1976). Thus, his interest in language is primarily in the role it plays in the body's processing of meaningful experience through perception. The primacy of perception is fundamental to his philosophy and to his approach to language (Merleau-Ponty, 1964a).

At the same time, he recognized that our formal language system enables us to go into the prelinguistic realm of primary perception, with its inchoate feelings and sensations, and to cast that experiential reality into a communicable verbal form. These formal linguistic structures thus provide a means for ordering experience and making it meaningful at an interpersonal, intersubjective level. He also recognized that this formal linguistic system, with its established meanings and syntax (*la langue*), allows the speaker to say something new, drawn from his or her own personal preverbal experience, and express it in a form that members of the same linguistic community can understand. This process enables the person to *think* about the *felt* meaning of the preverbal experience and to express it in a form that allows others to think about it without having to actually experience it themselves. One can see this working in the communal-discursive reminiscing Casey talks about.

Thinking, from this perspective, is always done in language, unlike perceiving and imagining, which can remain preverbal and unspoken. Even in solitary thought we "speak with ourselves" as we access the meanings in our bodily felt experiencing at the perceptual level. Actual thinking moves back and forth between experiencing and intellectual construction in language (Merleau-Ponty, 1964b). This is at the heart of true reflective thought, according to Merleau-Ponty.

Now, it is possible to express oneself in a rather unreflective way, which in fact is done much of the time. This is because once cognitive-linguistic structures have been acquired they tend to constrict or channel expression to those meanings that are already established and sedimented in formal language (*la langue*). We will often use these structures to express ourselves in very standard and unoriginal ways and restrict our meanings to those that seem perfectly apparent on the basis of common usage. Merleau-Ponty (1964a) has referred to such sedimented thought and speech as a "humming with words" and as less than authentic because authentic thought "transcends itself" by articulating prereflective experiencing.

This particular insight by Merleau-Ponty spoke directly to my experience as a participant-observer of reminiscence. There were some individuals who, when they were reminiscing, caught and held my attention and interest because they seemed to be relating their experiences in a truly reflective and expressive way. It was clear that they were "in touch" with what they were saying, and it was "authentic" in Merleau-Ponty's sense of the term. Far too often, however, the reminiscing—even about inherently exciting or meaningful events—would be expressed in terms of stock expressions, clichés, and common usage that left them uninteresting and impoverished in the telling and hearing. This had nothing to do with the vocabularies of the speakers. Indeed, some of the richest and most interesting reminiscing to listen to, even about the most banal subjects, was done by persons with limited vocabularies and education. This contrasted with some of the dull and uninteresting reminiscing expressed in the more highly educated but sedimented speech of others. This is why, in the words of one phenomenologist, "We must go beneath the sedimented expressions of *common usage* to their experiential roots" (Edie, 1976). The value of doing this is well expressed by Merleau-Ponty (1964b): "For the speaking subject, expression is a *coming to awareness*; man does not express himself only to others; he expresses himself in order to discover what he means himself."

EXPERIENTIAL LANGUAGE IN REMINISCENCE

The basic phenomenological experience of self in the world is in this body which is "here" (spatially) and "now" (temporally) while others and the things of the world are "there." "Here" is the orientation point of the self, and our presence in relation to other beings and things is always from this standpoint, whether we are in motion or at rest. Even time is experienced and expressed from this standpoint in spatial metaphors, as when we speak of the "distant" past. The statement "I am here" is ontologically fundamental and is the basis for the experiential approach to language that will be laid out here and drawn upon throughout the remainder of the book.

The linguistic I is very much an embodied one, and it is embodied in the "here." This is so not only ontologically and linguistically but also socially, so we speak of "close" and "distant" relatives, friends, and so on. Cognitive psychologists have found strong evidence that the first-person-singular also has a unique epistemological position as well (Seligman, 1975; Maier & Seligman, 1976; Bandura, 1977). It appears that a sense of agency, of a self as an active agent with some freedom of action, is associated with the sense and usage of "I" (the experience of I as an active agent). Also, cognitive therapists have been aware of the need to pay particularly close attention to the use of "I" by the person in treatment. The person's predications, especially verbal forms such as *to be, must, can, to need, to be worth*, and so on, when used after the pronoun "I" provide valuable clues about the person's self-concept and self-esteem as well as his or her cognitive constructions or attitudes toward significant others and reality, all of which can assist in clinical assessment and treatment planning (Guidano & Liotti, 1983).

The existential centrality of the linguistic "I" became poignantly clear to me when I heard a man try to relate a particularly tormenting personal experience from World War II. This was a man who had survived the Holocaust despite being put in several different concentration camps. He was being interviewed by a woman who was doing research on the Holocaust experience, and he related an incident in which he and his brother were marched, along with hundreds of other inmates, from one concentration camp to another. They had to march a terribly long distance, and many of the inmates were so malnourished and weak that they could not go on. Each time one would collapse and fall out of line he or she was summarily shot by the SS guards who were forcibly marching them.

This man was trying to hold up and support his brother, who was faltering badly because he was much weaker physically. However, he was having trouble holding on, and at one point, when his grip gave way, his brother toppled out of line and collapsed alongside the road. When he tried to pick his brother up, an SS guard aimed a rifle at him, ordered him back in line, and proceeded to shoot his brother through the head. At this point in his narrative he said with heavy and careful emphasis, "He tried to save him, but he couldn't. He really tried . . ." The "he" was himself, and he could not bring himself to say "I."

There is strong empirical evidence to show that when human beings are denied agency (the experience of I as active agent) and the freedom of action to support it they lapse into helplessness, hopelessness, and other signs of depression (Seligman, 1975). There is no doubt that this man was denied agency and had no true freedom of action under the circumstances surrounding his brother's death, and this was expressed in the language he used. The helpless and hopeless state he found himself in, which he has reexperienced ever since, has been called "psychic numbing." Robert J. Lifton (1976), on the basis of his studies of the survivors of Hiroshima and the Holocaust, gave it this description: "Psychic numbing is a form of desensitization; it refers to an incapacity to feel or to confront certain kinds of experience, due to the blocking or absence of inner forms or imagery that can connect with such an experience." This man's experience was so horrible, in fact, that there were no viable inner ways in which he could connect with it. His use of the third-person-singular was the only way he could handle it, to distance himself linguistically and existentially from the experience and still talk about it.

When Eugene Gendlin and his research collaborators eventually operationalized the experiencing construct into the Experiencing (EXP) Scale, they found that the absence of an "I" was the basic linguistic indicator of the lowest level of experiencing (Klein et al., 1986). Also, I found that the lack of first-person pronouns in reminiscence cannot be overemphasized in terms of its importance or significance. If, in fact, the person is engaged in *self*-narrative, whether in reminiscing or in relating a personal life story, the absence of a first-person pronoun can be highly significant. It can be indicative of an attempt to block, forget, or disown an experience from the past. This has, of course, important implications for gerontological practice as well as for the study of late-life narratives.

There are several other linguistic features of the EXP Scale that have proved to be most helpful in our understanding of felt meanings in reminiscence, life reviews, and self-narratives when analyzing these as forms of recorded discourse. In addition to the grammatical criterion of use of first-person pronouns, there are expressive-stylistic indicators of remoteness and impersonality at Stage 1 on the EXP Scale. At Stage 2 first-person pronouns are used, and there is manifest interest in the content of discourse, even though the interest is rather intellectual and more about ideas, events, and actions than about persons. Stage 1, by contrast, is remote and impersonal in expressiveness and about impersonal matters or about others' activities or events in terms of content.

Expressive-stylistic indicators of remoteness versus immediacy of feeling are relevant throughout the scale with evidence of direct sensing and changing experience at the top end in Stages 6 and 7 (Klein et al., 1986; Mathieu-Coughlan & Klein, 1984). There are also indicators such as fluency and disruption of speech including pauses, groping for words, and other indicators of dysfluency, particularly at Stage 5 but also at Stages 6 and 7.

The content of discourse and the speaker's perspective on the content also change throughout the scale. Whereas Stage 2 discourse is apt to be a narrative of events or a somewhat abstract and intellectual presentation of ideas, Stage 3 shows brief references to feelings and some limited situational or behavioral elaboration. Stage 4, as noted in Chapter 3, is the fulcrum and obvious turning point of the scale, with the focus on the speaker's subjective account and with the "story" primarily about personal feelings and associations and only secondarily about events or actions. Thus, there is a distinct change of perspective, from referring outwardly to referring inwardly. Then focusing becomes the essential element for Stages 5 through 7, although there are qualitative differences at each. In Stage 5 there is a directly sensed but unclear inner referent that the person is attempting to identify or "label." At Stage 6 there is a felt shift and emergent experiencing, with an increment of resolution of an issue. This culminates in Stage 7, where focusing comes readily and provides the connections for all discourse.

To recapitulate, the progression from one stage to another on the scale involves a shift in frame of reference on the part of the speaker. In the words of several of its most prominent researchers, the EXP Scale shows the following progression:

> Stages 1–3 define the progressive ownership of affective reactions. Stage 4 marks a transition that is especially important for most psychotherapy, that is, the point where content and focus shift from outside to inside, where the speaker's purpose is to describe phenomenology. Beyond this crucial transi-

tion, Stages 5–7 define the progressive expansion and integration of this perspective. (Klein et al., 1986)

The upper (5–7) levels of the scale became somewhat problematic when we applied it to our study of reminiscence. Since those stages are so "inward," they are also intensely private, and their linguistic derivatives are difficult to follow unless you are trained in therapeutic focusing as well as in the research application of the scale. Indeed, two or three days of intensive marathon instruction, followed by practice application and then by more instruction, is usually needed to learn focusing. Learning to apply the scale for research purposes is equally intensive. Actually, trained clinical researchers are now able to apply a Therapist Experiencing Scale to assess how effectively the therapist is able to stay in tune with and enhance (or detract from) the patient's level of experiencing in therapeutic sessions. The following excerpt should serve to give some idea of how this works and how different the upper EXP stages are from the usual form of discourse or dialogue. This excerpt follows an interruption in a therapeutic session in which the patient had been focusing on and attempting to keep in touch with an inner bodily felt referent related to his clinical problem:

		EXP Stage
Therapist:	Are you tapping it again?	5
Patient:	Yes, it's restless again when I don't feel the pain.	5
Therapist:	Maybe there's a place where you can be closer to the painful spot, but not be in it. (*minutes of silence*)	5
Patient:	It's OK now! I put the restlessness down, and I put the pain far away, and you know what made it OK? I was imagining playing !	6
Therapist:	Oh . . . yes . . . sure. That's neat.	6

The following observation was made by the researchers who presented this excerpt: "These moments [above] are the results, the endpoints of efforts at experiential focusing, where the effort involved in staying experientially with conflict, pain, confusion, and vagueness pays off" (Mathieu-Coughlan & Klein, 1984). Granted, this excerpt was taken out of context, but including all of the earlier part of the session would not have made the discourse much more intelligible to an outsider. This is because a great deal more experiential focusing had gone on in many prior sessions, so the patient had learned and was now able to use focusing to enhance his experiencing and the therapist was able to so closely parallel it, but this is a largely silent, unarticulated process for both of them.

However, these upper EXP stages are relatively rare, even in psychotherapy, to say nothing of the unusually close empathic correspondence the therapist's stages showed to the patient's in this case. Indeed, these upper

stages are probably only relevant to extended and intensive psychothera-
peutic situations, and there is some evidence that EXP is somewhat ele-
vated when people are in psychological distress and seek help for it,
whereas non-help-seeking normal people often have low levels (Klein et al.,
1986). This certainly seemed to be true of the "dissonant" people in our
Group Project who sought help with the conflicts that appeared to be
emerging in the course of life-review processes. They did show higher EXP
levels, but it should be recalled that for the most part their emotional functioning and morale later improved and that they showed a greater capacity
for experiencing in general. Thereafter, this enhanced capacity was in the
service of positive instead of just negative affective content and moods.

There is, in fact, a general trend for "healthier" people to have higher
EXP levels (Kiesler, 1971). This is largely true at the lower (1–3) EXP levels
where most people are most of the time under just about any circumstances. For example, in the pretest phase of our Group Project the mean
average EXP level for the whole sample of 104 people was near 2 (1.88).
However, by the time of follow-up testing the experiential group participants had shown an increase from 1.85 to 3.08. Most of them showed commensurate increases in measures of morale and self-concept. This did not
turn out to be a *statistically* significant relationship because some of those
gains were offset by some participants who appeared to be in the throes of a
life-review process and dissonant status and whose EXP would go up to 4
(even 5 in a few rare instances) while their morale and self-concept measures went down. These were people experiencing transitional difficulties,
but the key point here is that for most people the difference between Stage
2 and Stage 3 is a qualitatively significant one in the normal course of
events in everyday subjective experience.

It should be added that the EXP Scale is not an evaluation or clinical *outcome* instrument; it is a clinical *process* instrument. What it can do in this
study is tell us what the experiential level is in any one instance or segment
of reminiscence or self-narrative. It can sensitize us to some other things,
such as who is more open to new experiencing in reminiscence, who is remote and cut off, and so on. In this regard we found it to be a very effective
tool. Recall that a primary objective of this study was to learn what the experience of reminiscence was like—that is, from the inside, subjectively,
and from the point of view of the reminiscer. Consequently, EXP Stage 4
turned out to be a treasure chest of rich new data because at that stage the
speaker's purpose *is* " to describe phenomenology" (i.e., the phenomenology of one's own personal reminiscence.).

Recall also that the crux of Stage 4 is "What is it like to be me?" So if we
extend this into "What is it like to be me reminiscing?" it can be seen why
Stage 4 was the most fruitful one for answering one of our key research
questions. It was not subject to the more socially self-conscious reminis-

cence characteristic of Stages 2 and 3 as these occurred in group reminiscence situations. To the extent that the person is reaching inward at that moment (Stage 4) trying to describe what it is like "to be me" subjectively, not to be the objective persona or public self that is usually presented to others, the more authentic that description of the reminiscence experience should be.

Overall, I have found the first four EXP stages to be descriptive of most of the discourse I have encountered in both practice and research. In research we found that when EXP ratings of 3 and 4 were assigned to segments of reminiscence and personal narrative in analyzing audiotapes, the discourse itself sounded more lively, engaging, and imaginative. When I say "imaginative," I do not mean that they sounded "imaginary" rather than "true" or "real." Actually, when our participants described their experience of reminiscence, they tended to do so in terms of imagery. That is, they would describe the experience as consisting first of quick, brief, and usually partial images (pictures, smells, sounds, etc.) of persons, places, and things that would then set off a train of recollection, which they would proceed to express in the language of oral reminiscence. This was especially true when their descriptions were at Stage 4 on the EXP Scale. Then they would often turn to figurative and metaphorical language in an attempt to articulate the experience more fully (e.g., "I suddenly got a picture of myself—the way I must really have looked then. It as a real awakening, I can tell you . . . a shock of recognition"). At times, when they appeared to be moving toward Stage 5, they would silently ponder and grope for words to fit the images that had triggered the reminiscence or to complete the picture in their mind and then describe it, usually haltingly, in words.

IMAGERY IN REMINISCENCE

This sequence of imaging first and then articulating the experience in words was prominent not only in the participants' description of personal reminiscence but also in the use of focusing in life-review therapy. This shows in the third step of the focusing procedure. It will be recalled that the first step is to "clear a space," in which the person is asked to get in touch with each concern that comes in the body and to put each of them aside for awhile. In the second step, called the "felt sense," the person is asked to pick one problem to focus on and is given the following directions: "Don't go into the problem. What do you sense in your body when you recall the whole of that problem? Sense all of that, the sense of the whole thing, the murky discomfort or unclear body sense of it." Then in the third step, to "get a handle," the person is asked: "What is the quality of the felt sense? What one word, phrase, or image comes out of this felt sense?"

At this point, after asking this last question, it has been my experience that the person is apt to come up with an image rather than a word or phrase. Although Gendlin (1981) recognizes that quite a few people have an image come out of the felt sense, he prefers that they "get a handle" on it with a word and asks, "What quality-word would fit it best?" While I have followed this procedure in practice, I have had occasion to ask people about this step after all of the focusing steps have been completed. As they describe it to me afterward, it is an image rather than a word or phrase that seems to capture a "sense of the whole thing." Then they try to describe this (usually vague) image that gives the whole sense in a word or words. There are, of course, some people who initially come up with a word or phrase and are not aware of a preceding image, but this has been the exception rather than the rule in my experience.

This was also true of the reminiscence experiences as described by the Group Project participants in follow-up interviews. It should be added that it seemed to make no difference whether the participants had been in a conventional, experiential, or control group. As best they could recall, their reminiscing would seem to begin with a "flash," a "picture," or an "image" of something experienced in the past but not yet in words. This image could be triggered by what someone else had said or reminisced about, and this was usually the case when they reminisced in the groups. In private, on the other hand, they claimed their reminiscing could be triggered by a train of thought or even a random sound, smell, or visual experience. Then they would find themselves trying to recapture more of the image or memory trace that had been triggered. This did not necessarily have to be a visual recapturing. For example, one woman described a reminiscing experience by exclaiming, "I can still hear her yelling at me like that!" She had no initial "picture" of her mother yelling or even of the words her mother might have yelled out. Imagery does not, of course, have to be visual. Yet she was able to fill in some of the sensory context of the memory, including some partial visual imagery. From that point on she was able to elaborate on the past experience in words and sentences. This seemed to be a prototypical sequence of the reminiscing experience as described by the participants generally.

Most of the participants had not really thought about the actual form or sequence of their reminiscing experiences before being interviewed by us, and they became rather intrigued with the subject. One married couple reported that their reminiscing in the groups had usually been triggered by the memories shared by other group members, but it was different when they were together at home by themselves. There it frequently began with either one of them getting a "flash" of a particular place they had both visited during the course of their marriage or courtship. The "flashes" seemed to be partial images or "impressions," as they described them, but the flash would set off an interactive sequence between them that was repeated many, many times in the later years of their marriage. The one getting the flash would give the incomplete image or impression of the place, and then between them they would fill in more of the details of the location, appearance, surroundings, and so on in recollecting or reconstructing it in their "mind's eye." This in itself gave them a great deal of pleasure, but in addition it would often lead to mutual reminiscing about the pleasurable times they had spent together at each place.

The prominent role imagery seemed to play in these reminiscing experiences raised questions about why this was so and its place in the experiential/phenomenological approach to language taken in this study. Beginning with the primacy of perception, Merleau-Ponty attempted to show how the most fundamental structures of perception reappear in more complex form in higher-order activities, going from sensing, imaging, and speaking to reasoning and so on. Although this progression of activities is consistent with his basic theoretical and philosophical position, there is a good deal of independent experimental evidence to show that imagery and perception are foundational and are neurophysiologically similar processes that share the same experiential qualities (Leuba, 1940; Perky, 1910). Also, the locus of image excitation corresponds to the locus of sensory functions of the brain, which would help to explain the repeated connections between sensory and imagery phenomena in the reminiscence experiences reported by our group participants in the follow-up interviews (Penfield, 1963).

It appears that imagery represents the core of perceptual response and retrieval mechanisms, and although spoken language very often loses direct contact with experience, direct contact is always implicit in the "concrete modality-specific imagery system" that is the source of extensive details about past occurrences (Singer & Pope, 1978). This would help to explain why certain sensory modalities are prominent in the imagery related to specific reminiscence experiences and why going back to those modality-specific or sensory-specific images enables the person to elaborate upon them in reminiscence.

There are also certain features about imagery that account for its prominence in the focusing experience of those few participants who opted for life-review therapy after their group experiences. It has been said that "images may have a greater capacity than the linguistic mode for the attraction and focusing of emotionally loaded association in concentrated forms" (Sheikh & Panagiotou, 1975). It has also been observed that "the imagery system increases the likelihood that we will experience more fully a range of emotions" (Singer, 1979). So, even if focusing and all of its six steps are not used as specific therapeutic procedures there are good reasons for drawing upon and using imagery in life-review therapy generally.

When people are going through an active life-review process, reminiscing and its related imagery tend to arise spontaneously, and according to Robert Butler, the reminiscences are meaningful for the review work the person needs to do. Therefore, in life-review therapy the practitioner will use the occasions of these spontaneous reminiscences for therapeutic work. This usually happens very naturally because the memories are troublesome and self-indicative of the need for work and resolution. When such spontaneous memories are not forthcoming, the practitioner can move to asking for images of persons or situations that are known to be problematic in the older person's life. It is not only possible to evoke memories from images but also to use guided imagery in helping the person resolve the issue involved in a problematic form of reminiscence.

Based on my practice and research experience, there seem to be two kinds of reminiscence in which the imagery is spontaneous. The first is the one just described, which is part of a larger life-review process. The second is apparently independent of such larger issues, and it simply arises unexpectedly and spontaneously. It is usually pleasurable rather than troublesome, and it is also sometimes ineffable and sufficient unto itself. Those experiencing it have the feeling that there are no words to express it and no *need* to express it in words. It is just a self-contained, enjoyable, or aesthetic experience that is sufficient unto itself. There is no sense of purpose or goal, as there is in life-review reminiscing. The imagery in this type can be partial, impressionistic, or totally vague and indescribable, but despite this there is no compulsion to fill in the details or to clarify it any further. It is simply to be experienced and savored as is, as we shall see in Chapter 9.

Then there appear to be two types of reminiscence in which the imagery needs to be evoked with the help of the practitioner because it is not occurring spontaneously on its own. One instance or type is when the imagery is used in place of words that do not seem to come out of the reminiscence experience, as, for example, in focusing, when the person cannot come up with a word or phrase to capture the felt sense of the "whole thing" or the whole of the problem. The other nonspontaneous type occurs when the practitioner uses guided imagery to address the problematic core of the reminiscence experience.

The above discussion and illustration of imagery and its role in the language of reminiscence might give the impression that images always precede words in this process. Actually, words can elicit images, as is often the case in mutual reminiscing and memory sharing, in which one person's words describing a past event evoke an image or memory trace of a similar event in the listener's experience. However, when words elicit images, the emotional responses, and consequently the meaning, are from the images rather than the words (Bugelski, 1970). That is why images make it possible to retain an emotional attitude toward a lost or absent object (Arieti, 1976). Of course, it is possible, as illustrated in some earlier examples, to hear the actual words of an absent loved one in some instances of reminiscing, but in these instances the words are themselves an aural image of an earlier experience. Indeed, there seems to be an inseparability of images from words, sentences, and whole narratives related to human experience. As Susanne Langer (1957) once put it, "the first thing we *do* with images is to envisage a story."

METAPHOR IN REMINISCENCE

When trying to describe their reminiscing experiences, our respondents had to resort to figurative language, particularly metaphor, to give a sense of what it was like for them. Since metaphor is the substitution of one thing for another or the identification of two things in language (e.g., "Time is money"), it certainly enhances description of subjective experiences such as reminiscing. We found that this ability to find and express resemblance in apparently disparate things was a major asset for those respondents who could do so. There was a clear relationship between the capacity for metaphorical expression and the capacity for experiencing, which makes sense in light of the fact that "the essence of metaphor is understanding and experiencing one thing in terms of another" (Lakoff & Johnson, 1980). It has also been said that "no metaphor can ever be comprehended or even adequately represented independently of its experiential basis" (Lakoff & Johnson, 1980).

This statement, made by George Lakoff and Mark Johnson in their book entitled *Metaphors We Live By*, reflects what they call their "experientialist approach" to language, understanding, and meaning in everyday life. Their approach turned out to be highly compatible and helpful in this experiential study of reminiscence. Lakoff is an eminent expert in the semantics of natural language, and Johnson is a philosopher who has explicated an embodied conception of language that is consistent with Merleau-Ponty's but draws upon recent findings from experimental work in cognitive psychology (Johnson, 1987). He writes of "embodied schemata" or "image schemata" that are grounded in our motor-perceptual experience. Any given image schema emerges first as a structure of bodily interactions, but "it can be figuratively developed and extended as a structure around which meaning is organized at more abstract levels of cognition (Johnson, 1987). Most often, this figurative extension and elaboration takes the form of metaphorical projection, and it begins with the most fundamental structures of linguistic expression in common language. Since they are derived from the lived experience of bodily processes, from perceptual and sensory experiences, and from lived space and time, they lead to the metaphorical use of such terms as above-below, in-out, near-far, large-small, open-closed, before-after, and so on. These have had such long and pervasive use that they are no longer recognized as metaphorical. Therefore, they have been referred to as hidden, or *root*, metaphors. These metaphors turned out to be quite important in this study because they are so fundamental and pervasive that they were common to the language of all of the people studied here, regardless of their educational backgrounds and linguistic abilities. This point will be elaborated upon and illustrated as we proceed.

Metaphor is a special form of imagery construction in its origins, and it provides the linkage between the enactive and symbolic forms of representation in human experience. Jerome Bruner's (1966) experimental work on cognitive development indicated that there are three main forms of representation: enactive, iconic, and symbolic. He described their development as follows:

> At first the child's world is known to him principally by the habitual actions he uses for coping with it. In time there is added a technique of representation through imagery that is relatively free of action. Gradually there is added a new and powerful method of translating action and image into language, providing a third system of representation.

The first, or enactive, form includes the action or motoric sphere and is represented behaviorally in gestures, postures, and facial expression. The iconic, or imagery, form represents our sensory-perceptual reactions and actions, and these sensory-bound images carry forward much of the action in our imagination. These are then projected into more general, abstract, and symbolic representation in our formal language system. Within this scheme metaphor can play a powerful transformative role between the iconic (image) and symbolic (linguistic) forms of representation (Ricoeur, 1977). Prerequisites for its effective use in this role are a common language (and associations within it) among people and a more individuated resonance for each person in the imagery mode of experience. In this way metaphor becomes a nexus between the public-private and explicit-implicit dimensions of meanings between individuals. Metaphor is therefore an imaginative interchange in which one person must have enough imagination to generate a metaphor, and the other person must have the capacity to understand and respond to that metaphor.

The capacity to move from literal to figurative speech in metaphor did indeed prove to be a valuable asset among the elderly persons we studied. As Aristotle put it, "Ordinary words convey only what we know already; it is from metaphor that we can best get hold of something fresh" (Lakoff & Johnson, 1980). Or as one phenomenologist put it, "We must go beneath the sedimented expressions of *common usage* to their experiential roots" (Edie, 1976), and metaphor is one of the best ways of doing this. Ernst

Schachtel (1959), a psychologist, pointed out that as people are socialized they come to rely increasingly on empty verbal clichés or abstractions and thereby lose direct contact with experience. Unfortunately, such clichés and common (nonexperiential) metaphors did abound in much of the reminiscing that went on in the early stages of the group project, and they remained the same for many participants right through the project. However, a number of the participants were able to get beyond these, and their imaginative use of metaphor increased with their EXP ratings.

As one writer put it, "Experience makes connections and enlarges itself through the use of metaphoric processes that link together experiences similar but not exactly the same" (Polkinghorne, 1988). Thus, metaphor enables us to take experiences and construct them into larger meaningful wholes. This important integrative function of metaphor will be illustrated shortly, but we observed repeated instances in which the use of a metaphor in reminiscing led to valuable new linkages or integrations with other life experiences. Therefore, we would have to agree with Lakoff and Johnson (1980) when they say, "New metaphors are capable of creating new understandings and, therefore, new realities."

It is important to point out that metaphors can be positive or negative and functional or dysfunctional. An elderly person accepting a conventional or stereotyped metaphor that is negative and dysfunctional can be helped to find a more fitting and functional one. Thus, one elderly man in our group project, who appeared to be in a state of despair, made the following statement on more than one occasion: "Life is a battle, and I'm a loser." He did not opt for any follow-up service or life-review therapy; but if he had, it would have been essential to help him come up with a new and more functional life metaphor that would still be consonant with his actual life experience.

One gerontological practitioner reported a most successful use of such a fitting and enabling metaphor in the case of a very depressed 82-year-old woman who was particularly resistant to engaging in life-review therapy (Erlich, 1979). Based on two prior group reminiscence sessions in which she reluctantly engaged in some rather negative reminiscing, the practitioner identified what he felt was a theme running through her reminiscing, plus what he knew of her background, which included many moves and dislocations in Europe and America. In the third session, as she was again recalling some negative experiences from the past, he interjected with the observation that as she was talking he had an "image" of her as a "traveler in life." She immediately stopped, looked at him intently, and then with a brightened expression and voice she picked up on his statement and said emphatically that indeed she was "a traveler in life." Following this she began to reminisce with real enthusiasm around that theme, and he was able to engage her in a thorough life-review process. Over the following weeks, in various new social situations, she was heard to refer to herself as "a traveler in life."

As Lakoff and Johnson (1980) state, "A large part of self-understanding is the search for appropriate personal metaphors that make sense of our lives." The practitioner had hit upon a most appropriate metaphor for the depressed elderly lady, who in turn was prepared to accept it, own it, and build upon it. His identification of a theme was the key element in this, and he recognized this theme as the central thread in what he saw implicitly as her life narrative. Indeed, the blending of metaphor and narrative appears to be one of the most effective routes to self-understanding and constructive life reviews, based on what we learned from an experiential approach to the subject.

SELF-NARRATIVES

The case of the 82-year-old woman described above illustrates quite well the narrative function of reminiscence that was discussed in Chapter 2. Even though she engaged in the first two sessions of group reminiscence reluctantly and with negative content, she had inadvertently begun a personal narrative containing a tacit theme that the practitioner sensitively responded to in the form of imagery and apt metaphor. Her need to tell about herself, to narrate, came through almost despite herself. It has been said that people must talk about themselves until they know themselves, and we could add that they do it even if they are not aware or conscious of doing it.

There is another feature of this narrative impulse that needs to be mentioned; it shows a distinct tendency toward unity or integration. This became quite apparent to a social anthropologist and a professor of English who undertook an experimental life-history class with the elderly (Myerhoff & Tufte, 1979). They were particularly struck by the tendency of the elderly participants to attempt to integrate their life narratives, to make their life histories cohere into a unity. They were so impressed by this that they saw it as a clear "need among the elderly to make a life review." The whole question of the correspondence or relationship between life review and life narrative is one that remains to be explored, but the important point here is the integrative thrust of narrative toward unity. It is one of the basic ingredients of a true narrative. The essential ingredients of a narrative are concisely summed up in the following quotation:

> The narrative attends to the temporal dimension of human existence and configures events into a unity. The events become meaningful in relation to the theme or point of the narrative. Narratives organize events into wholes that have beginnings, middles, and ends. (Polkinghorne, 1988)

This identifies the ingredients of unity, events, theme, and organization into beginnings, middles, and ends. It is important to note that the temporal dimension and the organization into beginnings, middles, and ends are not one in the same. Lived time and the way it is experienced and narrated by the person is not necessarily in the linear mode of beginning, middle, and end. The narration of lived experience and time may be picked up in the middle, go back to the beginning, return to the middle, and work its way back to the end. In short, it is often recursive and keeps moving back and forth so as to integrate events with the theme or point of the story. A personal life narrative in oral unrehearsed form, which is what we undertook to obtain here, is not apt to be told in the strict sequential form of a *chronicle*. However, there is a need and tendency ultimately to organize events into a whole that has a beginning, middle, and end. Thus, in the end there is a temporal narrative unfolding. Again, this does not come about in purely linear fashion, for it is a synthetic type of integrating process that leads to the coherence of a narrative It is complex, figurative, metaphorical, and synthetic. This is consistent with Paul Ricoeur's observation that both metaphor and narrative use synthesis to bring about innovative meaning and unity (Ricoeur, 1984).

His observation is based on the fact that narrative meaning consists not only of events but of the significance of those events for the narrator in relation to a particular theme. Now, simple recollection of past events or reminiscence will not serve to provide a narrative, although it was mentioned earlier that events or episodes related in group reminiscence were sometimes thematic in terms of a life narrative. It was also mentioned that much reminiscing is simply enjoyable and an end in itself, without any necessary connection to an overall theme. If we are interested in eliciting life stories, we need to move from specific episodes and events to more general stories that contain a theme or themes that provide self-identity and unity to the person's whole existence. This is what we set out to do in the Integrity Survey, the last in the series of studies reported here.

What we were interested in doing during the interview phase of that study was to obtain what has been described as the "self-told life narrative" or simply the "self-narrative" (Bruner, 1987; Gergen & Gergen, 1983). We used Jerome Bruner's (1987) approach to te self-narrative, both in the interviews and in the analysis of the tapes afterward. There were several things that recommended his approach to us. First, he was already engaged in systematic research on the self-narrative, and if we used his interview procedures, we would have some basis for comparison of our results with his. His procedures were simple and straightforward, which also recommended them to us. He and his colleagues interviewed their subjects by asking them to "tell the stories of their lives" and "to keep it to about half an hour." They told the subjects that they would not be "judging" or "curing" them but were very interested in how the subjects saw their lives. Although they acknowledged to the subjects that telling one's life story in a half hour is an almost impossible task, most of their respondents had little trouble in staying within the time limits. Another half hour or so was spent asking questions designed to get at *how* the respondents' stories had been put together. Our experience with his procedures indicated the same ability on the part of our respondents to stay within the time limits.

Another point that recommended Bruner's approach to us was the fact that he was very much attuned to the characteristic figurative language, particularly the root metaphor, his respondents would use in their self-narratives. We knew we would have to get beyond the more conventional surface expressions and language that our respondents would largely use so as to get at unexpressed themes. Bruner's analysis (1987) of respondent language in selected case illustrations demonstrated the usefulness of this approach quite clearly. This enabled us to carry out a similar analysis, as will be seen in some of the case illustrations in Chapter 8.

A third point that recommended Bruner's approach was his close attention to the matter of *agency*, that is, to the agent or protagonist of the story. Since the concern is with *self*-narrative, it is important to see how the agent characterizes or portrays herself or himself in the narrative. Bruner (1987) notes that literary forms of narrative "have moved steadily toward an empowerment and subjective enrichment of the Agent protagonist."[1] Agency in narrative began in narrative with the folktale, in which the protagonist is "neither found by nor owns experience" (a *figure*), to the protagonist as one who is defined by roles and responsibilities and who gets rights and a social identity in return (a *person*), to one who has to compete for roles in order to earn his or her rights and achieve an identity (a *self*), and finally to one who has to transcend or resist society in order to create or "rip off" rights as well as an identity that expresses the essence of the person's self (an *individual*). This progression of empowerment and subjective enrichment of the self as protagonist in a life narrative is not unrelated to the experience of self in relation to events in the past, which is the central focus of this study. The experiencing construct as operationalized in the EXP Scale provides one means of looking at the subjective side of late-life stories and life reviews. Bruner's focus on agency provides another valuable way to look at a related dimension of these same phenomena of old age. The results of our application of some of Bruner's procedures and perspectives will be evident in Chapter 8, where our findings and more detailed case illustrations from the Integrity Survey will be presented.

The portrayal of agency in language within the self-narrative is, of course, most apt to be expressed in the first person "I" and its predications, and it was illuminating for us to follow this usage in the self-narratives that we tape-recorded. Not only did it aid our understanding of how the respondents viewed themselves as agents in the trajectory of their life histories, but by paying close attention to self-portrayals of agency in terms of the past we also learned a great deal about how the self is seen as agent in the present and the future. Bruner is of the opinion that we tend to become the self-narratives we tell and the autobiographies we write, or as Mark Johnson (1987) puts it, "We also experience, understand, and order our lives as stories we are living out." In his own autobiography Jean-Paul Sartre (1964) put it even more succinctly in saying that a man "tries to live his life as if he were recounting it." There is a great deal to be said for this, and I have certainly seen dramatic instances in which the self-fulfilling prophecy of self-as-portrayed-in-the-past comes to haunt the present and the future in very problematic ways. The fact that older persons in their sixties through nineties have already lived out most of the life cycle does not reduce the significance of their portrayals, for their "being" is in the present and their "becoming" is in the future. This has obvious implications for gerontological practice, and these will be drawn out later in the book. At this point it should be quite appropriate to turn from the self-narrative to the subject of the next chapter, "The Aging Self," which will be the agent and protagonist in the memories and life histories to be portrayed in the latter half of the book.

The following case will illustrate the use of this type.

Mrs. J. was referred to a family service agency where I volunteered some of my time to work with elderly individuals and their families. She had been referred from a clinic at a local university that specialized in stress and anxiety disorders. The clinic's services were part of a demonstration project with an upper age limit of 65 for its patients, so Mrs. J. had to be referred out when she turned 65 after receiving the usual round of treatment. She had been in treatment at the clinic for six weeks prior to turning 65, but she had not responded with much progress on her anxiety problem through the cognitive-behavioral treatment techniques they were trying with her. She continued to feel very anxious, and she wished to be transferred elsewhere rather than have her case closed. She was diagnosed as suffering from "generalized anxiety with panic attacks" at the time of referral.

Mrs. J. had much to be anxious about, for she had undergone a series of major physical problems over the past six years, two of which nearly killed her. Six years earlier she had suffered a massive stroke that paralyzed most of her right side. It took many months before she got any movement back in her right arm and leg. She still needed a walker for short distances and a wheelchair for longer distances. The stroke had rendered her speechless for a while, and she had to be fed through a tube for months afterward because the right side of her throat was also paralyzed. She literally had to learn how to swallow food again, but most of her speech did come back without therapy. She also suffered from diabetes and diverticulosis and had a very serious case of emphysema for which she had to be constantly on oxygen. When her husband would bring her to the family agency for her appointments, she would come in a wheelchair with a portable oxygen container with plastic tubing running from it to her nose for direct inhalation. Her speech was somewhat breathless because of that, and her voice was also hoarse because of the remaining damage to her throat from the stroke.

As though this were not enough, Mrs. J. had suffered cardiac arrest a year earlier and again nearly died. She was comatose and in intensive care for over two weeks and then remained in the hospital for many weeks thereafter. She was particularly shaken emotionally by this last experience. Her generalized anxiety had been building with all of the physical disorders, beginning with the stoke, but it was after the cardiac arrest that her panic attacks started. Although her anxiety and panic attacks were the most prominent and pressing of her problems, it was also clear that Mrs. J. was depressed and had very low self-esteem. Her body image was particularly poor because of all the recent physical insults to her body and because of her appearance with the plastic tubing in her nose as well as her difficulties in walking and talking. She said her small grandchildren would stare at her as though she was "something strange," and this hurt her deeply even though she could understand their behavior.

In the first few sessions we were able to adapt some of the relaxation techniques she had learned at the clinic with some other approaches that seemed to fit her capabilities and preferences a bit better. She had difficulty with cognitive procedures and attempted to explain this by saying, "I don't comprehend too good." She had dropped out of school in the ninth grade to work full time at age 16. She also felt the stroke had affected her ability to "concentrate," but on the other hand she felt that her ability to read and write had returned to its former level. At any rate, she showed a very good capacity for imagery, visual and olfactory in particular. Therefore, she was able to use calming imagery, such as being at a warm and restful seashore, while tensing and relaxing her major muscle groups in progressive relaxation exercises that I have put on tape for her use at home. This helped to reduce the occurrence of her panic attacks, but much of her generalized anxiety remained after about three weeks. Nevertheless, she felt that she could now cope somewhat better with that.

We then turned to her depression and her feeling that she had nothing to live for any longer. She and her husband had raised eight children, and she had been the central person in their nurturing and upbringing, while her husband tried to support this large family with two jobs. Now, because of all of her physical handicaps, her husband became the center of the family. All eight children and the many grandchildren continued to live in the area and visit their parents frequently. However, she was usually indisposed in bed, and when she was in the room with them, she would become tense and anxious in the presence of her very young and active grandchildren. She said that she felt they all saw her as a "strange and cranky old woman" who was no fun to be around. Her husband, on the other hand, was very popular with their adult children because he was a good mechanic and would gladly fix their cars and appliances for them. She said, "It's always 'Dad this and Dad that, but no 'Mom' anymore." Then she would feel guilty about being jealous of her husband for this and because she was "such a burden on him" with all the care and assistance she needed from him. Despite his protestations to the contrary and the protestations of all of her children that she had been a marvelous mother to whom they "owed everything," she was feeling very isolated and undesirable. She did not seem to be able to give herself credit for all she had done as a mother and wife.

It seemed that life-review therapy might be indicated, to go over and reinforce all she had done and accomplished in the course of her life and also to enhance her self-esteem and provide a sense of meaning and achievement. She would say, "Why do I go on living? I'm no good to anyone, including myself. Sometimes I pray to God that he will just let me die, peacefully, and it will be all over." She was certainly in despair, and it was hoped that the life review would tip the balance in a more positive direction.

The plan was to try focusing with reminiscing in the life-review process because Mrs. J. was already very preoccupied with her ailing body, and it was thought that she would respond quite directly to the focusing procedures. However, this did not turn out to be the case. She could not get any working space or distance from her problems in the first step, "clearing a space" by attempting to put the problems at a distance. In the second step she would get stuck on a specific bodily *symptom* rather than a body sense of the problem, and in the third step ("getting a handle") she could not come up with a quality word or phrase. She would just say the "feeling" (rather than the felt sense) was "awful" or "terrible," and she could not carry it any further in words. It is possible that her verbal ability had been somewhat impaired by her stroke, which had occurred in the left hemisphere of the brain and therefore might be more apt to affect the language function.

The life-review process was further complicated by the fact that Mrs. J. claimed that she "had no childhood to speak of." It too was "awful" and "bad." She claimed her mother was unhappy and depressed, and her father was just a poor farmer who worked hard, long hours and had nothing to give to his unhappy wife and children. Mrs. J.'s bare descriptions of her childhood family life would hover between EXP Stages 1 and 2, where it was expressed in distant and detached terms or in simple behavioral words like "sad" or "unhappy." Again, there was the same problem of finding the words that would connect with experience, as there had been in the focusing procedures.

Since she had been able to use imagery with some success in her relaxation exercises, it made sense to try guided imagery to enhance the reminiscing in her life-review process. I asked Mrs. J. if she could imagine herself approaching her old childhood home, and when she closed her eyes and attempted to do so, she had good results. She imagined herself traveling up the old dirt road on the open back of the old Model A Ford truck her father owned. She could not only see the house more clearly as they approached it, she could smell and feel the dust from the road in her nostrils. Therefore, I asked if she could imagine herself walking into the house and seeing her mother there, and she was able to do so without difficulty. She saw her mother as sitting at the kitchen table with her head in her arms, crying. This was a very familiar scene from her childhood, as she described it.

Mrs. J. could also imagine herself a little girl (she pictured herself about 8 years old) being with her mother this way, but she was not able to imagine talking to her mother at that age. She could, however, imagine what she would like to say to her mother today. It would not be to ask her what was making her cry; Mrs. J. felt she knew that only too well already. It was that her mother felt lonely and isolated on that farm. She had been "a city girl who had a good education." She had gone to a teacher's normal college for two years, and when she graduated, the only teaching job she could find was in a rural school about 50 miles outside the city in which she had been raised, Albany, New York.

Mrs. J. went on to say that her mother was also a very religious woman, a Roman Catholic, who had to teach in a very Protestant rural area. In her loneliness she responded to the interest shown by Mrs. J.'s father, allowing him to court her, and they were married despite the fact that he was a Methodist. Mrs. J. went on to explain that her mother was "raised to be a lady," so she was "terrible" at housekeeping, cooking, and caring for the children. She said her mother never ironed the children's clothes, and she would dress them in very old-fashioned dresses and shoes, so they constantly felt ashamed in school. She could recall desperately wanting to go off and get a job so as to buy clothes that would let her look like other young women, which she did the moment she turned 16.

However, Mrs. J. said she understood her mother, and she could imagine herself as an adult telling her mother that she understood why she was so unhappy. She would tell her she knew that it was sad to be so lonely, to be married to a man with a different religion and no education, who had to work hard, long hours and who "really wasn't much of a talker, anyway." She also imagined telling her mother that she understood how it was to have only two little girls for company, who were just more of a burden than a help, instead of another adult. Mrs. J. summed it up by saying that she still felt very guilty that she had not been able to do more for her mother, to make her feel better, then. She recognized that her mother was "a depressed woman and probably needed a psychiatrist," but Mrs. J. still felt she should have done more.

The only light points from her childhood, which she had forgotten but got back in touch with through the guided imagery, were two-week visits every summer to her older (14 years) sister who lived in Rochester, New York. This sister would treat her and her younger sister to new clothes, candy, and other things they did not get at home. Then Mrs. J. began to reminisce about how good she felt when she finally left home, came to Albany, got a job, and bought herself "all new clothes." She found to her surprise that she was an attractive and popular young woman when fashionably dressed. Quite a few boys asked to date her, but it was her husband to whom she was immediately and unquestionably attracted.

She said she knew nothing about sex, given her very religious mother and distant father, so marriage came as a revelation to her. She chuckled for the first time in our sessions when she recounted the fact that they had their first child nine months and one week after they were married, and they had seven more children plus three miscarriages within the next ten years. When talking about the raising of the children and her husband's skilled renovation of their little house to accommodate all of the children, her mood began picking up. She brought in a photograph of her whole family, grandchildren and all, taken about a year before her stroke. She and her husband were standing in the center of the picture, looking proud and happy, surrounded by their children and grandchildren. When I asked her to imagine herself back to the time of that picture and what it was like to be there in the center of the family, she was able to do so and said it was "great"; so it was agreed that she would look at that photograph from time to time when she was feeling particularly down and worthless. This and the structured life-review reminiscing helped considerably with the depression.

However, Mrs. J. experienced an upswing in her anxiety when she began having some abdominal symptoms accompanied by constipation. She became particularly anxious about going to the bathroom and sitting there awaiting a bowel movement. She actually began to experience attacks again at those times, but she could not say what brought them on. Gentle questioning did not help to clarify it for her or me, but when I asked her if any images came to her at those times, she realized that there were images of her mother. In fact, her mother had died ten years earlier in her (Mrs. J.'s) home in the *very same bathroom*! She had somehow blocked this out, but it now came back to her in full force and in the form of manifest death anxiety.

Mrs. J. recognized it as such but she would say, "Why death anxiety? I sometimes pray to die." There were obvious connections with her mother and the fact that her mother had been in a similar semi-invalid status when she was in Mrs. J.'s home and being cared for by her. We attempted to explore these connections but without much success, since they tended to make Mrs. J. a bit more anxious. Then, in an effort to find a good calming image from her past to work with, I asked if there was any time in her life in which she could remember feeling totally calm and at peace. Mrs. J. thought carefully about it and then suddenly exclaimed, "Yes, when I had my stroke!" She then went on to describe what that experience was like. She said that the peaceful feeling occurred when she was in the hospital shortly after suffering the stroke at home. She was just lying in her hospital bed and feeling totally at peace. I asked if she was fully conscious at that time, and she said: "Yes, I was. I knew I had a stroke and that I almost died . . . but I didn't really care. You know, I remember thinking if death was like that . . . then, that's really good."

She went on to say that she could not speak, but that did not bother her either. She also realized that she did not have movement in her right arm and leg, but that too did not upset her at the time. She said, "I realized I had this body . . . (*pause*) but still . . . I thought . . . it's not really me. . . . It was almost like somebody else's body. It was wonderful!"

Fortunately, with guided imagery Mrs. J. was able to go back and get in touch with the sentient nature and context of that experience. This enabled her to use a technique called "dis-identification," in which the person is instructed in how to dis-identify with one's body, one's negative emotions, and so on by identifying with the kind of aware but detached consciousness that Mrs. J. had actually experienced after the stroke. Consequently, she did not require as much instruction in it since she could evoke it through memory and imagery. It not only enabled her to deal with her death anxiety, since death now seemed peaceful and pleasant, but also enabled her to detach herself from time to time from her prior preoccupation with her body when in an anxiety state. She was able to say to herself, "I am *not* this body. I have this body, but I am not it. I am I, this center of consciousness and not the body I am conscious of." It seems unlikely that she could have used these self-instructions so effectively if she had not had the actual poststroke experience with such disembodied consciousness.

Although Mrs. J.'s anxiety and depression lessened in the course of life-review therapy and guided imagery experiences, it could not be said that she was "resolved" and had attained ego integrity. She had not worked many things through and still felt a good deal of guilt and regret, and probably unexpressed rage, about her mother. She was not at all content with her current physical state and the limits it put on her existence, but she was able to cope with them better and gain some respite from time to time. Her morale was clearly improved but far from idyllic. At any rate, Mrs. J.'s case illustrates a number of different uses of imagery in reminiscence and life-review therapy and some instances in which imagery enabled her to articulate her experiencing in a language she had not been able to use until then.

NOTE

1. Bruner was specifically influenced in his thinking here by Amelie Rorty (1976) and her characterizations of personal identities in literature.

5

The Aging Self

There is a change in the subjective experience of self over the life-span that is manifested and expressed in such phenomena as reminiscence, life review, and even foreclosure. To explore these phenomena in their many facets through the actual reminiscences and narratives provided in the remaining chapters of this book, it is necessary to delineate here a conception of the nature and evolution of the self across the life-span. This conception will provide the framework by which the description and analysis of these reminiscences, life reviews, and personal narratives will be carried out in the remainder of the book.

The embodied self, within the framework of this experiential study, represents the origin and foundation for the development of the self in its various stages throughout the life cycle. We begin with it because it is the first subjectively experienced sense of self in the life cycle. It is also quite compatible with most major theories of human development. Freudian psychoanalytic theory posits the "body ego" as the foundation and precursor of all further development of the ego, or "self," within that theoretical framework. Even current object relations theory would find the concept of embodied self to be quite compatible with its basic premises, which enables us to accommodate and reflect upon some of the findings from that body of theory and research as it relates to the phenomena of reminiscence, life review, and personal narratives.

Discussion of the embodied self will be followed by an examination of the development of a socialized self. Following this will be a sketch of the older self and issues of identity and ego integrity based on findings and formulations from gerontological research and theory. Much of this research and theory comes mostly from a quantitatively oriented social science perspective that gives a picture of the objectified dimensions of the aging self as obtained through psychological testing and self-report.

This will be followed by a discussion of the self-as-process based mostly upon the phenomenological and existential formulations of self to be found in more experientially oriented thinkers in psychology, sociology, and phenomenology.

The most comprehensive compilation and discussion of the subject of the self in the gerontological literature was presented in the most recent edition of *The Handbook of the Psychology of Aging* (Bengtson, Reedy, & Gordon, 1985). The authors of that section recognized the complexity and difficulty of the subject in making the following observation:

> The terms "self" and "self-concept" invoke some of the oldest, most enduring, and yet most perplexing themes in social psychology; these themes originated in philosophy—especially phenomenology. Their nature, their social and intrapsychic determinants, and their development over time have been the sources of continuing debate for almost a century.

After having reviewed the relevant literature on the subject, these authors found themselves going back to William James (1890) and the distinction he made between the self as subject (the "I") and the self as object (the "Me") in his *Principles of Psychology*. James (1961) differentiated these two aspects of the self as follows:

> Whatever I may be thinking of, I am always at the same time more or less aware of *myself*, of my *personal existence*. At the same time it is *I* who am aware; so that the total self of me, being as it were duplex, partly known and partly knower, partly object and partly subject, must have two aspects discriminated in it, of which for shortness we may call the Me and the other the I.

Those authors went back to James's conception of the self because it has shown such enduring descriptive and operational value. It has served to structure much of the later empirical work on the self and the self-concept in the social and behavioral sciences. James's distinction between pure experience and the contents of experience has been useful in identifying the existence of conscious activity and the objects of that consciousness. The I as the experiencing subject makes a great deal of intuitive sense to most of us, and as two prominent social psychologists noted, "It is probably this capacity for experiencing that the individual recognizes as most basic to being a self" (Gordon & Gergen, 1968). Because of their compelling descriptive power from both an experiential and empirical point of view, James's concepts of the I and the Me will be used throughout this analysis and subsequent sections of this book. Now it is important to emphasize that James sees the I and the Me as aspects of an embodied self.

THE EMBODIED SELF

James (1890) had the following to say about embodiment: "We feel the whole cubic mass of our body all the while; it gives us an unceasing sense of personal existence." Not only does it give us a sense of existence, it gives us a place or center of existence from which we approach all things:

> Where the body is is "here"; all other things are "there" and "then" and "that.". . . The body is the storm centre, the origin or coordinates, the constant place of stress in all that experience-train. Everything circles around it and is felt from its point of view. The "I" then, is primarily a noun of position just like "this" and "here." (James, 1971)

This statement by James is remarkably similar not only to Merleau-Ponty in the *Primacy of Perception* but also to contemporary psychologists and sociologists who share a phenomenological perspective (Berger & Luckmann, 1966; Giorgi, 1970). As a matter of fact, there is now a resurgent interest in the work of William James in the human sciences in general and a recognition of this work as essentially in the tradition of modern phenomenology (Edie, 1978).

James's conception of the self fits extremely well with the experiential view of reminiscence presented in Chapter 3. For him there is an intimate relationship between what is remembered in reminiscence and the embodied self:

> Remembrance is like direct feeling: its object is suffused with a warmth and intimacy to which no object of mere conception ever attains. This quality of warmth and immediacy is what . . . *present* thought also possesses for itself. So sure as this present is me, is mine, it says, so sure is anything else that comes with the same warmth and intimacy and immediacy, me and mine. What the qualities called warmth and intimacy may in themselves be will have to be matter for future consideration. But whatever past feelings appear with those qualities must be admitted to receive the greeting of the present mental state, to be owned by it, and accepted as belonging together with it in a common self. This community of self is what the time-gap cannot break in twain, and is why a present thought, although not ignorant of the time-gap, can still regard itself as continuous with certain chosen portions of the past. (James, 1890)

It is hard to imagine a more vivid description of what was referred to as embodied reminiscence in Chapter 3. His statement that the "community of self is what the time-gap cannot break in twain" speaks directly to the point of how reminiscence can be such a valued resource in late life. It enhances and strengthens the sense of continuity, the sense of a common self in the span of a single life.

THE SOCIALIZED SELF

If we begin with the embodied self, which is, after all, a very egocentric point of origin, how do we get to a socialized self? Consistent with the experiential and phenomenological focus of this study, I would like to turn now to a prominent phenomenologist, one who undertook perhaps the most extensive phenomenological study of the self (Natanson, 1970). It is Maurice Natanson (1973) of Yale University who has been foremost among phenomenologists in attempting to bridge phenomenology and the social sciences. He began with a conception of embodied self that was almost identical with James, words and all.[1] In addition, he articulates James's point about the central feature of consciousness, which is that consciousness can reflect upon itself. Natanson says: "It is perhaps the central feature of consciousness that it is capable of reflection, and within that generic attribute it is a decisive fact that consciousness is able to reflect upon itself, to take its own activity as an object of examination" (1970).

Natanson found that the social psychology of George Herbert Mead contained a number of ideas that could begin with the concept of an embodied self and trace its development into a socialized self. Mead had taken Cooley's (1902) concept of "the looking-glass self," the idea that a person could perceive himself or herself in the way others see him or her. Although as embodied selves we are "here" in our bodies, we are also capable of imagining or projecting ourselves from "here" to "there" where another person is. We can put ourselves into the position of the other person and temporarily take it as our own so as to know how to interact with that person. Mead felt that all intelligent social interaction was a matter of putting oneself in the role of the other and acting accordingly.

Mead went further and claimed that we can symbolize ourselves to ourselves—that is, become objects of our own reflection—by learning to symbolize the roles played by others and to take the role of the other in determining our own conduct. We learn by communicating with others that symbols, particularly linguistic symbols, can arouse in us the same sort of responses they can arouse in others. Through the internalization of others' roles, as well as by adopting the generalized social attitudes of one's society and culture, we become socialized and are able to interact meaningfully with others. This is the essence of Mead's theory of "symbolic interactionism" (i.e., human interactional experience mediated by language and other symbols). This organized set of social roles, expectations, and social attitudes was called "the generalized other" by Mead, and he felt that it accounted for generalized feelings about the self.

Natanson utilized the phenomenological concept of sedimentation to show how such generalized expectations about feeling, thinking, and behavior could come about and be passed on. At the individual level only a fraction of human experiences can be retained in consciousness. The ones that are retained become "sedimented," that is, "they congeal in our recollection as recognizable and memorable entities" (Berger & Luckmann, 1966). This has an important bearing on reminiscence and will be covered later, but for the moment we are more interested in social or intersubjective sedimentation, which takes place when common experiences have become congealed and incorporated into a common social stock of knowledge. Language has become the chief depository of a large aggregate of such collective sedimentations. Thus, we can be told or read about the many roles and related social expectations that have been sedimented in usage over time in the history of a society.

Mead also used the concepts of the I and the Me, just as James had done in his paradigm of the self. Like James, Mead saw the I as the subject of all action, whereas the Me was the object. The Me in Mead's conception is the repository of all past actions and of individual and social sedimentations. It thus represents both individual and societal stability and continuity. Furthermore, as Natanson notes, "the Me articulates itself through roles." This, of course, makes the Me aspect of the self even more of a social creation, given the plethora of already sedimented social roles available to individuals in any society. However, there is a difficulty in all this. It leads to what Dennis Wrong (1961), a sociologist, has referred to as the "oversocialized conception of man."

Even before he made use of the concepts of the I and the Me, Mead recognized that his symbolic interactionist framework ruled out the possibility of individual creativity, novelty, or innovation. Yet he believed that individual humans were capable of an originality and a creativity that is not socially scripted. Consequently, he took the I and made it *into* the spontaneous initiator of action:

> It is because of the "I" that we say that we are never fully aware of what we are, that we surprise ourselves. . . . The "I" gives the sense of freedom, of initiative. The situation is there for us to act in a self-conscious fashion. We are aware of ourselves, and of what the situation is, but exactly how we will act never gets into experience until after the action takes place. Such is the basis for the fact that the "I" does not appear in the same sense in experience as does the "me." (Mead, 1964)

Natanson (1970) expands on this to say that the Me is the reservoir of everything the person has done. However, the I and the Me are not separate regions of the self; they are functional aspects of the self. Natanson speaks of them as polarities and adds: "To speak, as we have, of their dialectical relationship is to recognize that the integrity of the self is sustained in dynamic fashion by its temporal development . . . in which each 'I' of a present becomes incorporated into the 'Me' of a later state of the self."

This dialectical relationship between the I and the Me is central to the concept of self-as-process, which will be treated in much more detail at the end of this chapter. At this point it is important to call attention to the experiential nature of the I. As noted above by Mead, the experience of the I does not appear in the same sense as the Me. It is out of awareness and pre-verbal and very much like the felt sense in Gendlin's experiencing construct. This is an essential point for this experiential study of reminiscence, for the method Gendlin developed can be used to explore the possible role of this elusive phenomenon of the creative and spontaneous I in old age.

It is also important to underline the temporal nature of the relationship between the I and the Me, for we will have occasion to come back to it repeatedly throughout this study. Natanson (1970) draws certain conclusions from this relationship that have clear implications for the study of reminiscence and the self in old age. He observes: "If the Me is the reservoir of the past, it includes the spontaneities of former moments of action which have been fulfilled in action and are now remembered events. In these terms spontaneity is destined to a middle age of stability if not respectability." Given this type of process, how much more stable or "respectable" would the self become in old age? Some would say the self is destined to become more rigid in old age, and this is an issue that will be addressed now.

THE OLDER SELF

There has been a good deal of debate in the gerontological research literature about whether there is change or stability, flexibility or rigidity, in personality functioning in late life. Some research on cognitive functioning shows greater rigidity in the cognitive processing of perceptions as persons grow older, whereas other research has shown the evidence on this to be inconsistent (Chown, 1961; Schaie & Labouvie-Vief, 1974; Zarit, 1980). Part of the dilemma lies in the fact that there are different aspects of personality, and some aspects show change while others show remarkable stability.

The overt aspects of personality that have to do with sociability, interpersonal behaviors, and life-style tend to show stability and continuity over the life span. In other words, if you were an extrovert when younger, you will probably remain an extrovert through old age (Bengtson, 1973). These overt aspects of the personality are clearly observable to others, and they lead to such observations as "That's good old Dave, all right" when speaking of a man named Dave who exhibited his own particular characteristic kind of behavior in some situation.

On the other hand, the areas in which personality seems to change in old age are in covert functioning that can be picked up only in certain kinds of psychological testing and in-depth interviews. What this research seems to show is that there is an increased saliency of the inner life and an "increased interiority of personality" in old age (Neugarten, 1969). There is more focusing of thought and feeling on inner issues in relationship to external or environmental issues, and much of this has to do with an inner sorting out of experiences, persons, values, and things that are most central to the self. One group of gerontological researchers reported that there are developmental factors in aging that seem to make for greater continuity in personality and life-style than had previously been thought. These researchers found that "those characteristics that have been central to the personality seem to become even more clearly delineated, and those values the individual has been cherishing become even more salient" (Neugarten, Havighurst, & Tobin, 1968). Now, it is possible that, in the process of delineating core values and characteristics, older persons can come to premature closure and not be open to new perspectives or values based on new experiences. We know such older persons by the fact that they are critical and rejecting of anything new and different. This is clearly reflected in their reminiscing about the "good old days," which are much preferred over the present in all of its aspects (Lieberman & Tobin, 1983). The fact is that we frequently see this rigidity in older persons, but it would be a mistake to equate this with the adaptive simplification or paring down to what are deemed the essentials of the self. To do so would be to confuse foreclosure with integration. We will encounter this issue again, but the difference will become apparent in the reminiscences and narratives to be presented in subsequent chapters.

Another change that has been found in gerontological research dealing with the older self is a change from an active or aggressive to a more passive and accommodating relationship of self to the outer world. David Gutmann (1977) referred to this as a shift from "active mastery" to "passive mastery" in his cross-cultural study of older men. Other gerontological investigators have found this shift in women as well as in men. Bernice Neugarten (1969) found that older persons generally (those over 60) began to feel that the environment could no longer be reformed in line with their wishes, so they tended to see themselves as accommodating more to the demands of the outer world. The middle-aged (forties and fifties), on the other hand, tended to see themselves as having enough energy to overcome obstacles in the outer world and to take advantage of opportunities.

So among older persons there is a perceptible change in the way they see themselves in relationship to their surroundings and circumstances. Rather than aggressively trying to remake or reshape their physical and social environments, they attempt to deal with each circumstance more reflectively and thoughtfully so as to minimize stress, conserve ego energy, and ensure a better "fit" or balance of self with environmental factors. Some of this is a protective or defensive device to ensure greater security and accommodation in what is perceived as a more complex and perhaps fearsome environment, but it also marks a shift in attitude toward greater acceptance and valuing of what one actually has. Gutmann (1977) has described this as a turning toward the elemental and sacred aspects of life and away from competition and achievement. This goes hand in hand with the increased interiority of old age. More passive activities of thinking, praying, imagining, and remembering—all inner activities—begin to replace some of the more external physical activities that impact more directly on the environment. Thus, the phenomenon of increased reminiscence in old age is also a reflection of increased interiority in which memories and images of the past, now internalized, become salient and meaningful in the present, frequently in new ways.

IDENTITY AND INTEGRITY IN OLD AGE

This shift toward greater interiority is a normal, if not universal, phenomenon in the dialectical relationship between the self, particularly the embodied self, and the outer world. The inevitable physical decrements that are part of the aging process call for a reassessment of how much one can actually do to remake the outer world to one's liking. Many older people stay very active and productive far into old age, but even they have thoughtfully considered how to conserve their energies so as to expend them on the things that are most meaningful to them.[2] There are those who will deny, suppress, or try to overcome those decrements by exerting themselves, but there may be a price to pay in terms of stress and exhaustion. Along with this experience of reduced physical and energy levels is a subtle but inexorable need to redefine one's self or, more precisely, one's identity. Klaus Riegel (1976), probably the most prominent developmental psychologist to study the dialectical processes of aging, has clearly delineated how this subtle change in identity comes about. He notes that because of the human capacity to develop abstract ideas and symbols it is possible for a person to think about his or her own appearance, body, and even mind and to interpret feedback from within as well as from others outside in defining the self. In the course of aging, the person attempts to orchestrate all of these perceptions, experiences, and ideas into a coherent identity or ongoing concept of self. Actually, this delineation by Riegel is quite consistent with the symbolic interactionist conception of George Herbert Mead and the phenomenological conception of self by Maurice Natanson, as these were presented earlier. If anything, Riegel more consistently and emphatically emphasizes the dialectic of self and world. Riegel also emphasizes somewhat more the material and physical dimensions of world, along with the social, in the self–world relationship, and this is an important addition to any study of developmental processes in later life.

Another investigator in the developmental psychology of later adulthood, Susan Whitbourne (1986) has taken a similar dialectical approach in describing identity processes on the basis of Piaget's concepts of accommodation and assimilation. Identity accommodation is the process that accounts for change in adulthood, whereas identity assimilation is the process responsible for stability (Whitbourne & Weinstock, 1986). In accommodating to the perceived realities of the world, the older person's identity or conception of self changes accordingly, as noted above. In assimilation, on the other hand, the changing realities of the world are reinterpreted in terms of the preexisting identity or conception of self. This process would be operative in the closure of self-concept that was discussed earlier. Whitbourne and Weinstock propose that these are the two overriding identity processes through which individuals come to define and redefine themselves, their priorities, and their experiences. The resulting personal identity is what gives a sense of continuity to the adult's experiences, linking them to the common denominator of "me" and "mine." It is significant that Whitbourne (1986) equates the word *me* with identity and refers to identity as "the Me I know," much as William James would have.

Although it is primarily the process of assimilation that facilitates the sense of continuity of identity, when there is a major dislocation in the person's world, such as the death of a spouse, then the process of accommodation is called for in order to retain a viable and realistic sense of identity. C. Murray Parkes (1971), a social psychiatrist who has extensively studied bereavement and the crises of identity in the wake of the death of loved ones, has clearly identified the need for accommodation to avoid mental illness, specifically depression. He too notes the human tendency to link experiences and objects with ourselves. He emphasizes the tendency to identify "my house," "my car," "my wife," "my child," "my success," and so on with ourselves, as parts of our identity. These are also parts of what he calls our "assumptive world," and when one of them is lost in the outer world (e.g., death of a spouse), there is a need to restructure that assumptive world in line with the new reality. He uses the term *psychosocial transitions* to describe these major changes in a person's life space that take place within a relatively short period of time but affect large areas of the person's assumptive world and are also lasting in their effects. Such transitions are apt to occur more commonly with the elderly because of more such losses among them than among any other age group, and it is largely because of these loss experiences that a life-review process occurs in older adults.

Whitbourne has commented that it is difficult to imagine an older person *not* reviewing and asking questions about the meaning of the losses they have sustained and who they are as a result of those experiences. All of the object losses, along with the loss of social roles (spouse, parent, breadwinner, homemaker, etc.) one could *identify* with, would seem to require such a review. Yet she and her colleagues, in their study of ego integrity statuses mentioned earlier, found the largest single group in their sample to be the "foreclosed" elderly who had not gone through a life-review process (Walaskay et al., 1983–84). These individuals seemed to have reasonably positive self-concepts and seemed not to admit they were aging. Unlike the integrity-achieving group, they tried not to think too much about existential or philosophical questions regarding life's meaning or whether it was worth it to "keep going," a question the dissonant group raised.

It would be helpful at this point to step back and look at the Eriksonian framework that Whitbourne and her colleagues used in arriving at the four ego-integrity statuses of integrity-achieving, foreclosed, dissonant, and despairing. They described it as follows:

> The developmental theory of Erikson suggests that the approaching end of life precipitates a period of intense reflection in older adults. This period, which is the eighth and final psychosocial stage or crisis, is referred to as Ego Integrity versus Despair. During this time the individual is involved in reminiscence, the recollection of memories, dreams, and thoughts and attempts to reconstrue the meaning of life while coming to terms with impending death. (Walaskay et al., 1983–84)

This is a good brief recapitulation of the reflective processes that would be involved in achieving ego integrity as set forth by Erikson. Now it is interesting to see what they found with respect to the foreclosed individuals. Was there "a period of intense reflection" in which they attempted to reconstrue their lives? No, there was no clear evidence of such a period in their lives, based upon their own reports. Was there a "coming to terms with impending death"? Yes, in fact there was. Most of the foreclosed individuals in their study had come to terms with the eventuality of their own deaths by making arrangements for their own burials and for the dispersal of their possessions.

This latter finding was rather perplexing to the investigators at the time. Somewhat later, Whitbourne and Weinstock observed that foreclosed individuals seemed to interpret the new experiences of aging in terms that are old and familiar. They "may even transform potentially deep questions of the meaning of existence into relatively trivial, mundane matters such as to whom to leave the family silver" (Whitbourne & Weinstock, 1986). It seemed as though the foreclosed "were able to survive into old age without having contemplated the meaning of their past and future, despite the loss of their friends and the activities involved in preparing for their own death." Whitbourne and Weinstock felt this could be done only after a great deal of "practice in avoiding confrontation with psychologically challenging issues."

In other words, the foreclosed did not experience the losses and changes, as life crises or as true psychosocial transitions in Parkes's sense. By sticking to interpretations of things as they were in the past (assimilation) they were able to avoid changing their old assumptive worlds—but at the cost of not integrating their experiences of loss and change into a larger sense of meaning in their lives or into a sense of self as part of a larger scheme of things.

A number of other gerontological investigators have found this same kind of foreclosed late-life adjustment pattern (Neugarten et al., 1968; Maas & Kuypers, 1974; Reichard, Livson, & Peterson, 1962). This raises questions concerning not only Butler's claim about the universality of the life-review process but Erikson's concept of a bipolar resolution of the psychosocial crisis of old age into either ego integrity or despair. In fact, the equivalent of the foreclosed status in the Chicago study by Lieberman and Tobin outnumbered their integrity-achieving counterparts. They seem to be a large (a majority of the Chicago subjects) and relatively unexamined group of elderly in terms of resolution of life crises and transitions. This was the primary reason for my undertaking the Integrity Survey, the last in this series of three studies.

Now, with the advantage of hindsight from these studies, I would like to go back to Erikson and pick up on some other observations he made about ego integrity. He said that one major feature of it would be an "acceptance of one's one and only life cycle as something that had to be and that, by necessity, permitted of no substitutions (Erikson, 1963). Now what does he mean by this? Does he mean "Whatever will be, will be," or that people have to accept rather passively whatever "happened" to them in their life cycles? Does it mean they really had no choices at key junctures of their lives and that therefore their lives "permitted of no substitutions"? It is quite clear from reading Erikson that he did not take such a simple, fatalistic view of the matter. He did not see the individual as a mere passive recipient of whatever society or circumstances meted out.

Erikson (1976) made another statement about the struggle for ego integrity. He noted that the fruit of that struggle would be "wisdom," which he defined as "the detached yet active concern with life itself in the face of death itself, and one that maintains and conveys the integrity of experience, in spite of the decline of bodily and mental functions." They key words here are *integrity of experience*, and the maintenance of that in the face of declining physical and mental capacities is the *essence* of ego integrity.

This is not the same as identity, which has to do with the incorporation of past roles, achievements, and experiences and then redefining them in the light of later life events and experiences. As Natanson would say, there is probably already a rather stable, sedimented Me (i.e., identity) by middle age. Integrity, on the other hand, is more of an ongoing process if only because the physical and mental changes will continue right up to the time of death. Thus, identity has to do largely with the dialectic between the self, particularly the Me part of the self, and the world. The integrity of experience is more of an inner dialectic between the I and the Me of the self, if you will. Furthermore, it is an inner dialectic that goes on throughout the

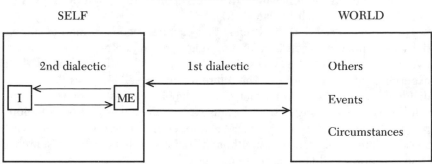

Figure 1
Two dialectics of the self.

life cycle and that may become amplified in late life with increasing interiority.

So what I am proposing here is a terminology and framework that can serve descriptive and perhaps heuristic purposes for the remainder of this study. The framework consists of two basic dialectics: (1) self–world, which has to do with identity formation or the Me; and (2)I–Me, which has to do with the process of experiencing throughout the life cycle and ultimately with integrity of experience (from a life-span perspective) in old age. These two dialectical processes are depicted in Figure 1. It is the Me that faces out toward the world and is the part of the self most directly interactive with the world in all of its varied social and cultural manifestations. There is apt to be decreased dialectical interaction between self and world in old age due to loss of significant others, retirement, and so on; but there is apt to be increased dialectical interaction between the I and the Me with the increased interiority of later life. How the inner dialectic between the I and the Me works within this whole framework is the subject of the following section on the self as a process.

THE SELF AS PROCESS

Any attempt to draw the boundaries and domains of the self is apt to show some theoretical bias, and this attempt is no different. This study does, after all, take an avowed experiential perspective, which necessarily leads to exploration of certain domains in preference to other theoretically possible ones. The I–Me dialectic serves the experiential perspective of this study.

Two recent writers on the psychology of the self remarked on the recurrent centrality of the personal pronoun "I" in the inner descriptions of various theories of the self. They go on to say that even common and mundane sentences such as the following express this centrality: "I am not myself today" (Young-Eisendrath & Hall, 1987).

They go on to say that the I refers to a particular construction of subjectivity that apparently acts as a kind of judgment on another state of subjectivity—"myself"—which is recognized as more familiar than the immediate experience of I. Furthermore, the reference to "myself" implies that the individual has a personal construct of self that is seen as characteristic and valid, as well as ongoing in time, because it is evaluated as part of a temporal process "today." The other thing that is implied in this simple statement is a sense of self as coherent unity, although "today" in this particular sentence is an exception to this usual sense of unity.

The "myself" in this statement is, of course, very much related to the Me of our earlier discussion. It is familiar, well known to us, and has to do with a sense of *identity*. The I is less familiar, but by implication is certainly "there." As noted earlier, Mead was not satisfied that the Me could be the totality of the self. It was too much of a social product or artifact, which at best could be a self-reflecting-on-self based on how we think we look in the eyes of others (looking-glass self), which is still a highly socialized conception. Therefore, he turned to the I as the spontaneous aspect of the self. However, because of his emphasis on social behaviorism he never systematically explored or delineated the implications of his I concept (Coulter, 1979).

Natanson, as an existential phenomenologist, emphasized not only the spontaneous feature of the I but also that it was the locus of *choice* or authentic decision making in the self. Thus, a person might chose to act in a socially approved manner in a particular situation because of how it would look in the eyes of others, which would be a choice of the Me, or looking-glass self, rather than an authentic choice of the I. Natanson (1970) goes on to say that when the person has to reflect on a choice for action, it is always over the backdrop of the Me, which also handles the procedure of enactment, but "the *deed* is sprung by the I." The I is thus the subject of all action, and the Me is the object. Since choice is so central to existentialist thinking, Natanson's focus on the I is understandable.

Erikson was also interested in the personal pronoun "I" and the extent to which it expressed Freud's meaning of ego. Although Freud's use of the German *Ich* has consistently been translated as "ego" in psychoanalytic literature, Erikson (1981) thinks Freud used *ich* most clearly at times to mean "I", particularly in the sense of its experiential "immediacy, spontaneity, and certainty." Erikson (1982) later went on to say:

> I am, of course, aware of the linguistic difficulty of speaking of *the* "I" as we do of *the* ego or *the* self; and yet, it does take a sense of "I" to be aware of a "my-

self" or, indeed of a series of myselves, while all the variations of self-experi-
ence have in common (and a saving grace it is) the conscious continuity of the
"I" that experienced and can become aware of them all.

Although Erikson was fascinated with the role of the I in human experience, it does appear that his descriptions of *ego* integrity sound much more
like manifestations of the Me rather than the I. Operationally, these descriptions sound like conscious reflective views of self as object in terms of
social experiences, roles, achievements, failures, and so on. In fact, it seems
much more like an integration of *identities*, or series of myselves. The fact
that the term *ego* tends to be used much more frequently in the sense of Me
in the psychoanalytic literature has led one expert on autobiographical
memory to note that the ego is that "aspect of the mind that moves through
space and time" and that accounts for "personal memories" but that it is
only part of the larger entity of the self (Brewer, 1986). So the use of the
term *self* will be broader than, though inclusive of, the ego for the purposes
of this study.

Although the I was an integral part of William James's conception of the
self, he was troubled by it because it was wholly subjective and could not be
seen. The Me is a much more observable part of the self, and since he was
interested in the empirical study of the self, James devoted much more attention to the "Empirical Self" or Me. The Me is more observable because
so much of it is identified with objects. James (1890) noted:

> *In its widest sense*, however, *a man's Me is the sum total of all that he can call
> his*, not only his body, and his psychic powers, but his clothes and his house,
> his wife and children, his ancestors and friends, his reputation and works, his
> lands and horses, and yacht and bank account. All these things give him the
> same emotions. If they wax and prosper, he feels triumphant; if they dwindle
> and die away, he feels cast down — not necessarily in the same degree for each
> thing, but in much the same way for all.

All of "these things" were not of the same order in the hierarchy of the
self, as far as James was concerned. He posited the "self-as-known," or Me,
as being composed of the *Material Me* (e.g., my body, clothes, immediate
family, home, property, creative products, etc.), the *Social Me* (e.g., affilia-
tion, recognition, reputation, fame, honor in the eyes of significant audi-
ences, etc.), and the *Spiritual Me* (consciousness of active states of thinking,
feeling, and behaving). This ordering of Me's by James is a meaningful one
in terms of priorities in the course of aging, as we shall see, and it is clear
that James saw the "spiritual Me" as the more foundational and prior Me.

Although James wrote more about the Me aspects of the self, he was
aware of and wrote that conscious content of the self (Me phenomena)
could not exist in the absence of consciousness (the I) any more than a pure

and abstract form of consciousness can exist without a content. As he put it, we should not let our language trick us into dividing the phenomenon of self into two *separate* things. They are only separated aspects of the same *process*. The point to be emphasized here is that the I and the Me are integral parts or polarities in a dialectical process called the self.

Eugene Gendlin (1981) also refers to the self as a process, and it is clear that his experiencing construct is very much in line with this dialectical conception of the I and Me. The inner, felt sense and felt meaning belongs to the I part of the dialectic; the verbal articulation belongs to the Me part. The reflective dialectic between these two gives explicit meaning to the implicit felt meanings that constitute lived experience.

It is not only possible but quite common for people to go through a series of events in their lives without these events becoming truly *lived* experiences. This is because there was no true experiencing of the events in terms of a bodily sensed meaning. It is those events in which one had a gut reaction that are remembered as lived experiences. There are people who in telling about their life experiences show that they have been in touch with the felt meaning of those experiences, especially when pivotal life choices were involved. Such a person can say, "I *lived* my life," and we would take it to be an authentic and valid statement. However, with other persons we would feel it more valid for them to say, "My life lived me." In other words, there are older people who in reminiscing and engaging in self-narrative will present a picture of someone who more or less went along with what they were presented with or what happened *to* them in life. There is little evidence of proactive choice in the events and circumstances of their lives and also very little evidence of reflecting on (experiencing of) the meaning of those experiences. They will tell their stories in matter-of-fact terms as to the roles, statuses, and external circumstances in their lives, but the felt meanings will be lacking.

We will see illustrations of this sort of narrative in the chapters to come. They can be fine diachronic narratives that are well integrated in terms of chronology, but they will lack the "integrity of experience" Erikson spoke about. On the other hand, there will be narratives that are reflective of just such integrity because it will be evident that they are about *lived* experience.

In the course of a long life older persons have gone through many experiences, some of which have been explicated in terms of their felt meaning either at the time (in a spontaneous I-initiated action) or afterward. However, many if not most of their experiences will not have been explicated or integrated until old age arrives. Butler would claim that this is what the life review is intended to accomplish, and Neugarten and her colleagues would claim it is what the increased interiority of old age is all about (Neugarten,

1969). It is in late life and often after retirement that the person reflects upon and explicates the felt meaning of those experiences.

It is important to point out that this increased interiority occurs in extraverts as well as introverts. As noted earlier, the extraverted person will remain an extravert, which is one of those consistent and overt aspects of the personality, but there will be more of an inclination from time to time to reflect inwardly on the felt meanings of those earlier experiences.

It is also important to point out that this interiority is not simply introspection in the sense of thinking to oneself. Such introspection would not lead to ego integrity. As Butler noted about the life review, it means going over painful as well as positive feelings attached to memories and objects, and this calls for a combination of thought and feeling. It is significant that two prominent researchers in life-span development of the personality have found repeated empirical evidence of integration of the feeling and thinking dimensions in older men, even though other aspects of personality (such as introversion and extraversion) seem to stay remarkably consistent from about age 30 through old age (Costa & McCrae, 1976; McCrae & Costa, 1988). They felt that these findings provided some support for Jung's concept of individuation in late life, in which the thinking and feeling (as well as the sensing and intuition) dimensions of the personality become integrated or synthesized in a more balanced way (Jung, 1971). There is, of course, much more to Jung's concept of individuation, which also has to do with integration of unconscious and conscious aspects of the self. These other aspects of individuation will be drawn upon later. However, it is important to note here that the integration of thought and feeling, together with increased interiority, can provide the older person with a capacity for experiencing that can be a remarkable creative resource for reminiscences, life review, and the ongoing integration and reconstruction of life experiences into a meaningful whole.

Rather than speaking of ego integrity or even identity as resolved or realized end-states, it would be more appropriate to speak of a continuing overall integrative *process*, a process of experiential integrations in old age. These integrations involve both the self–world and I–Me dialectics as well as the past, present, and future. From this perspective we can speak of the self as an ongoing, even emergent, process into very old age. I hope this will be amply illustrated to the reader's satisfaction in the remainder of the book.

SELF-INTEGRATION VERSUS EGO INTEGRITY

A process view of the self alters the way one interprets a number of the recurrent phenomena and empirical findings encountered in the study of aging. Rather than interpreting the last task of life as one of attaining a final state of ego integrity over despair, it appears more that the person is involved in an ongoing process of integrating various aspects of the self and experiences of the self-in-the-world. It is as though the person is attempting a number of different kinds of integrations in the process of constructing a cohesive sense of self and meaning in life.

Thus, the concept of ego integrity as laid out by Erikson seems to have too many dimensions and requirements to be more than an ideal. His ideas about those dimensions are provocative and promising, and his language in describing them is evocative and compelling. However, fundamental questions have been raised about the concept. It assumes attainment of a sense of self-continuity and cohesion; acceptance of self, significant others, and life; good morale characterized by contentedness and equanimity; and a sense of meaning, to name a few. It would seem more realistic to propose a number of integrative processes to attain some of these ends, rather than an overwhelming task of achieving all of them as the only way to avoid despair.

It has already been noted that four ego-integrity statuses have been offered as one alternative to the simple polar resolution of the task in favor of ego integrity or despair. However, another objection to the ego-integrity concept concerns Erikson's "epigenetic" model of ego development, whereby there has to be a positive resolution of each of the seven preceding psychosocial crises or stages of the life cycle, beginning in infancy, in order for ego integrity to be the resolution or outcome of the last stage of life. Some gerontologists do not see ego integrity as defined by Erikson as a very likely outcome. Based on her life-span studies, Vivian Clayton (1975) came to the conclusion that many people simply do not complete the life cycle as he defined it and that most people seek foreclosure or prolonged moratoriums after adolescence. She felt that, rather than complete resolution between conflicting forces in each major life stage, people most commonly and "realistically" opt for compromise. However, she proposes that the ability to deal with the conflicting forces in psychosocial crises and to come to some sort of compromise, actually a synthesis, is one of the strengths or virtues necessary for individuals to attain a "sense" of integrity rather than an idealized state of ego integrity.

One of the difficulties with the epigenetic model is that Erikson poses the tasks and crises of each life stage in terms that have a universal and perennial quality about them: trust versus mistrust (infancy), autonomy versus shame and doubt (early childhood), initiative versus guilt (play age), industry versus inferiority (school age), identity versus identity confusion (adolescence), intimacy versus isolation (young adulthood), generativity versus stagnation (adulthood), and finally integrity versus despair (old age). Take, for example, identity versus identity confusion, or identity "diffusion" as Erikson sometimes refers to it. This can be a recurrent dilemma in life and not because it was not "resolved" once and for all in adolescence. Erikson was aware of this, of course, and the rash of literature on mid-life crises is largely posed in terms of identity crises for both men and women.

Let us go back to the central ingredients that comprise the adolescent crisis of identity and then see where they stand in terms of old age. Erikson defined ego identity as a sense of oneself and one's place in society as well as a feeling of continuity with the past. A sense of identity requires that a person be able to define himself or herself in terms of the entire life-span. The adolescent is required to synthesize childhood identifications in such a way that he or she can establish a reciprocal relationship with society and still maintain a feeling of continuity within the self. Further, the adolescent has to arrive at a commitment to an occupation and an ideology in order to achieve a sense of identity. This ideology, or "ideological worldliness," as Erikson calls it, should be a synthesis, rather than a thoroughgoing acceptance or repudiation, of parental values and newly experienced countervailing values in order to achieve a sound identity of one's own.

The crisis in this stage refers to the adolescent's period of engagement in choosing among meaningful alternatives in ideology and occupation, whereas commitment refers to the degree of personal investment the individual exhibits. An adolescent in a state of identity diffusion shows a lack of commitment in terms of ideology and occupation, whether or not a crisis has been experienced. The "foreclosed" adolescent, on the other hand, has not experienced a crisis, yet expresses a commitment. This foreclosed state, identified in a research study of adolescents, was actually adopted by Walaskay, Whitbourne, and their colleagues as the prototype for the elderly foreclosed integrity status discussed earlier. The researcher in that study described the foreclosed adolescent as follows:

> It is difficult to tell where his parents' goals for him leave off and where his begin. He is becoming what others have prepared him to become as a child. His beliefs (or lack of them) are virtually "the faith of his fathers living still." College experiences serve only as a confirmation of childhood beliefs. A certain rigidity characterizes his personality perconsistency of form. (Marcia, 1966)

One could substitute *life* experiences for college experiences in the quotation above, and it would fit well the foreclosed elderly person. As a matter of fact, Erikson (1982) raises the question of what kind of alternative there is to this sort of rigid ritualization of an ideological world view, and he answers as follows: "I think it is *philo-sophical*; for in maintaining some order and meaning in the dis-integration of body and mind, it can also advocate a durable hope in wisdom. The corresponding ritualistic danger, however, is *dogmatism*, a compulsive pseudointegrity." So there needs to be the development in old age of a philosophical perspective, or wisdom, as Erikson puts it, to replace the ideological world view of the adolescent with one's *own* sense of integrity.

Let us go back to the occupational aspect of identity for a moment. What happens when the older person loses that essential piece of identity through retirement or disability? Some sociologists have held that the lack of a clearly defined and valued status of "retired person" has made for a sense of anomie or unclear identity among large numbers of the elderly (Rosow, 1973). Volunteer activities might serve to maintain self-esteem and morale, but they do not replace a strong vocational identity. The answer lies in Erikson's statement that the person has to be able to define himself or herself in terms of the entire life-span to retain a sense of identity. Thus, the older person can review and identify with past occupational and social-role commitments and accomplishments as an essential and valued part of the self within that whole life-span. In addition, however, it will be necessary to develop a philosophy that will sustain and guide the older person in the present and future. That might involve a recommitment or new commitment to certain religious, spiritual, or humanistic values and perspectives that will enable the person to face and deal with a future of likely physical and mental deterioration, or "dis-integration" as Erikson would have it, as well as the certainty of death.

Thus, there are certain integrations that have to take place in the older person in order to sustain a sense of identity, and thus self-integrity, in terms of the total life-span. There are also certain integrations that have to take place to sustain a sense of self-worth and self-esteem. One of the features of our society that has created problems of lowered self-esteem as well as loss of identity among the elderly is what has been referred to in the gerontological literature as the "functionalistic ethic" (Bengtson, 1973; Kuypers & Bengtson, 1972). This is an ethic by which the individual evaluates his or her own *self*-worth in terms of his or her functional value in society. In a society such as ours, with the highest premium put on the consumption and production of goods and services, the person is frequently evaluated in terms of productive or professional (service) functioning, monetary value, and the quantity and kinds of goods consumed within a market economy. This is not a valid or emotionally sound standard for self-evaluation by elderly individuals when they are no longer able to produce or consume in the quantities or style expected by such an ethos. Yet so ingrained is this ethic that large numbers of older persons continue to evaluate themselves in terms of their functional value within society.

When we did a survey of retired elderly in a metropolitan area of the northeastern United States, we found that about one-third of the 229 men and women studied clearly identified with and evaluated themselves in terms of the functionalistic ethic, and another 20% were somewhat mixed about it (Sherman, 1985a). Those who identified with it strongly agreed with the following statements: "A person isn't worth much when he or she is no longer able to carry on as a productive member of the community" and "Unless I feel that I have accomplished or done something that other people value, I feel quite worthless." They strongly disagreed, in turn, with the following statement: "A person's worth does not depend on how good a citizen, parent, or worker he or she is, but simply that he or she is a human being."

The latter statement speaks to a broader alternative ethic that underlies both religious and humanistic thinking concerning the inherent and basic value of human existence. Nevertheless, a large proportion of the elderly (though probably less than younger age groups) choose instead to evaluate self and others in terms of their functional value to society. This is at a serious cost to themselves, because they showed significantly lower measures of self-esteem than the other elderly persons in the study sample. This was particularly, almost devastatingly so when those who identified with the functionalistic ethic also believed themselves to be no longer healthy or competent. Their measures of self-esteem were among the lowest, and they were a generally demoralized group.

Self-esteem has been conceptualized and measured a number of different ways in the psychological literature, but one of the more prominent ways (especially for the elderly) is to conceptualize self-esteem as the degree of congruence between the individual's self-concept and self-ideal (Bengtson et al., 1985; Butler & Haigh, 1954; Friedman, 1955). In this conceptual scheme the self-concept is the cognitive element in that it is what the person *thinks* he or she is like. The self-ideal represents a composite of standards for behavior, performance, and achievement based on precepts and examples acquired from parents, teachers, and other role models who were available in the larger social and cultural milieu. It is what the person thinks he or she "should" or "ought" to be like, whereas self-esteem is the affective or emotional element in the scheme in that it represents how the person *feels* about him- or herself. That is, how much does the person feel he or she is actually (in terms of self-description, i.e., self-concept) like the person he or she ideally wishes to be? In its operationalized form, self-esteem is measured as the congruence or discrepancy between the (self-rated) self-concept and self-ideal. The more the concept and ideal are alike, the higher the self-esteem; the more discrepant they are, the lower the self-esteem.

Taking this back to the subject of the functionalistic ethic, it is evident that social roles are central to the ethic just as they are prominent in the development of the self-ideal. Expectations and standards for behavior associated with social positions are what constitute social roles, and how one performs one's social roles has an ongoing impact on one's self-esteem. Positive feedback from self and others for meeting or exceeding these expectations and standards can thus be essential to maintenance of self-esteem. Therefore, the loss of social roles or reduction of activity or performance in social roles, which may be an inevitable part of aging, become direct threats to self-esteem. Also, since self-esteem is emotional or affective in nature, it tends to be responsive to inner moods and bodily states as well as to performances or behaviors in the external world. Given the bodily changes inherent in the aging process, there are bound to be differential effects on self-esteem in old age.

In the course of aging there should be a dialectical process going on in the self between the self-concept and the self-ideal such that, through life experience, the expectations of the ideal and the definitions of the self in the self-concept are more in tune with inner and outer reality. This is clearly an important integrative process that can provide a stable and consistent sense of self in the face of losses and role changes in later life. What usually happens is that the self-ideal becomes more realistic in the course of life experience, and the older person becomes more accepting of self and others. As one prominent gerontologist put it, part of the process of growing old is a shedding of illusions and earlier grandiose ideals with respect to the self (Birren, 1964).

This type of integration or synthesis is a kind of incorporation, acceptance, and accommodation of reality and involves a willingness to let go of the grandiose and unrealistic. There is another kind of integration with respect to the aging self that is of a more active and searching nature. It is a search for what one writer has called the "existential self" or the "really me" (Tiryakian, 1968). He points out that some aspects of "reality" are more basic than others, and

> this qualitative differentiation of reality into what is "more real" and "less real" is given directly in experience when we are aware that some of the things we do or say do not represent the "really me." At the same time we do not feel that the "not-really-me" is illusory or nonexistent, but rather that it is in some way peripheral or epiphenomenal; yet, and paradoxically, it is the "not-really-me" that we know and are familiar with much more than the "really me."

This familiar not-really-me is apt to consist of the persona, the faces and "looking-glass" behaviors we exhibit in carrying out our everyday social roles and interactions (Goffman, 1959). In late life, with the increasing interiority, there is apt to be an attempt to get at and retain the sense of really-me as the core of continuity in the self. This is very much like James's "spiritual me," and it involves the inner I–Me dialectic referred to earlier. We will see examples of this kind of search in some of the reminiscences and self-narratives to be presented later.

This kind of integration is related to the idea introduced earlier in the expression "I am not myself today." If we can call this a sort of existential integration, it can be differentiated from the kind of *emotional* integration that is involved in the life review. There it is the feelings of grief, regret, anger, desolation, and so on that accompany the losses of late life that have to be confronted and worked through. In this process, the person integrates the reality of these losses into his or her assumptive world, which will therefore provide a more realistic and viable basis for living in the present and future. As a result of this process there is a kind of emotional integrity about the person and the likelihood that demoralization or outright despair will not be the outcome.

However, this does not necessarily mean that the person has addressed or answered the earlier question, "Who am I, really?" Nor does it mean that the person has addressed another existential question, "What does it all mean?" Although the person who has gone through such a life-review process is more likely to raise these questions than is the foreclosed individual, there is no guarantee of it. This was borne out in the Integrity Survey, and I have certainly seen it in clinical practice. There are some older persons who have gone through what appears to be a life-review process, at least as described by Butler, but have not consciously or purposefully addressed these other existential questions. Consequently, despite their emotional integrity and the likelihood of good mental health in late life, we could not say that such persons have necessarily met Socrates' twin injunctions to live an examined life and to "know thyself."

Another form of late-life integration that differs somewhat from the life review, as well as from the other self-review processes already mentioned, is the personal life story or self-narrative. Some gerontologists have observed and studied the autobiographical impulse among the elderly, an impulse described as a seeking of integrity or internal harmony (Myerhoff & Tufte, 1975). There does appear to be a need among many older persons to sustain a sense of continuity of the self with the past, which was one of the elements Erikson included in both his ego identity and ego-integrity concepts. There is little doubt that a cohesive life story, or the integration of a series of story lines with beginnings, middles, and ends, can provide some sense of continuity. That it is a need seemed evident in the group reminiscence project when individuals would relate different narrative episodes in their lives and then try to integrate them later in the groups or in the follow-up interviews. This seems quite consistent with recent findings from cognitive psychology and the newly developing area of narrative psychology concerning the predilections of the elderly for the narrative mode of learning, knowing, and acting.

These are just some of the integrations of self that might serve as alternatives to despair, although no one of them can be said to be the equivalent of Erikson's global conception of ego integrity. Just how they manifest themselves, how they fit together, or how they substitute for one another are questions that will be addressed in the remainder of this study. All of these questions were triggered by that initial excursion into group reminiscence that in turn prompted more questions of an existential and ontological nature about the experience of old age. Now, with all the recorded material that came out in the Individual Reminiscence and Integrity Surveys, we can explore these questions in greater depth in Chapters 7 and 8. First, however, it will be necessary to explore the role of time and objects in the dialectical processes of the aging self.

NOTES

1. See Natanson (1970), where he states the following: "I find my body as the central point at the source of the Here. In fact, Here is where my body is. There is where my body is not."

2. See especially the "focused pattern" of aging in which the old person focuses diminishing energy on a few highly valued activities and pursuits, as described in Neugarten et al. (1968).

6

Of Time and Objects

Over time, from infancy through old age, the human being has a changing relationship with objects in his or her life. Erikson's developmental model (1968, 1963) is quite clear about the fact that relationships between the self and selected objects evolve over time. Some aspects of these relationships may be lost, while others develop into something different, but a basic core is maintained over time that makes them identifiable (i.e., the core of ego identity).

Object relations theorists, in line with Margaret Mahler's (1979) findings of early childhood development, do not see the beginnings of a distinct self emerging until about the age of 2 in the course of a separation/individuation process. Until then the symbiotic relationship of the child to the mother or primary caregiver is such that, perceptually and experientially, clear boundaries between self and object (mother) are not possible. In the course of normal development from age 2 onward, the child is considered to be on the way to object and self constancy. Separation between self and the primary object becomes a greater perceptual reality, and a functional degree of individuation of self becomes possible.

Perhaps more than any other object relations theorist D. W. Winnicott (1971) has been able to provide a descriptive reality to these evolving relationships to objects in early life. He observed that many infants develop intense attachments to certain material objects, and these attachments are very much related to the beginnings of independence or individuation. These external objects function as comforters in the earlier months of development, and at first they are apt to be the child's thumbs or fists. However, the child will later substitute a piece of blanket or cloth sheet and later still perhaps a teddy bear, doll, or other soft toy. It can and frequently does happen that the object (blanket, bear, cloth, etc.) becomes extremely important to the child as a defense against anxiety, particularly when going to sleep. In this case the object is a comforter that acts as a substitute for the secure attachment figure of the mother herself.

These objects represent transitional stages between the child's attachment to the mother and the child's later attachment to other objects (i.e., people whom the child comes to depend upon and love). For this reason Winnicott called these "transitional objects"; they enable the child to progress through different stages of development in the process of separation and individuation. Also, although the objects act as substitutes for the mother, this is not because the mother has been somehow inadequate. In fact, in order for the child to invest these objects with supporting and loving qualities, the child must have experienced these qualities in the mother.

Consequently, the development of transitional objects is not at all pathological and is very much a feature of normal and healthy development. This capacity to invest objects with special meanings, particularly meanings related to secure and supportive relationships, can become an important resource in later life. Several of us who have researched this area among the elderly have come up with comparable evidence to show that certain objects can function as transitional objects of late life (Csikszentmihalyi & Rochberg-Halton, 1981; Sherman & Newman, 1977–78).

It would be a mistake to view this as some kind of infantile regression, just as it would be a mistake to view transitional objects themselves as somehow pathological. We have already noted in the writings of James, Mead, and Parkes the human propensity for identification of self with objects. We also noted that this was specifically so for the Me aspect of the self. Thus, over time there is an accretion of meaningful objects in a person's life, so it is commonplace to hear of elderly people who are loath to let go of many of their accumulated possessions.

OBJECTS AS SYMBOLS

Since the above observations about transitional objects came from Winnicott, a psychoanalyst and psychiatrist, and from others like Parkes, also a psychiatrist with an object relations orientation, they may seem to have a distinctly clinical flavor to them. However, there seems to be a remarkable unanimity across disciplines about objects as symbols, as distinct from objects as useful or consumable items. So fundamental are they for our very sense of being that Hannah Arendt, a philosopher, made the following observation: "The things of the world have the function of stabilizing human life, and their objectivity lies in the fact that . . . men, their ever-changing nature notwithstanding, can retrieve their sameness, that is, their identity, by being related to the same chair and the same table. (1958)

Clifford Geertz (1973), an anthropologist, writes that the "view of man as a symbolizing, conceptualizing, meaning-seeking animal . . . has become increasingly popular both in the social sciences and philosophy over the past several years." From this view, Geertz says:

Thinking consists not of "happenings in the head" . . . but of a traffic in what have been called . . . significant symbols—words for the most part but also gestures, drawings, musical sounds, mechanical devices like clocks, or natural objects like jewels—anything, in fact, that is disengaged from its mere actuality and used to impose meanings on experience.

Thus, material objects can have a central role in thinking and, as we shall see, most certainly in feeling.

A centerpiece of phenomenological thinking is the concept of intentionality, which states that human consciousness is always consciousness *of* something, of its object. It is essentially directional (i.e., intentional) in nature, and much of this intentionality is directed toward the "objectivity" of material things. Thus, in his study of the phenomenology of the self, Natanson (1970) can say:

Rather than speaking of mind "inside" and the world "outside" the body or the individual, the phenomenologist maintains that there is an integral relationship between man and the world, between consciousness and reality. In its dynamic, consciousness and its object are polarities of a unity, world-as-meant.

Natanson felt that Mead's symbolic interactionism operationalized the dynamics of this unity very well. Symbolic interactionists view people as constantly in an interactive process of interpretation and definition as they move from one situation to another in the world. Some situations are unfamiliar, such as chance encounters with strangers, or very familiar, such as one's parents or own bedroom, place of work, and so on. However, all situations consist of the actor, others and their actions, and physical objects. Whatever the juxtapositions of these elements, a situation can have *meaning* only through people's interpretations and definitions of it. This is the essence of Natanson's phrase "world-as-meant."

The pervasiveness and importance of objects in the development and existence of the individual are reflected in this statement by Mead (1934):

Any thing—any object or set of objects, whether animate or inanimate, human or animal, or merely physical—toward which he acts, or to which he responds, socially, is an element in what for him is the generalized other; by taking the attitudes of which toward himself he becomes conscious of himself as an object or individual and thus develops a self or personality.

So, from this perspective, objects, including physical objects, are part and parcel of the individual's very identity as a person.

In addition to the creation of self, there is an ongoing creation of meaning within this perspective. There are three components in the creation of symbolic meaning. The object acts as a sign (first component) that stands for something (second component) by creating an interpretive thought or emotion (third component). The range and pervasiveness of this interpretive process becomes apparent when we study the kinds of objects or possessions that the elderly cherish or consider special. The meanings and referents of these objects are extremely rich and varied as are the roles they play in reminiscence as well as the sense of continuity of the self, or Me. This rich diversity will be reported in the next two sections of this chapter, but it would be helpful to give a brief example of the interpretive process in the creation of symbolic meaning from one of the studies to be reported (Sherman & Newman, 1977–78).

One elderly widow in a nursing home identified a gold cross as her most cherished possession. She said, "It was a gift from my son when he was a youngster. He had a paper route and worked and saved very hard to get it for me. It means a lot to me." The cross was a sign (first component) standing for the love her son demonstrated for her by all he went through to get it for her (second component). The interpreting emotion (third component) was the love she felt for him in return and the mutuality of their love. She articulated this third component as she went on to describe what she meant by the statement "It means a lot to me." She added that each time she looked at the cross it evoked memories, thoughts, and feelings about her son. As she reflected on the object, most of the time she would reexperience the same memories and feelings, but sometimes there would be new memories or the old ones would be reexperienced somewhat differently and with a richer nuance of meaning. Thus, objects like this can develop and even take on new meanings, particularly so in the very last years of life. This is an extremely important point to keep in mind as we continue to explore the experience of reminiscence and the role objects play in it.

It is also important not to view this reflective and interpretive process as a totally abstracting one, distant in time, feeling, and thought. Sometimes it has an emotional immediacy that is overwhelming. Take, for example, the situation of a recent widow whose husband died unexpectedly of a heart attack in his mid-sixties. A number of months had passed, and although she was still in the mourning process, she was able to give away or dispose of a number of her husband's personal possessions. However, there was one object she simply could not part with. It was a beach ball that her husband had inflated by mouth a short time before his death. The intensity and immediacy of the emotions and meaning of that ball for her was evident in her expression, gestures, and words as she spoke about it. The ball contained an actual part of him: the very breath from his body!

The reader probably also recalls the earlier instance of the woman who could almost smell the presence of her dead husband in his clothes that she kept in the closet. Although both of the above instances involve a recently deceased loved one, there are other instances of spontaneous, intense, and vivid imagery and feeling attached to certain objects and to certain memories in reminiscence, as we shall see. In fact, people frequently personify objects through what have been called personification metaphors, in which the object will be identified as a friend, protector, companion, and so on (Lakoff & Johnson, 1980). This is particularly true for certain cherished possessions in old age.

CHERISHED OBJECTS IN LATE LIFE

Cherished objects are those possessions that are considered special by the person. Any *thing* can serve as a cherished object: a photo, a recording, a book, a chair, etc. The relative importance of cherished objects for the elderly has been associated with the fact that they provide a sense of continuity, security, comfort, and satisfaction and also that the fear of their loss is a common preoccupation among older persons (Butler & Lewis, 1983). Simone de Beauvoir (1973) went so far as to claim that ownership of certain possessions acts as a guarantee of ontological security for the elderly, for "thanks to his possessions the old person assures himself of his identity against those who claim to see him as nothing but an object."

Personal possessions take on different meanings from childhood into old age. In perhaps the most comprehensive empirical study of personal possessions heretofore, two investigators from the University of Chicago found that in childhood objects most often serve the purposes of action and use, whereas in later life they more often serve to reflect meanings related to the past and to integrate former experiences: "For an adult, objects serve the purpose of maintaining the continuity of the self as it expands through time (Csikszentmihalyi & Rochberg-Halton, 1981). By the time the people reach old age, they are apt to have certain objects that they cherish above all others because of the meanings associated with those objects from the past, whereas younger people are apt to prize certain possessions for their *current* meanings, usefulness, or enjoyment.

We found in the study of cherished possessions referred to earlier that 81% of the 94 elderly persons we interviewed could readily identify at least one cherished object, and those objects were related much more to the past than the present. (Sherman & Newman, 1977–78). We also found that those who could identify a most cherished possession generally evidenced significantly higher morale, as measured by a life-satisfaction instrument, than did those who could not. This led us to recommend strongly that aged persons going into nursing homes and other long-term-care facilities be encouraged to bring these cherished possessions with then into the facilities. This echoed a similar recommendation made by Butler and Lewis (1983) somewhat earlier, based on their practice experience. Our research findings served to validate their practice experience.

There were a number of different referents and meanings associated with the objects identified by our elderly respondents. Objects were cherished primarily because they referred to certain persons or experiences in the lives of our respondents. Referents included the self, when the object referred to a personal experience, or to any other person. Among those who claimed to possess at least one cherished object, the persons they identified as referents occurred in the following order of frequency: self (25), child (18), spouse (15), parents (5), grandchild (4) friend (1), grandparent (1), aunt (1), other relative (1), other nonrelative/nonfriend (1). Different kinds of objects tended to have different referents. Photographs most often had a child as a referent, whereas symbolic jewelry (e.g., rings, necklaces, etc.) were most often associated with a spouse. Religious objects most often had the self as referent, as did personal performance (musical instruments, tools, etc.) and consumer (TVs, radios, etc.) items.

The particular personal meanings of the objects varied considerably, but the following representative responses should help to give some sense of their nature and range (Sherman & Newman, 1977–78).

> (Female respondent): My Bible—it has been my guide and has sustained me through life.
> (Male respondent): Violin—I am a musician, and the violin means everything to me.
> (Female): Pictures (photos)—they mean I was a woman. I had children and built my life around them. Happy memories.
> (Female): Pictures (photos)—you renew your life with your children's pictures. They can appease your loneliness.
> (Female): Ring—it was my mother's wedding ring. She gave it to me before she died.
> (Female): Bracelet—my husband gave it to me sixty years ago. My feelings add much meaning to the object.
> (Female): Paintings—painting keeps my mind off the nursing home.

Women tended to have more frequent referents and meanings associated with significant others, whereas men tended to identify somewhat more with personal performance and consumer items, such as tools and TVs, related to the self. However, women also indicated a substantial number of self-referent objects, and men identified a substantial number of objects that had significant others as referents. Overall, then, cherished objects were quite prominent in the lives of these elderly respondents. So it would be quite appropriate here to explore the role objects, particularly cherished objects, play in late-life reminiscence.

REMINISCENTIA: OBJECTS IN REMINISCENCE

Edward Casey (1989) coined the term *reminiscentia* in his phenomenological study, *Remembering*, to refer to objects that act as *inducers* of reminiscence. He observed that they could include anything that survives from the epoch reminisced about and could include photographs, letters, relics, and souvenirs, "indeed any object or trace of an object that remains and is presently available in perception" and that "has a special aptitude for arousing a reminiscent state of mind."

We attempted in the course of the Integrity Survey in 1989 to obtain data on the kinds of objects or memorabilia that tend to induce reminiscing more than others among the elderly. We asked about such reminiscentia as well as any special or cherished possessions they could identify in a questionnaire distributed to over 100 elderly respondents. We found that 96% of them could identify at least one kind of object that would set off their reminiscing more than others, and some could identify as many as seven. Among the most frequent objects that served as reminiscentia were photographs, which accounted for 36% of the identified objects, followed by books (12%), symbolic jewelry (11%), and music (7%) in the form of recordings, tapes, dances, and music boxes.

Although photographs were the most frequently identified cherished objects (24%), they were not as predominant among cherished possessions as they were among reminiscentia. Symbolic jewelry was almost as frequently identified as a cherished object (22%) as photographs, and these two types of objects far exceeded the next most frequent type, which was religious objects (6%). We also found in our interviews with the respondents following the completion of their questionnaires that when symbolic jewelry was identified as a reminiscentia item it was identified as such specifically because it was a particular cherished possession of the respondent. This was not as much the case with photographs. When interviewed, quite a few of the respondents reported that seeing photographs in magazines or newspapers would trigger reminiscences about the era or epoch of the photo, just as Casey had described the process. These photographs were not related to specific persons or experiences in the lives of the respondents. However, quite a few others (about one-third of those interviewed) reported that they had specific cherished photographs in mind when they mentioned photographs as reminiscentia. With symbolic jewelry, on the other hand, respondents were almost invariably referring to a specific piece of cherished jewelry in their listing of reminiscentia, and these objects were usually given by or associated with a spouse or parent.

It has been my experience that when elderly persons reminisce with the aid of a cherished object, or an aide-mémoire as Casey calls it, they are apt to give much "thicker" descriptions in their reminiscences. Phenomenologists refer to thick description as the kind that captures the meanings and experiences that have occurred in a rich, dense, and detailed manner and creates the conditions for interpretation and understanding (Denzin, 1989). Thin description, on the other hand, is factual in a purely descriptive sense and is often incomplete or glossed over It provides little in the way of interpretation or understanding. We shall see some examples of this in the following chapters, but for the moment it might be helpful to give an illustration of thick reminiscence that was evoked and then sustained by a cherished object serving as a piece of reminiscentia. This illustration comes from an 81-year-old woman I interviewed in a nursing home who identified as one of her most cherished possessions a photograph of the home she had to leave. It triggered a whole series of memories and associations and led to much thicker description in her discourse than she had demonstrated earlier in the interview when she described her childhood.

The photograph was a colored one of a modest little one-story brick house on a corner lot with ample green lawn, bushes, and flowers around it. It appeared to be solid, clean, and very well cared for. When she showed me the photograph, she began by saying, "My husband and I spent the happiest years of our lives in that house. It meant a great deal to us, and every time I look at this [photo] I know I'll never forget those times. We had that house for thirty years, and the funny part of it was that we bought it as an investment—to make it into a business instead of a home."

She went on to describe the purchase of that house as a demarcation point in their lives. She said that she and her husband had to struggle during the first decade of their marriage because it began with the advent of the Depression. Because of large stretches of unemployment for her husband, they had to leave their own apartment to live for a number of years in a single refurbished room in the attic of his parents' home. It was not until 1941 that her husband got a good job as a toolmaker in an aircraft factory, after serving several years of apprenticeship at low pay. He took evening courses in engineering and mathematics concurrent with his job and became a tool procurement engineer at good pay with the same aircraft company just as America's war economy went into full swing in late 1942.

Although they had more money, they could not buy or maintain a house because her husband was constantly traveling by plane to different parts of the country evaluating and purchasing tools for his company. She described this as "one of the lowest points in my life." She had the major responsibility of raising the children in a second-floor apartment at a time when she had some physical complications leading to a hysterectomy in her mid-thirties, while he was "constantly on the road."

She said:

> I vowed that when the war was over we would have a life *together*, one way or another. At the end of the war his company made plans to move their head-

quarters out west to Denver, and they offered him a good job if he would move. He wanted it badly, but it meant that he would have to continue traveling a lot. There was no way I was going to have any of that! . . . Besides, it meant the two of us leaving the town we were both born and raised in . . . and neither of us really liked the thought of that. So I convinced him that we should take the money we had saved during the was and invest it in a grocery store in our hometown, where we could work together as a family.

She then described a number of moves and changes in their life that were making her husband increasingly unhappy. Not only did he give up a good-paying job to go into the grocery business but that business did not do well. They next purchased a delicatessen, which did no better after two or three years. This was the beginning of the era of supermarkets, and they simply could not complete. Furthermore, their children had grown and left home, so their help in the store was gone. They then purchased a tavern, which they ran for three years, but it did not yield much profit for all of their effort. Her husband, in frustration and some disgust, took a job as a toolmaker in a local factory but he still harbored the hope of "making it big somehow."

They decided they might try to make it in real estate. They then proceeded to buy a house every year or two, improve it, and then try to sell it for a profit. After doing this with about six houses, they got their real estate licenses and decided to find a home where they could set up their own real estate business. That home turned out to be the house in her cherished photograph.

She explained what happened as follows:

Without knowing it we came to love that house little by little. My husband began building things and improving things around the house, while I began to thoroughly enjoy the gardening and canning and other things that could be done there. We began losing interest in the real estate business, and we kept our regular jobs. I had a temporary job as a file clerk for the state, so I took the civil service exam, passed it, and made the job permanent. We ended up by making that our retirement home . . . but, looking back on it, I can see why. It meant stability for the first time in our lives. It meant warmth, security . . . and love. My husband and I became much closer there. It was the one place where we really felt at *home*. . . . We had peace of mind there.

Our children would come from out of town for visits, and our grandchildren would play in the backyard or in the big clean basement we had. We did some traveling ourselves after we retired, but we always looked forward to coming back to the house. When my husband had a stroke and had to be in a wheelchair, I was able to keep him there for the next four years until he died. I am so thankful he died there instead of somewhere else. It was impossible for me to keep it up after he died, though, because *my* physical condition became so bad. I hated to give it up—not the house so much—that was something we had *together*—being alone there was not the same. It was the whole process of getting rid of our furniture and so many other things we were fond of. It was heartbreaking.

This whole narrative was unsolicited by questions from me, other than some encouraging nods, and it appeared to be prompted solely by her recollections while looking at the photograph and attempting to recapitulate the way in which that house was so central to her life. She would look at the photograph from time to time and reminisce about what had happened at various times in conjunction with different parts of the house — her husband working with his tools in the basement, their grandchildren playing in the back yard, and so on.

Toward the end of the interview she pointed out where the living room was located and what was in it. She described the furniture, the fireplace, and a picture on the mantle over the fireplace. It was a copy of a Spanish Renaissance painting showing the interior of a manor, a large room in which a family was gathered to hear one of their young daughters perform on a harp. It also had a fireplace in it, and she said the picture "gave off the warmth of a family gathering." She said that when she broke up the house she gave that painting to a favorite niece who had expressed a great liking for it. She said her niece had just sent her a letter telling her how much she treasured the painting and how grateful she was for it. My respondent then offered to show me a letter she had started to write in response to her niece. In it she had written, "I am so glad you like that picture because I've loved it right along. So, I'll always know there's a little part of me somewhere."

This last statement suggests so much about the meaning of that painting for her at this stage and place in her life. It touches on the issues of mortality and continuity of the self. There can be no question, on the basis of her whole reminiscential discourse, about the meaning and experiential qualities attached to the house and where it fit into her life as a whole. The discourse was redolent with expression of her thoughts and feelings about the house and its furnishings. Although she no longer had the house, she had the cherished photograph that enabled her to retain and reexperience much the house had meant in her life.

TIME AND THE OBJECT SELF

It should be evident at this point how central objects are to the aging self. The progressive losses of objects such as beloved homes and of the loved ones from those homes in the course of aging calls for a greater and greater need to retain those valued places and persons symbolically. While many material possessions are lost or shunted off over time, through the process of interiority in old age certain remaining objects (which represent the most valued persons and experiences) gain greater and greater inner salience. These, then, become the cherished objects of old age.

There is a shrinking of time in old age that makes this whole process take on a greater urgency. This has been no more poignantly expressed than by Vladimir Nabokov (1966) in his remarkable autobiography, *Speak Memory*, when he says:

> Initially, I was unaware that time, so boundless at first blush, was a prison. In probing my childhood (which is the next best thing to probing one's eternity) I see the awakening of consciousness as a series of spaced flashes, with the intervals between them gradually diminishing until bright blocks of perception are formed, affording memory a slippery hold.

He was fortunate to possess an uncanny capacity for detailed recollection in his reminiscences and for drawing upon reminiscentia, combined with his literary gift for richness of description. As he put it, "The act of vividly recalling a patch of the past is something that I seem to have been performing with the utmost zest all my life, and I have reason to believe that this almost pathological keenness of the retrospective faculty is a hereditary trait" (Nabokov, 1966). After which he goes on to demonstrate this trait in the following passage:

> I see again in my schoolroom in Vyra, the blue roses of the wallpaper, the open window. Its reflection fills the oval mirror above the couch where my uncle sits, gloating over a tattered book. A sense of security, of well-being, of summer warmth pervades my memory. That robust reality makes a ghost of the present. The mirror brims with brightness; a bumblebee has entered the room and bumps against the ceiling. Everything is as it should be, nothing will ever change, nobody will ever die.

There is not only a shrinking of time in old age, there is also a shrinking of space. From the middle of life, when most people are at the peak of their vocational and financial power and the space perspective is one of "the world is my oyster," there is the common experience of progressive loss of this through retirement and declining physical (and perhaps financial) capacity for extensive travel. Since it is no longer necessary (for raising children) or possible (for physical or financial reasons) to keep one's house, this often necessitates a move into the smaller confines of an apartment. With further physical or mental deterioration it frequently becomes necessary to move into an adult home, a nursing home, or some other long-term-care facility. There, personal space is reduced to a room or part of a room. The kinds of cherished objects one can keep in such a setting are drastically reduced in numbers and size. This is probably why about a third of the nursing home respondents in our cherished-objects study claimed to have no cherished possessions, as compared to less than 1 in 20 of the community elderly.

Along with the shrinkage of time and space there is a shrinkage of memory. Granted that the elderly appear to retain long-term memory much more effectively than short-term, even those memories from the distant past dim and fade. Objects can help reverse some of this. That is why the use of memorabilia, of reminiscentia, in group reminiscence in long-term-care facilities continues to increase. However, after awhile even these props are not sufficient. As old age moves on into its very late years, symbolizing through objects is sometimes not enough to retain images and experiences from the past. As memories dim, there is sometimes a need to dramatize the significant persons and objects from the past, to make them stand out as figures; in fact, to give them mythological status. Two investigators of this phenomenon found that their more elderly respondents (going all the way to 103 years of age in their sample) revealed significantly greater dramatization and mythicizing of significant figures than did a comparative group of younger, middle-aged persons (Revere & Tobin, 1980–81). For the most part this dramatization was positive; for example: "Mother was one of the most wonderful women in the world. Everyone loved her." Or "My father was the greatest provider." But this dramatization could also be negative: "I had a mother, the most selfish creature on earth." Sometimes these descriptions of significant figures would be accompanied by apparently exaggerated examples of personal feats, accomplishments, or behaviors by those figures. Parents and spouses were frequently described in heroic terms. The investigators concluded that the reasons for this dramatization and mythologizing of figures from their pasts was a need to keep the respondent's own sense of self vivid and unique. It thus served an adaptational purpose. As they put it, "Later in life the past becomes unique, and in the myth becoming the reality, one's life becomes justified."

Without this sort of dramatization, the progressive loss of real objects and memory function can be a demoralizing process. Probably the most devastating of all is the massive loss of memory and the capacity to symbolize objects that results from organic brain disorder, particularly in Alzheimer's disease and the other organic dementias of old age. The progressive losses of memory from dementia occur in the following sequence: First, disorientation about time—the day, the house, and they year; second, the loss of sense of place—where am I, what is this place, what country am I in; next, the ability to recognize other people including one's own spouse and children; and finally, the person cannot remember who he or she is. So it can be seen that there is a total loss of self or sense of identity—of being an identifiable person to oneself.

All of this is to emphasize the fact that the capacity to symbolize some one or some experience through a thing, a material object, is a precious one in old age. The loss of this capacity robs the person of something that is uniquely human, the sense of an identifiable self, of being an existential entity. Another important existential aspect of what happens in the course of dementia is an increasing process of literalism. Language becomes extremely literal, and the use of figurative language, particularly metaphor, is lost. Consequently, there is no ability to distance thought from thing. The object no longer represents something — it *is* the thing. For example, an 83-year-old woman in a nursing home who was diagnosed as having advanced Alzheimer's disease almost invariably had a doll named Johnny in her possession. She insisted that the doll itself was her son Johnny. So firmly did she believe this that she would insist that the doll was her son, even in the very presence of her own son Johnny during his visits. Of course, by this time she had lost the capacity to recognize other persons. Consequently, the material object (doll) that was in her actual physical grasp was the reality, not her real son. Unfortunately, this is all too common in the later stages of Alzheimer's disease. However, it should be recognized that Alzheimer's disease, which is by far the most common of the dementias, afflicts only about 4% of those over 65 years of age. It is a disease predominantly of very old age (Butler & Lewis, 1983).

Since we are concerned in this study with adults of 60 years and older, few of them (under 4%) will have primary degenerative dementia. It should also be recalled that we are concerned here with the phenomena of reminiscence, life review, and the related issue of integrity versus despair. Reminiscence for the purposes of life review and ego integrity is predominant in the earlier stages of old age (sixties and seventies), and as Erikson (1982) noted, achieving ego integrity through reminiscence and life-review processes serves to maintain "some order and meaning in the dis-integration of mind and body" of very old age. Although the very old still reminisce, we have empirical evidence of the fact that reminiscence is significantly more frequent in the young-old than in the old-old.[1]

The accumulation of objects, both real and symbolic, is a process that continues throughout the life cycle, and it occurs in the context of self–world interactions, or the "first dialectic of the self" depicted in Figure 1 of Chapter 5. The external or "objective" world provides the stage on which the self encounters, relates to, and identifies with the various significant objects, persons, things, and circumstances of the individual's life cycle. However, as noted earlier, there is usually a pattern of loss of significant objects, persons, and possessions the further one moves into old age. Whatever integration of objects and experiences into the self occurs through symbolization in old age comes less from the dialectic of self and the current external world and more from an inner dialectic involving symbolization and integration of *past* objects and experiences. The shrinkage of time and space discussed earlier shifts the emphasis on integration to the I–Me dialectic of Figure 1. Integration of self in terms of identity is not going to come as much from the outside world, except for reassurance and reinforcement from remaining friends and relatives that one has been and remains an identifiable and valued personal entity. The older person is less apt to identify self with current "objective" possessions, positions, accoutrements, and so on. This is not always true, however, for there are those elderly who cling to and accumulate more possessions, some to the point of extreme hoarding behaviors. This is, of course, an unusual attachment to and identification of material objects with the self, so in a very literal sense those elderly can be said to have an "object self."

Such behavior is not normative in old age, and as noted earlier, in the normal course of late-adult development through the process of greater interiority there is a sloughing off of extraneous things, postures, attitudes, and so on, that do not reflect the core self or identity of the person. This process is never complete in any one person to the point of pure integrity of self, but some people accomplish it to a greater extent than others do. Actually, the extent of its accomplishment is very well represented by William James's model of the self, which we have adopted here for descriptive and analytic purposes. His model seems to correspond well to and describe what we have observed empirically, so it would be best to recapitulate it here and show how it applies.

It will be recalled that James posited three constituents of the Me, or the "Empirical Self," as he called it: the Material Me, the Social Me, and the Spiritual Me. He referred to the body as the "innermost part" of the Material Me in everybody and noted that certain parts or aspects of the body seem more intimately ours than the rest. Clothing and other adornments and extensions of the body would also be objects of the Material Me. Then, the Social Me has its identifiable objects. James writes that a person's Social Me "is the recognition he gets from his mates." However, there is a distinction as to which "mates" are closer and more intimately related to the Social Me. One's immediate family, parents, spouse, children, and siblings usually are included in the innermost circle, with friends, extended family, and broader social groupings radiating out from it. Finally, the Spiritual Me he defines as "the entire collection of my states of consciousness, my psychic faculties and dispositions taken concretely." Any object from "this collection can become an object to my thought . . . and awaken emotions like those awakened by any of the other portions of the Me" (James, 1961). However, even within the Spiritual Me some objects are experienced as more external than others. For example, sensations are experienced as less intimate than emotions or desires, and intellectual processes are seen as less intimate than our "volitional decisions" or active choices. He puts it as follows: "The more *active-feeling* states of consciousness are thus the more central portion of the Spiritual Me. The very core and nucleus of our self, as we know it, the very sanctuary of our life, is the sense of activity which certain inner states possess" (James, 1961).

James goes on to identify some of the objects that appear to be more extraneous, frivolous, and sometimes even dysfunctional for each constituent Me. For example, objects of adornment, "foppery," and objects of sheer acquisitiveness would be extraneous among those of the Material Me. Objects of emulation, envy, pride, and snobbery would be extraneous among those of the Social Me, and thoughts of moral or mental superiority or purity would be extraneous among those of the Spiritual Me. These are the objects of the Me that would be most expendable in the honing-down process that should occur in old age. The Spiritual Me seems to be the locus for making those decisions about what is expendable and what is essential for the self. It is there, James puts it, that "the seeker of his truest, strongest, deepest self must review the list carefully, and pick out the one on which to stake his salvation" (James, 1961).

It is interesting to note that the primary referent of religious objects in our earlier study of cherished possessions was the self rather than a significant other. This suggests that such objects, with their obvious spiritual connotations, were identified by the elderly respondents with the Spiritual Me. It is also worth noting, as James did, that close family ties and lifelong friendships (the Social Me) have been broken because of deep religious or philosophical (the Spiritual Me) differences. Also, people have been known to die (the physical, Material Me) for their beliefs (Spiritual Me). Now it is possible that a person could value family or friendship above everything else and some other person could value survival above anything else, but if so, the locus of this evaluation is in the Spiritual Me. James (1961) is quite clear about these priorities and states them as follows:

> Unless our consciousness were something other than cognitive, unless it experienced a plurality for certain of the objects, which, in succession, occupy its ken, it could not long maintain itself in existence; for, by inscrutable necessity, each human mind's appearance on this earth is conditional upon the integrity of the body with which it belongs, upon the treatment which that body gets from others, and upon the spiritual dispositions which use it as their tool, and lead it either toward longevity or to destruction. *Its own body, then, first of all, its friends next, and finally its spiritual dispositions, MUST be the supremely interesting objects for each human mind.*

If the Spiritual Me is the locus of evaluation, it is quite possible, through symbolization, for material objects to become identified with that spiritual aspect of the self. This was expressed by one elderly man as follows:

Things grow into the soul. This remarkable phenomenon can be best observed as part of the general process of aging. The older people get, the more they are attached to their things; as their passions, their hopes, their hair, their teeth desert them, the more they cling to what they are left with. But even the young keep back what they can from the days that rush past: what child hasn't once kept a broken toy? It is as if each cherished object were a photograph capturing a moment irretrievably gone. Things embody something of the years that drift away and evaporate like smoke. Possessions are proof, concrete evidence of all that has disappeared; to rob a man of what he has is to rob him of his past, to tell him that he didn't live, that he only dreamed his life (Vizinczey, 1963).

OF TIME AND TRUTH

Barbara Myerhoff's book, *Number Our Days* (1979), is a moving portrayal of Jewish old people in the urban ghetto of Venice, California. It effectively captures a sense of continuity and survival in an unhospitable environment, yet the title of the book suggests a linear view of time—the relentless ticking of a clock with an image of the Grim Reaper in the background. This reflects our concept of physical time, and as one writer put it, "poor ole physical time just ticks along, stuck in the passing present, mindlessly, monotonously, causally" (Wilber, 1973). However, humans have the capacity to transcend this mechanical conception of time and "can span and scan the past and future, anticipate and remember, reminisce and envision, and thus allow mind to escape its bondage to the merely passing present of bodily sensations and perceptions" (Wilber, 1973).

Robert Ornstein (1986) observes that there has been a confusion of the linear, mechanical conception of time with other legitimate conceptions of time. He states: "This confusion stems from the underlying, implicit belief that a 'real' linear time exists somewhere outside of man." Paradoxically, this conception of a "real" (external and linear) time comes from the internal experience of duration which seems "to be constructed on the remembrances of things past—retrospection" (Ornstein, 1986). However, in addition to this retrospective experience of time, there is a mode of time experienced mostly by its intention. This is narrative time, the time that marks the history of one's own life story or self, that carries hopes and ideals, plans and ambitions, goals and visions. It is a subjectively experienced time that can speed up or slow down, expand or collapse, transcend or concentrate, according to our interest and intention.

We will be looking in much greater detail at narrative time as it is enacted in the personal histories to be covered in the next two chapters. At this point it is important to expand our conception of time, particularly when it comes to reminiscence, which because of its retrospective nature can be confused with the linear concept and therefore appear to be stuck forever and unmoving in the past. There are *different* modes and experiences of time that can be captured in reminiscence, and one of these has been aptly expressed in the following: "Time is not a dimension. . . . You don't look back along time but down through it, like water. Sometimes this comes to the surface, sometimes that, sometimes nothing. Nothing goes away" (Atwood, 1989). This statement was made by Elaine Risley, the fictional narrator of Margaret Atwood's novel *Cat's Eye*. Ms. Atwood's books are particularly interesting in that in them she approaches the sense of time through objects—furniture, knickknacks, and other domestic memorabilia—but in the statement by Elaine Risley she has captured one quality of time in the experience of reminiscence that is somewhat different from narrative time. It does not have the consistency of a story, and there is the unpredictable element of one thing or another, or nothing at all, coming forth, uninvited and unannounced.

The phrase "nothing goes away" seems to speak to what phenomenologists call the "sedimentation" of the past. The metaphor here is doubly apt in that anything or nothing can come to the surface from the "sediment" below. What comes to the surface, though, tends to be a function of what caused it to be sedimented in the first place (i.e., because it was meaningful and of special interest to the person at a certain time in the past). However, the reason it is "dredged up" at this time is much more likely to be a function of what is going on in the present. It is the present experiential context that will usually tell us the most about the comings and goings of particular memories in reminiscence. From a phenomenological perspective the past is experienced, as Natanson puts it, through our current "schemas of understanding" (Natanson, 1970). What this means is that it is not possible to talk about a "real" or "true" past that is divorced from and uninfluenced by the present. George Herbert Mead (1932), who viewed this issue from the dynamic and emergent perspective of the I–Me dialectic, made the following statement:

> It is idle, at least for the purposes of experience, to have recourse to a "real" past within which we are making constant discoveries; for that must be set over against a present within which the emergent appears, and the past, which must be looked at from the standpoint of the emergent becomes a different past. The emergent when it appears is always found to follow from the past, but before it appears it does not, by definition, follow from the past. It is idle to insist upon universal or eternal characters by which past events may be identified irrespective of any emergent, for these are either beyond our formulation or they become so empty that they serve no purpose in identification.

Recent findings from cognitive psychology and experimental work on autobiographical memory clearly support this phenomenological view of the relationship of past to present (Rubin, 1983). These findings show that our present moods and physical condition strongly influence not only the kinds of things we remember from the past but also the types of memories we store for the future. Thus, when we are feeling happy, we are more apt to remember earlier happy times; and when we are feeling sad, we are more likely to remember earlier times of sadness. We are often unaware of how our moods affect the emergence of certain memories in reminiscence.

One of our respondents in the Integrity Survey said that "anything and everything" can trigger reminiscing for him. It did not have to be certain specific objects or memorabilia; it could be a drive in the country, seeing the fields and the trees and then going off into a reverie about an earlier pastoral/idyllic experience. He was aware, however, that he was always in a peaceful and contented frame of mind when he would have such reminiscences or reveries. He was not alone in this, for quite a few of our respondents said without our solicitation that they reminisced most of the time without the aid or presence of certain objects or reminiscentia. This is quite consistent with Edward Casey's (1989) observation that "such *reminiscentia* are rarely, if ever *necessary* to reminiscing." What apparently happened was that the reminiscing of our respondents was set off by the immediate experiential context in which they found themselves.

Israel Rosenfield (1988), a neurobiologist and psychiatrist, indicates that Freud was right in saying there is no recollection without context, and "since context must, of necessity, constantly change there can never be a fixed or absolute memory." Rosenfield goes on to say not only that "memory without the present cannot exist" but that we actively engage in *creating* memories out of fragments of the past. He says, for example, that obsessional neurotics "redo" unpleasant experiences in a variety of obsessional rituals, and these "rituals are memories *par excellence*—new creations, the past reworked—doomed to failure as *pleasant* feelings, and hence the sought-after agreeable sensations remain elusive" (Rosenfield, 1988).

It is not that these memories of the obsessional are *false* memories. If anything, they are only vague fragments or traces recognized more for their feeling tone than for concrete events. The current experience of unpleasant feelings prompts the attempt to redo the past. What is missing in the obsessive's strategy is not that he or she has not really worked through the feelings associated with the earlier experience—in short, it has not been effectively reexperienced.

The cognitive research is quite consistent in showing that most of the time we remember only bits and fragments of experience. What we then do with these pieces is to create more complete and coherent memories, and we usually do this without realizing that a reconstruction is taking place. Recent gerontological thinking appears more and more to view memory as an "active construction" (Scheibe, 1989). These findings have led some investigators, particularly those with a dialectical approach to cognition, to regard memories as epiphenomena of various cognitive activities (Kvale, 1977; Meacham, 1972). The activities (i.e., the processing) are therefore seen as primary, while the processors (memories) are secondary. For example, there is an important current purpose for the life-review process, and it is the process itself (i.e., the reconstruction of memories) rather than its constituent memories that is more important for personality development in the areas of identity and self in old age (Meacham, 1976). So ego integrity is not so much a matter of what "really" happened in the past, a matter of veracity or validity; it is more the result of a reconstructive process that is nevertheless experientially grounded.

It is evident that people use memories of events from their lives to build an ordered and continuous sense of time and self. This sense of time is more in the nature of narrative time than of historical time as it would be in the form of a chronicle. Also, the sense of self is more in the nature of a narrative self than a historical one. This has led Donald Spence (1982), who takes a psychoanalytic view of the matter, to distinguish between "narrative truth" and "historical truth." What is important from a therapeutic perspective is narrative truth. Since many patients seen in psychotherapy have both a fragmented memory *and* sense of self, it is essential that they be helped to reconstruct a viable life story or self-narrative that will enable them to go on with their lives in a more "constructive" manner. This is because "in the end, we *become* the autobiographical narratives by which we 'tell about' our lives" (Bruner, 1987).

Again, the issue is not veridicality or truth, although it is important that the narrative be as contradiction free as possible. The primary issue is that it be a *generative* narrative, enabling us to get on with our lives effectively and in a manner we choose. One psychotherapist who uses the generative life narrative in his practice is so impressed with its therapeutic value that he calls it a "healing fiction" (Hillman, 1983). For him, the issue of truth is indeed secondary when it comes to the pragmatic concerns of psychotherapy.

The major point in all of this is to emphasize the immense importance of self-narrative for life-review processes and what its potential role in late-life adjustment and the attainment of a sense of integrity can be. With this in mind we will take a close look at such narratives in the next two chapters.

NOTE

1. We obtained the same finding of significantly less frequency of reminiscence among the very old (80 +) in our Integrity Survey as Lieberman and Tobin report in *The Experience of Old Age* (1983).

7
Life Themes in Reminiscence

It is important to put the content of this chapter into the context of the three studies that provided the basic material for this book. The exploration of life themes in reminiscence was conducted during the follow-up interviews with 88 of the 104 Group Project participants, which was referred to earlier as the Individual Reminiscence Survey.

We attempted several things in that survey. First, we wished to get at the subjective experience of reminiscence (i.e., what both group and private reminiscence was like for them as individuals). Second, we wished to follow up on possible instances of life review that might have begun during the group experience. Chapters 2, 3, and 4 have covered the essential findings and illustrative case materials concerning these two areas of inquiry.

The third area concerned the exploration of life themes. It will be recalled that certain thematic elements would show up in remembered life episodes that individuals would share in their reminiscence groups. We wished to find out whether a life theme would emerge from these elements if the individual had the opportunity to tell his or her life story in the follow-up interview, without having to be concerned about limited time or personal inhibitions in a group context. The results of this exploration will be presented here along with the life stories of two individuals whose self-narratives represent two basic types of life themes: discovered and accepted. These two narratives also include illustrative content concerning self, identity, cherished objects, and other material covered thus far in this book. It is hoped that they will help to integrate as well as illustrate some of this earlier content for the reader.

LIFE THEMES: THE CONCEPT

The term *life theme*, as it is used here, has a particular applied meaning that was developed by Mihaly Csikszentmihalyi and Olga Beattie (1979) at the University of Chicago. Csikszentmihalyi was prominently mentioned in the previous chapter in reference to his work on the meaning of things, of material objects in the lives of individuals in the course of human development (Csikszentmihalyi & Rochberg-Halton, 1981). He and Beattie defined the life theme briefly as "a problem or set of problems which a person wishes to solve above everything else and the means the person finds to achieve solution" (Csikszentmihalyi & Beattie, 1979). The theme itself is the affective and cognitive representation of the problem or set of problems that are either consciously or unconsciously perceived or experienced. These problems constitute a fundamental source of psychic stress during childhood or adolescence for which the person wishes resolution above all else and which thereby triggers adaptive efforts based upon a perceptual set or definition of the problem that provides "the basis for a fundamental interpretation of reality and ways of dealing with that reality. Life themes [then] are an important aspect of the adaptive strategies people develop through their life cycle" (Csikszentmihalyi & Beattie, 1979). Therefore, although these problems are most often experienced in childhood and adolescence, it could be expected that their effects and their recollections could show up in the reminiscences and self-narratives of the elderly.

Another writer who has applied the life-theme concept in his work with older populations has described it as "the human tendency to be absorbed over time with a central question or problem—one that infuses one's approach to living with meaning and purpose. The choice of a particular career, the tendency to avoid or seek out certain kinds of relationships, the desire to model oneself on someone special, or other such motives form a cognitive system, an outlook on life, that leads to a characteristic design for living" (Goldstein, 1984). Whether this design was the result of a "discovered" or "accepted" life theme was a major point for exploration in the Individual Reminiscence Study.

I would like to describe the original research done on the life theme by the two University of Chicago investigators so as to give a better idea of what we were looking for and how we went about it. We used their methods so as to be able to compare our findings and interpretations with theirs. Before doing so, however, it is important to note that the core problem would not have to be conscious and the solution would not have to be explicitly and actively pursued to qualify as part of a life theme. If in the course of providing an oral life story or self-narrative it becomes evident that the informant has invested more attention on that problem than on others, this would meet the definition of a thematic problem, according to the Chicago investigators, because attention invested is a good measure of the salience of the problem.

They conducted their study by collecting life histories from a sample of 30 adult males, from 36 to 75 years of age, who matched one another as clearly as possible in background characteristics. The major difference within the sample was that half of the men selected were very successful professionals, such as physicians and professors, whereas the other 15 men were largely blue-collar workers such as steel workers, plumbers, and policemen. However, the socioeconomic class of origin was the same for both groups of men. This was done purposely in the sampling to see if any systematic differences would emerge in the life themes of the two groups while holding socioeconomic status constant.

The interviews with the respondents lasted from one to three hours each and were geared toward eliciting significant or salient experiences or events that the men considered to be formative in their lives. No indication was given by the interviewer that there might be a central existential problem or theme in such experiences.

The interview notes were transcribed and then analyzed to see (1) if the respondent described problematic events from childhood as influencing his future life; (2) whether he formulated these events as a problem; (3) whether he attributed a specific cause to the problem; (4) whether his later life addressed the problems directly (in particular, was his occupation related to the solution of the problem?); and (5) if he could identify experiences that contributed to the solution of his central existential problem.

Ten of the 15 men in the professional, or upwardly mobile, group and 10 of the 15 men in the stable lower-class, or blue-collar, group described problematic events or experiences that had a strong influence on their lives. Since both groups came from lower-class origins, they had a relatively equal exposure to problems of poverty, alcoholism, divorce, and death in their childhoods, which they recalled with vividness. Although there was no demonstrable difference in the objective nature of the problems confronting the two groups of respondents, the professionals tended to generalize their personal stress into a more universal type of problem than did the blue-collar workers, who tended to respond to the stress in more personal and concrete ways. For example, one man who came from a poor immigrant family was injured as a child by a negligent driver in an auto accident. However, his impoverished immigrant family had to pay for his medical expenses because they did not know they had a legal right to compensation from the negligent driver, who purposely kept this knowledge from them. The man saw the disadvantaged immigrant status of his family as the cause of the injustice done them. With this formulation of the problem he vowed to extend his knowledge of the law. He went on to become a lawyer who committed much of his time and energy to representing the legal rights of minority groups. Thus, he had generalized his personal problem and found a method of solution that merged his self-interest with a larger social interest. In fact, personal stress experiences in the professional group tended to become transformed in their minds into problems that affect other people, and this type of cognitive transformation appeared to have powerful consequences for the course of their adult lives.

Conversely, the blue-collar respondents tended to identify and formulate their problems at a more concretely personal level. For example, one blue-collar respondent remembered near-starvation poverty in his childhood and identified poverty as a central problem ins his life. He saw the cause of poverty as the lack of thrift, so thrift became the method of solution to the problem. He was preoccupied with saving, literally hoarding, money. In his later years this method of solution remained his main approach to life, saving money even when he was affluent and the problem was no longer there.

The attribution of causality to the central problem was found to act as a link in the life theme between the early stress and the later coping strategies, as can be seen in the above examples. However, most of the blue-collar respondents did not seem to attribute causes to their problems. Therefore, their occupational life activities seemed to lack connection with the problems they confronted in their early life experiences. Two thirds of them took jobs that gave them a degree of material security and pride, and the other third ended up in jobs their fathers held. Thus, their work activity was a solution to the issues of survival and personal worth, which made their lives meaningful. However, the solution was not the result of a personal *discovery* in their lives but more the *acceptance* of socially sanctioned solutions that happened to be available. As the researchers put it, "the work of the blue-collar respondents is *external* to them, while the work of the professional is *essential* in that it is an integral part of a life theme which the person had discovered and formulated on his own" (Csikszentmihalyi & Beattie, 1979).

This distinction between "discovered" and "accepted" life themes was a major finding from that exploratory study of the lives of those 30 men. There were those who had life themes that were not "discovered" or developed by the person himself but that were "accepted" from models readily available in the family or society. On the other hand, there were those who "discovered" a link between their personal problem and a more general human condition or concern.

This distinction between discovered and accepted life themes was important for any research on reminiscence and life review with the elderly because it clearly had implications for life trajectories, career choices, and self-identity in their life cycles. It also raised some interesting questions about the experiential aspects of aging. For example, What is it like to *be* an elderly person who has been living an accepted (or discovered) life theme? Does it make any difference in how older persons feel about themselves and their lives? This highly suggestive distinction could have considerable heuristic value for the study of life histories, self-narratives, and the reconstructive aspects of life reviews.

I was particularly intrigued with exploring the possible connections between cherished objects and life themes. In the light of Csikszentmihalyi and Rochberg-Halton's observations about objects acting as signs in complex interpretive processes, it seemed that it might be possible in some cases to triangulate the meaning of a cherish object with the significant elements and actors in a person's life theme. This did indeed turn out to be possible, and it will be amply illustrated in the two life stories in this chapter.

The interviews in the Individual Reminiscence Survey all began with an exploration of what the reminiscence experience was like for the informants before, during, and after the Group Project. Any possible instances of an ongoing life review that might have been triggered by the group experience were followed up. As noted earlier, it sometimes took three interviews to cover all this as well as the life theme material. When it cam time for that material, I began with the statement "Now, I would like to turn to your recollections about the kinds of influences that you think might have been critical in your life—the happenings, concerns, or stresses that might have been most important in shaping your life." Then I asked the same questions posed by the Chicago investigators, as follows:

> So that's the kind of thing I would like to hear from you. Thinking back on your life, what are the kinds of things you remember being influential? In order to help structure this interview, why don't you start with where and when you were born? Tell me a little about your parents—what they did and what they were like—and about your early environment. Work your way up to the present time in terms of influences in your life. (Csikszentmihalyi & Beattie, 1979)

With this type of structure the informants had little difficulty in covering the main stages and occurrences in their lives, usually in less than an hour. I did, however, ask some additional questions, usually for clarification and to pursue possible thematic events or problems. Therefore, the case illustrations of the two types of life themes to be presented here will contain substantial segments of the actual interview dialogue between the informant and me so that the reader can follow some of the key exchanges that touch on possible life themes. The first of these case illustrations will be that of a man who represents a discovered life theme.

A DISCOVERED LIFE THEME

Max Korvitz[1] was an 87-year-old widower who lived alone in a senior citizens' apartment dwelling and regularly participated in various activities at the Jewish Community Center. He was a member of one of the "conventional" (nonexperiential) reminiscence groups in the original Group Project. His case was selected for presentation here not only because it clearly represents a discovered life theme but because it illustrates elements of a late life review with related patterns of reminiscence and changes in levels of experiencing. Important issues concerning resolution and ego integrity are raised by the case as are differences between the concepts of ego integrity and identity. Additionally, Mr. K. identified and described one of his most cherished possessions and in the process revealed how such an object can act as a sign that captured the essential meaning of his life.

Although Mr. K. was interviewed for the purposes of understanding his reminiscence experience in the project and to explore a possible life theme, there was also evidence of dissonance and distress suggestive of a life-review process, which was unusual at his rather advanced age. For example, Lieberman and Tobin (1983) had found the majority of octogenarians in their study to be somewhat resolved, contented, and mellow but infrequent reminiscers. Frequent life-review reminiscing was much more characteristic of those in their sixties and seventies. Mr. K. was a very frequent reminiscer, both in terms of self-report and his participation in his conventional reminiscence group. He also had low life satisfaction and self-concept scores at pretest, well below the average for the study. He had the same low life satisfaction score for all three testing periods of the study. Furthermore, his self-concept score was not only low but became lower in the course of the project. His first group session revealed that his reminiscences were already characterized by a good deal of negative content. He began by saying that he didn't really have anything to say, and his experiencing level was quite low (EXP score of 2). He related events in his life as external and largely with concrete self-descriptions lacking expressiveness: "I was an orphan when I was 10." "I went through the First World War and was a prisoner of war." "I came from a poor family in Lithuania, the youngest of 11 children, so I didn't have an education." These brief staccato statements were characteristic of his early group self-descriptions, and although he claimed to reminisce "all the time," he did not particularly enjoy it.

Mr. K. liked to discuss politics and current affairs in the group whenever there was a chance, and he was one of the most verbally active members on those matters. However, as the group was nearing the end of its ten sessions, his reminiscences and his observations about current affairs began taking on an obsessive quality. He began expressing considerable personal distress about the current world and national situation in light of his own life. He had been a union organizer, leader, and social activist from the time he was a teenager in Europe. Two years after he came to the United States at age 21 he was jailed for his involvement as union leader in a long and bitter strike in an attempt to organize a cap and hat workers' union in Albany. After a lifetime of social activism based on "a certain philosophy and ideals," he found himself not only dismayed but truly demoralized over the current state of affairs during the Reagan presidency. He exclaimed that "the young people," instead of being idealistic and progressive as they should be, were all for "consumer materialism, individualism, and self-interest."

This became something of a litany in his group participation. However, at the follow-up testing he appeared more demoralized and made more depressed statements, such as "I didn't have a youth." There appeared to be more personal as well as social or political regret and a concern that time was running out. Consequently, he was not only quite willing but even anxious to be interviewed individually when I contacted him at the end of the group project. His comment at the end of the project was, "Going through this, recollecting from childhood on, made me want to tell my story to someone and to myself all the way through." He even started the interview with the statement, "What I am going to tell you now is going to sound like a novel, with everything that has happened to me and I have seen."

Mr. K. was a stocky, solidly built man with a deep voice who spoke slowly and with a rather thick accent. His English was quite formal and at times stilted. He proceeded to explain that he was the youngest of 11 children from a very poor Jewish family living in a small city near Vilna, the capital city of Lithuania, which was part of Czarist Russia when he was born. Because of their severe poverty his brothers and sisters all began emigrating to the United States as soon as they reached their late teens. Consequently, there was only one older brother left at home when Mr. K. began school. He attended what was called a "community school" (not a private yeshiva) in the poor Jewish working-class area in which the family lived. He was evidently a good student and was one of the few selected from that school to go on to the regular Russian high school, or gymnasium. However, his family had been reduced to just his mother, older brother and himself, his father having died when Mr. K. was 10. His brother was unable to scrape enough money together from his own lowly work to pay for the uniform that was required for the boy to attend the gymnasium. He felt this was an important event because he always had an inclination toward learning and would have relished a good education.

He explained that he had to get his education later through the labor movement. When he came to the United States in his early twenties, he became a devoted student in the Workmen's Circle, a worker's school organized by Jewish workers who came mostly from eastern Europe. He avidly studied history, philosophy, literature, and any other such offerings of the Circle. However, that came later in his life. At age 12 he found himself working in a leather factory because he could not afford to go to school. Thereafter he worked most of his life as a tanner.

While he was employed in that leather factory, World War I came and impacted directly on him and his family in 1915. The Germans had made inroads into Russia from the beginning of the war in 1914, and they had advanced to the outskirts of Vilna, so he and his family were in a "no-man's-land" between the German and Russian forces. Because the Russians were so desperately in need of soldiers, they tried to conscript the young boys and old men in his city on the spot to fight the Germans. However, he managed to escape from that situation and went further into Russia, to the city of Minsk. Unfortunately, the Czarist army was conscripting young men 17 (his age) and older there as well. He got caught there in a group of about ten boys who had attempted to avoid conscription by coming there from other towns.

They were inducted into the army and sent into training for about eight months, after which they were sent into front-line trenches in Romania against Bulgarian soldiers who were commanded by German officers. He said that they all knew they were just "cannon fodder" because the Russian forces were so poorly organized and commanded. They were ordered to make an attack on the opposing forces, and, after sustaining heavy losses, they were surrounded and captured. Then they were sent to a prisoner-of-war camp in Ruse (Rushuk), Bulgaria, which was on the Danube River at the Romanian border. There they were guarded by Bulgarian troops who were actually ethnic Turks, though Bulgarian nationals, and who were terribly brutal. He said life in the camp under them "was hell. That's the only way to describe it. I can't tell you the many atrocities I witnessed." The Turks had particular animosity toward Russians, and they took it out on the prisoners.

He related one incident when he went to the outdoor latrine one evening. As he stepped out of the latrine after relieving himself, a Turkish guard smashed him in the face with his rifle butt—without warning or provocation. On the following morning a German officer saw his face and demanded to know what had happened. He was made to identify the guard who had done it to him, and then the officer proceeded to beat the guard with a riding crop publicly and mercilessly. "From that moment on," Mr. K. said, "I was in mortal danger." The Turkish guards were on a constant lookout for him, and he would have to slip from one building to another in the evenings so they could not catch him in the dark.

Fortunately, he and a number of his fellow prisoners were transferred shortly thereafter to another prisoner-of-war camp in Varna, which was a port on the Black Sea in northern Bulgaria. He spent three years in Varna, from 1916 to 1919. Although the war was over in 1918, the repatriation of prisoners did not take place immediately. He was not repatriated until late spring of 1919. By that time he had learned to speak Bulgarian and had made many friends there. He related an incident that occurred there that was highly thematic of his life.

Upon arrival in Varna from Ruse he recognized a different kind of brutality that was going on there. Although there were no Turkish guards, the prisoners were made to transport crushed anthracite coal in bags on their backs from piles that had been dumped off freight trains to ships that were docked in the port of Varna. The crushed coal had shards that were very sharp and cut into the prisoners' feet as they walked from the piles to the ships. They had no decent shoes and some had none at all, so their feet would become bloody and infected. After experiencing this and seeing his comrades go through it for weeks on end, he felt compelled to do something about it.

He went to the German officer in charge to plead for some kind of improvement in these intolerable conditions. Although he did not know German, he felt he could communicate with the officer in Yiddish. After much insistence and persistence on his part with lower-echelon guards, he was allowed to speak to the officer, who looked at him severely all the time he was talking, without saying a word or even nodding. Finally, he proposed to the officer that he be allowed to have a detail of men work on making some work sandals with heavy leather soles that would protect the prisoners' feet. He, as a tanner, would know how this could be done. The officer glared at him for what seemed an interminable time without speaking and then demanded to know if he could *guarantee* this would work. When Mr. K. said that he could, the officer said ominously that it had better work, for his sake.

It did work and that made life in Varna much more tolerable. Mr. K. said that he often wondered why he was the one who put himself forward in that situation. There were others who could have done so because they could speak some German and could have cited prisoner-of-war conventions that were being violated. True, he was a leather worker and knew how to make the sandals, but he did not *have* to. So he had always asked himself, "Why me? Why did I put my life in jeopardy?"

After being repatriated in 1919 he came to the United States in 1921. He settled in Albany, New York, and obtained employment in a glove factory there. Again, he found working conditions in the factory that he considered to be intolerable, and before long he was attempting to organize a union to rectify those conditions. As noted earlier, he organized a strike in 1923 in an attempt to unionize his factory and was sentenced to jail for several months by an Albany city court judge. It should be noted that as he described the conditions and his reactions to them in the prisoner-of-war camps and later in industry the experiencing level of his narrative went up (from EXP 2 to 3 and 4), as it was expressed in much more personal terms. Instead of just a description of external events, Mr. K. began expressing personal reactions to those external events, including descriptions of his feelings.

Although Mr. K. had related a number of significant episodes in his eventful life, and although a theme of social action and leadership had emerged, the causal problems and turning point in childhood had not yet been identified by him—at least not in line with Csikszentmihalyi and Beattie's formulation of the life theme. Therefore, I pursued the matter more directly in the verbatim dialogue that follows:[2]

I: At this point I'd like to go back to the kinds of things you think might have been influential in your life, because one of the things that seems to come out as a common theme or common thread in your life is you were obviously affected by the historical events that occurred in your life . . .

K: That is correct.

I: But there were other people who also went through the same kinds of things, and it seems to me that in these various situations in which you found yourself you tended to end up in a kind of leadership or forward role. Right?

K: The question comes first. I *(pause)* formed a philosophy of life which includes a human aspect, humanity. I reaffirmed ideals that society which was in existence in the twentieth century, an intelligent era, that we would do away for good with the prehistoric inhuman activity that took place earlier in history.

I: Ok, I understand that. But I really want to get back to where does this come from. What were the formative kinds of things in your life that led you to adopt these? Now, you said that you came from a relatively poor family and a big family. . .

K: That's right.

I: You didn't have the advantage of a formal education where some people might study philosophy or politics and learn it that way.

K: That's true.

I: You were sort of thrown into the middle of things. However, there must have been something even before you went into the army . . . some kind of turning point. There must have been something formative or influential in your life that started you on the road toward the philosophy you have now.

K: True.

I: What do you think that was?

K: It began when I got into the leather factory where I was working as a young boy. I would say 12 years.

I: 12 years. Uh huh.

K: I believe so.

I: O.K.

K: And the minimal amount of money I was getting paid. As I mentioned, I believe 25 cents a week.

I: Right.

K: And then naturally I worked up some from that.

I: But you were struck by that . . . low wage.

K: I was struck by that. Then I realized, I began to think about how to better my conditions. I could not wait a number of years because the raises were too small.

So I began to think of how to better my conditions, and in order to better my conditions I realized that I cannot do it by myself but we can do it in an organized form of equal elements that are involved in the same situation that I am.

I: Mmhmm.

K: And it so happened that it was a matter of control, you see, between the older workers in that particular trade and all the other workers, adults and youngsters. The older workers gave up their desire for putting up a fight for a betterment of conditions. I said to the youngsters that we are not going to. We should stand for our principles and demand to better our conditions.

I: Uh huh.

K: So we organized and won.

I: In that leather factory?

K: In that leather factory.

I: Good. You got an increase in salary.

K: That's right, and that was a push forward toward the ultimate desire to achieve more and more of my way to improve my way of life.

I: That sort of verified, that verified and assured you that you were on the right track. Now let me go back even a little bit further because here you . . . you were with these other young people in the same situation right? However, you were the one that tended to be the spokesperson who said we won't stand for this.

K: That's right.

I: Now what that suggests to me is that there were already formative kinds of things in your thinking and your life that would have led you, as distinct from these other young people, to have taken on that leadership role. Now let me ask you this. Specifically, was there anything on the part of either your parents, or both, that would have given you some indication that you should be assuming this kind of responsibility or this kind of role?

K: No. Definitely no. Because my father died before I even started to work. My mother was a woman of no education or knowledge and so on. And she was a very working woman [sic], I mean as maintaining a family life. But something struck me from my brother who participated in the revolutionary movement. From him I drew my conclusion that in the organized form of people for the same cause would be proper. So I learned that not from my parents but it came to me from my brother. Not all my brothers. But one of my older brothers.

I: What do you remember him telling you about those issues that stuck in your mind? Do you remember?

K: No . . . I don't think we had any form of a conversation. There was such a difference in age . . . 13 or 14 years. . . . I was a child, so there was no such conversation whatsoever.

I: I see. . .

K: But what struck me most . . . he was arrested once, and his arrest was embedded in my mind because my mother took some food to him in jail . . . and when she was there a policeman . . . a cossack . . . resented her because my brother, when he was arrested, it was a . . . ah . . . a strike between them and the police-man who guarded the jail. So this cossack had one of those . . . leashes?

I: For the horses?

K: Yes, I think so. . .

I: A riding crop?

K: More of whip . . . and it had a leather pouch at the end of it . . . with some lead in it. So when you swing it, it causes real damage. Anyway, he hit my mother over the head, and split open her head . . . scalp. When she came home, she was bleeding . . . and that made on me a very deep impression, and I remember that . . . I remember that because . . . I couldn't understand why a human being should be so cruel . . . to hit an elderly woman for no reason at all. So that brought in me, also, a sense of how . . . how in . . . inhumane a person can be to another human being. The whole thing . . . my mother . . . my brother . . . made a feeling against oppression.

The above discourse by Mr. K. reveals all the essential elements for a dis-covered life theme. He described the problematic circumstances and events from his childhood related to poverty, denial of further education, and working-class conditions in an oppressive society. He definitely identified these as causative factors in his central existential problem, and he saw the solution to this problem as engagement in worker organization and solidar-ity in pressing for economic, social, and political change. Furthermore, un-like most of the blue-collar workers in Csikszentmihalyi and Beattie's study, he was able to generalize his personal problem and stress into a more uni-versal type of problem.

Mr. K. presented all of the above information related to his personal his-tory and life theme in two interviews. In the third interview we began dis-cussing his reminiscing experience during the project and since. He de-scribed this experience as increasingly unpleasant over the past two months. He was not sure whether the reminiscence group experience had caused it, but he felt it would have happened sooner or later anyway be-cause of a growing dissatisfaction. He was distressed by the state of the world in the mid-1980s. The philosophy, ideals, and hopes from his youth and manhood had not been fulfilled. Organized labor was dramatically weaker under President Reagan than it had been in Mr. K.'s organizing days of the 1940s, 1950s, and early 1960s. The conservatism of the current youth was particularly distressing to him because many of them came from more progressive unionized parents and "should know better."

Now, although he was upset about all of this, the experiencing level of his narrative was not particularly high (EXP levels of 2 or 3 at best) because he was talking about issues and content in a rather intellectual and abstract manner without expressing his internalized feeling state.

However, his experiencing level went up as his discourse became more personalized. He said he found himself reminiscing constantly about all he had gone through, about how much personal sacrifice and effort had all gone for naught. He said he could not stop "all these thoughts," and they might even be affecting his health. He was not sleeping well because of his obsessive reminiscing and concerns. His appetite was also affected, and he was eating less. He said, "Why should I feel this way? I used to be able to talk about and argue about these things and get them off my chest, but now I feel them . . . sitting right here (*pointing to upper part of his stomach*) and . . . it is a terrible weight." At this point I asked him if he could stay with that feeling in that place for awhile and see if anything further would come from it.

I did this because Mr. K. seemed to be focused inwardly, with his eyes closed, trying to express in words what he was experiencing in a bodily way. He had been in a conventional rather than an experiential reminiscence group, so he had no prior guidance in experiential focusing. What he was doing seemed to be quite natural and unpracticed, and he had no apparent difficulty in remaining unself-consciously focused for over a minute on the bodily feeling with his eyes closed.

As he did so, his demeanor and facial expression seemed to become less intense or pained, and his body shifted several times in his seat. I had put away the tape recorder early in this interview because it could be experienced as intrusive and disruptive of a very personal process. Thus, there is no verbatim record of it; but when he opened his eyes, he took a few moments before saying that he had been struggling with feelings of failure and disillusionment in himself. He added that he felt like a "failure," "a personal failure," because of the failure of social reform and lack of progress in society in general. He went on to say that he had just recognized that he had identified him*self* with "the movement . . . with history." Then he realized how mistaken that was, that he was only one person in "a larger scheme of things." He then paused reflectively and said emphatically, "I did what I had to do!" He hesitated and said again, more slowly, "I did what I had to do!" At this, his body went loose, and he practically slumped in his chair. He stayed in this slouched posture for while and then said that he had "lots of things to think about." He preferred to keep these for the next interview because he had to think about them in a "whole new way."

It certainly appeared to me that I had been witness to a natural, emergent instance of experiential focusing in the midst of a life-review process. Except for the mild intervention of asking him if he could stay with "that feeling," Mr. K. did it all by himself. From an experiential point of view he had moved from EXP Level 5 to 6 as he was sensing that feeling, and he was at Level 7 when he exclaimed, "I did what I had to do!" It was something that he now *knew*, for himself.

The next, fourth and last, interview with Mr. K. took place two weeks later. He looked better, more rested, and he acknowledged this by saying that he had been sleeping well and that his appetite was back to normal. He went on to describe his experience at the last interview as a "tremendous sense of relief . . . and letting go of a tremendous burden." He still seemed exhilarated from that experience and claimed that he had learned a lot from it. He said, "Who did I think I was . . . to identify the failures of the world as *my* failures, as my responsibility." Realizing that they were not his was a great relief. At the same time, he realized that what he had worked for was right and, more important, that it was right *for him*. It couldn't be any other way, regardless of what happened with society in general. He said, "I walked in the sun and it was worth it." All of this was said with the declarative and fresh expression characteristic of EXP Level 6.

Then Mr. K.'s discourse moved from the expressive to the thoughtful. He said that he had been doing a lot of thinking since the last interview, but not the "merry-go-round kind" he had been doing before. The essence of what he went on to say was that although he realized he had to be less critical and more accepting of himself he was still "not satisfied with life." There were many things he still felt critical about and that he wanted to see changed, and he felt that he had "earned the right to be critical." He was still critical of the lack of idealism and progressivism in the youth of today, the decline of the labor movement, and so on. He would continue to be outspoken on these matters, he said.

During a lull in this interview I took the occasion to ask him about some of the photographs in his living room where I was interviewing him. Most of them appeared to be family pictures of his children, his wife, himself, and perhaps extended family at various ages and stages in life. The pictures were located in various places in the living room, but the photograph that had the most prominent spot in the room was a picture of about two dozen men arrayed on a large mound of coal, with several men at the top linked arm in arm. Mr. K. was one of those at the top, and it was a photograph taken shortly after the hostilities had ended in World War I, so all the men were smiling. Mr. K. informed me that the photo was taken next to the docks in Varna. I remarked on its prominent place in the room and asked him if it was special to him. He readily agreed that it was and said, "I look at that picture and I know what I have been through. I can still feel the sharp coal on my bare feet."

I then asked if he would say it was one of his "most cherished possessions." He again readily agreed and said, "These are my old friends and comrades. It [the photo] says a lot to me . . . about what I did . . . my philosophy . . . what I worked for." In asking this question I was aware that "the home contains the most special objects: those . . . selected by the person to attend to regularly or to have close at hand, that create permanence in the intimate life of a person, and therefore that are most involved in making up his or her identity" (Csikszentmihalyi & Rochberg-Halton, 1981). This quotation from a study of domestic objects is reflective of the fact that "household objects constitute an ecology of signs that reflects as well as *shapes* the pattern of the owner's self." That photograph was surely central in the ecology of signs in Mr. K.'s living room—and his life.

Mr. K. certainly had a clear sense of self, of identity, and of its related life theme. This might not be the same thing as ego integrity, however. Although Mr. K. had gone through an apparent life review, there were elements still missing from the picture of ego integrity painted by some writers on that subject (Walaskay et al., 1983–84). It will be recalled that Mr. K.'s scores on measures of life satisfaction and self-concept were in the lowest quarter of the group project sample right up to the third and last testing after the groups ended. On the self-concept measure he had identified himself as a "failure" rather than a "success," "unsure" rather than "confident," "sad" rather than "happy," "tired" rather than "relaxed," and "extremely dissatisfied" rather than "satisfied."

As a result of the life-review process, especially during the third interview and immediately thereafter, Mr. K. came to feel much better about himself and would undoubtedly change his answers to more positive ones on the above items from the self-concept measure. However, he would *not* be apt to change "dissatisfied." Take, for example, his responses to the last Life Satisfaction From he filled out. He *agreed* with the following statements: "My life could be happier than it is now" and "Compared to other people, I get down in the dumps too often," but he *disagreed* with the following: "I am just as happy as when I was younger"; "These are the best years of my life"; "I would not change my life if I could"; "As I grow older, things seem better than I thought they would be"; and "As I look back on my life I am fairly well satisfied." Now, it is possible that he would change his responses on some of these statements as a result of the life review, but it is highly unlikely he would change his disagreement with "things seem better than I thought they would be" or with "I am fairly well satisfied."

Although he achieved a greater self-acceptance toward the end, there was still a sense of dissatisfaction and that "things were not as they should be." There was not the kind of contentment that some writers have identified with resolution and equanimity in achievement of ego integrity. Mr. K. would not be one to "go gentle into that good night." In fact, about five years after the group project I happened to read an article in a local paper about a current affairs discussion group at the Jewish Senior Center. A 92-year-old man, "the eldest member of the discussion group," was quoted as making the following statement: "I have been a worker all my life, a proletarian." The article went on to say this man was "angered when others praised the opening of a yeshiva in Troy. He dismissed orthodoxy as "mysticism, make-believe, and lamented its apparent ascendancy." It then quoted him as saying, "It took so many years to bring enlightenment to Jewish life. They're trying to dominate the Jewish community as a whole. Why turn back the clock?"

This man was, of course, Mr. K., Max Korvitz, who was not about to give up the good fight while there was still an ounce of breath in his body. He certainly had a kind of integrity, whether one calls it *ego* integrity or not, and there is no question about his identity (i.e., a worker, a proletarian), and all that stands for in 20th-century history.

AN ACCEPTED LIFE THEME

Ruth Gold was an 85-year-old widow who participated in one of the conventional reminiscence groups in the Group Project. She had been a very active and enthusiastic participant, and she welcomed the opportunity to follow up on her group reminiscence experience in the individual life-theme interviews with me in the subsequent study. She was a vivacious and petite woman, barely five feet tall, who looked fully ten years younger than her actual age. She was always neatly and formally dressed at all of the group sessions and later individual interviews.

The social worker who led her reminiscence group gave Mrs. Gold the highest ratings on the practitioner rating scales concerning reminiscence, morale, and self-esteem. She estimated that Mrs. Gold's reminiscing was a functional part of her present life experience to "a great extent." She also described Mrs. Gold's reminiscences as "very vivid." Furthermore, on the basis of her observations over ten sessions, the social worker evaluated Mrs. Gold as "very high" on both current morale and self-esteem.

Mrs. Gold said more than once in the group sessions, "I reminisce all the time, and I *love* every minute of it." Her reminiscing was invariably positive in content during the Group Project. In fact, in the pretest reminiscence exercise she said, "I try to remember only nice things." On the basis of that, her reminiscence was categorized as "selective avoidance" on the avoidance/engagement continuum in the pretest. This was because she gave clear evidence of excluding or avoiding negative or painful content in her reminiscing. She did progress to the next level, or category, called "selective engagement," in the course of her group reminiscence experience. This meant that she did not give any further explicit indication of avoidance of negative content, but her reminiscence was made up entirely of positive or neutral content. Negative content did not seem to get incorporated or integrated into her reminiscence or shared memories.

Two life-theme interviews were conducted in Mrs. Gold's tastefully furnished apartment in a well-kept senior apartment dwelling located in a middle-class residential neighborhood. She obviously took pride in the furnishings she was able to bring from her large house after her husband's death. Pictures of her husband, children, and grandchildren were evident on the tables and mantles in her living room, where the interviews took place.

She was the youngest of six children in a family consisting of four boys and two girls. She was born eight and a half years after the previous child, who was a boy. Her father came from Russia in 1871 and settled in Texas. Her mother was born in London, but they met in the United States and were married in St. Louis, Missouri, in 1882. Her father had been in a general store business in Mississippi and traveled the river boats to St. Louis to buy, which is where he met his bride-to-be. The family had apparently lived in the South during most of her childhood, and most of her siblings were born in Mississippi. Her parents were both Jewish, and she described herself as a "Reformed Jew."

The first interview with Mrs. Gold was taken up in part by a discussion of her experiences with a number of her elderly neighbors in the apartment house. She had mentioned these because of what she called her frustration at hearing the many complaints her neighbors had about the decrements and ailments of old age. She described how she told them, "This is it! You have to make the most of it," and in effect told them to stop complaining. I had noted in listening to the audiotapes of her group sessions that she had used this expression "This is it!" a number of times, so I asked her to expand on it at one point in the interview.

G: Sometimes, in reminiscing, they [her neighbors] are angry at this time of their life. They are very angry. And we hear so often people say, "I used to do so and so, but I can't do it now. I used to walk a great deal, but I can't now. I used to go to the theater a great deal, but I can't anymore," and they're angry at their age, which is ridiculous. We can't change how old we are. We can't change whether we have certain aches and pains that constrict our comings and goings and our activities. But we live through it, and so what! You're not going to change it, so laugh at it. If they could only laugh at themselves a little bit. We have to be able to laugh and say, "Oh boy, I used to do so and so, but so what? Now I can't, but so what? Now I'll do so and so, something that will supplement to make it a good today. Don't always say what's bad about today. Not everything is bad. Old age has good things. I find many things at my age that are very comforting. I find many people don't even buy a newspaper. They don't read what's going on in the world, what's happened today or yesterday. So that's why I say, reminiscing is only for the best. Live in the present and there is a future. It may only be tomorrow, but there is a future. Even the next hour is a future. So you have to live a little bit for the time that is coming. I like to reminisce. Perhaps I've been very fortunate. Oh, I've had things that are not so good, but most of my life has been good. I had a good family relationship. My parents were down-to earth people.

Mrs. Gold went on to provide much of her family history, which was described briefly above. She had gotten to a point in the history in which her father moved the family north because of her mother's poor health. I asked her to expand on this particular period, and she provided the following information.

G: Yes, My mother wasn't well, and the doctors in the South were not as well trained or taught as the doctors in New York, so my father gave up his business and came to New York, and that's where I was born . . . in New York City. I was pampered because I was the baby. I was spoiled. I know it. However, I did show talent when I was very young. I don't talk about it too much because it doesn't sound as though it's truthful, but it is. I started to play piano before I ever took lessons. And my mother recognized the talent. And in 1904 she took me to the World's Fair in St. Louis, and she was told there, by my grandfather and my mother's father, that I should have lessons. But my people were poor. We didn't know we were poor, but we were (*small laugh*). And the cost of lessons was more than my father could afford because he had lost all of his money when he had to come north here, through a business deal, and, uh, but we always had a clean house, plenty to eat . . .

My mother was not well for a number of years. It wasn't the kind of sickness that put her in bed all of the time, but she had had a heart condition, and in those days they didn't know too much about it, so she died when I was 18 years old. At that time I was hoping to go to Milano to study at the Milano Conservatory, but my mother died, and I was the only one home to take care of my father . . . not to take care but to run the house . . . and I didn't know beans about it. I didn't know how to boil water because I was never allowed to do that. We always had a European maid. They used to call them servant girls; they didn't call them maids then. They got about $20 a month and their room and board, and, uh, they were faithful and good, and that was just the time my mother died . . . that was in 1918 . . . when the First World War was on, and this German woman who was working for us was sent back, and I was left, really, not knowing what to do. Well, a few days after my mother died, after the funeral, I had a very nice neighbor, who came in. She said, "How are you doing?" I said, "All right, I guess." She said, "Do you cook for your father?" (*Mrs. G. laughs*) I said, "Cook! I never helped to boil water. I never had to be near the kitchen." She said, "It's time. What do you want? Your father to come home with a stepmother?" She said, "Do you have any money?" I had a little money . . . I don't remember what. She said, "Come on. We're going marketing." Well, we went marketing, and I thought she was going to cook the meal. Well, when we got home with all the things, she told me how to peel the potatoes and so forth. Well, she taught me how to scrub floors, how to wash and iron . . . we didn't have washing machines . . . and we didn't have automatic dishwashers, and she taught me a great deal, and I was very grateful to her.

I: May I ask you something to go back to. Just to fill me in. You started out to pursue music, but your family was poor and couldn't afford it. But somewhere along the line, somehow they must have gotten you . . .

G: Yes, I took lessons.

I: Beginning when?

G: I started taking lessons when I was probably 8 or 9 years old. Afterward, I was interviewed by a very famous teacher named Giuseppi. He was the teacher for Josef Hoffman, who was at that time a very great pianist, and Giuseppi was very interested in me because he felt I was talented, and he wanted me to . . . he said I was too young for him to teach me but that one of his younger teachers, or assistants, would take over. Then he would take over later. But the young assistant got $5 a lesson, but that was more than we could pay, so I didn't go to him. But later on, I did have a scholarship . . . I studied later on . . . I did have a scholarship to what is now called the Juilliard School. At that time it was the Institute of Musical Art. Frank Damarish was the head of it. I studied orchestration and instrumentation with Ruben Goldmark, who was the composer of the "Gettysburg Requiem," and that was in the same class with Aaron Copland.

I: Really!

G: For a short time he was in that class. I don't know if he would even remember me. He was in that class, and I envied him his very large hands because my hands were small, and I envied him, but he was showing great talent even in those days. He was very young, of course. So was I, but I studied with other teachers. Later on I studied with Maestro Pietro Ferivia. He was written up at that time in *Who's Who in America*. He had some sort of run-in with the Metropolitan Opera . . . the old Metropolitan . . . I don't know what it was, but they resented him even coming in to concert, but he was a very great man and I liked him very much. Of course, when I got married (*small laugh*), I didn't go ahead with any musical work, but I did do work with professional people . . . in between times. I worked a little bit with the Dolly Sisters. I don't know if you remember them. I wish I had a copy of it. My daughter has it. Adelaide Hughes was a great ballerina. She was second only to Pavlova. And she was really great. And I wrote music for her. I was supposed to be . . . supposed to be . . . the youngest composer in the country, and they have, my daughter has a copy of the original music that I wrote. She has it framed. I don't know why.

I: How old were you when that . . .

G: I must have been 19 . . . 18, 19, around that time.

I: Now then, your mother died when you were 18, so . . .

G: That's right.

I: How did that fit in?

G: I still kept on with this music, with the professional people. 'Cause I lived in a neighborhood where many of these professionals lived. I played for different singers. I taught diction. I played for a woman who called herself Marta Dulac. She pretended to be Italian. I don't believe she was. I think that was the name she took, but she did sing in Milan. She really did . . . with the opera company there. And I played for her. And then I played for different people, and I enjoyed what I did. But, uh, I have no complaints.

I: Would you say your musical career came to an end? You've always been involved in music.

G: I was, uh . . .

I: That is, if your career . . .

G: I wouldn't have wanted a career . . .

I: You wouldn't?

G: Because I didn't ever go beyond certain limits. I wanted to do what I wanted to do, where I wanted to do it. I wasn't interested in becoming a big celebrity. I was happy in my own little niche. Doing what I wanted to do. And then, of course, I met my husband. He was at West Point. I met him about two months before he graduated. We went out on dates. When he went to West Point . . . later on, I'll show you a letter that I have that I think you'll find interesting . . . he was appointed to West Point, and in that time, there were very few Jewish boys at West Point. When he graduated, there were only four kids that we knew of, in his class. There were others who didn't acknowledge their religion. We found that out in later years. But he was one of the four. In fact, the young man who graduated number one in his class was named Horowitz. He was a very brilliant engineer, subsequently committed suicide, but that was something else. I went to the graduation. Of course, to me it was something wonderful. You had to wear certain clothes. You were told what you were expected to wear for each function. When you were introduced to the superintendent, you wore a long dress with long white gloves, the other glove you held, and all that sort of non-sense. But it was very formal. And, believe me, we were chaperoned. No question about it. So after that, after graduation, he came to Brooklyn, and he was with that class that went to Europe on our tour of the battlefields. Now, this class that he graduated with was called the "Bastard Class." Originally, they were supposed to graduate in 1922. But the war came along, and they acceler-ated their course, and scheduled them . . . they had no time off . . . November 1918, but on November 11th, the Armistice was signed, so they graduated them, which I did not see, and they called the student officers and kept them for another year and graduated them in 1919.

Mrs. Gold went on to say that her husband proposed to her shortly after his graduation from West Point, and they were married in 1920. Mr. Gold had studied accounting at New York University prior to attending West Point, so after his discharge from the army he worked as a CPA for a large firm in Manhattan. However, her older brother, who was in the diamond business in Albany, convinced them to move up to Albany and start a jew-elry store. They took her younger brother, who was familiar with the jewelry business, into partnership with them. She said her husband "knew how to run things," and with her brother's knowledge of the business, they did quite well. She had an 8-month-old baby when they moved to Albany, but she got involved in the store to the extent she could. When their two chil-dren were both in school, she worked full time and claimed to enjoy every minute of it. The Depression presented some difficulties, but she said: "We didn't reduce anybody's [two hired people] salary, but *we* took less. We ate dried lima beans in more ways than I ever thought they could be cooked. But we weathered the storm; we paid our bills; and we stayed there for 60 years."

Mrs. Gold stayed on at the store for another year and a half after her husband's death two years earlier. Then she retired, leaving the store to be run by her brother, and moved into her present apartment. Since she had provided all of this background information in the first interview, I was able to devote much of the second interview to an exploration of the meaning and place of music in her life, which could have been a career line, given her apparent musical talent as a child.

I: Ahh . . . You were saying in the first interview that there was a time when your father really couldn't afford to have you get musical training, but then a point came along where apparently he got more established and you were able to get training, is that right?

G: Yes.

I: Would you like to go back and remind, er, refresh my memory about that?

G: Well, the reason that I couldn't have more opportunity to study with various good teachers was the fact that I was teaching music. I had a group of students, and I was being paid the huge sum of two dollars a lesson.

I: Oh, really? How old were you then?

G: I was fifteen, sixteen, and my earning this extra money, that was a big help for me to use that money. I didn't have to contribute to the home. In fact this money was mine, and I spent that for lessons for myself, and of course there were times when it was difficult because some of the students hadn't practiced that week, and their parents wouldn't let them have a lesson . . .

I: And you wouldn't get the money then?

G: I was out of that two dollars, and if there was more than one or two it was rather difficult. However, in retrospect, I managed to get the lessons, and I studied with some very fine, wonderful people. I don't know whether I mentioned the fact that I studied orchestration and instrumentation with Ruben Goldmark. I remember we paid fifteen dollars for that hour, hour and a half. It was a lot of money, but we managed somehow.

I: Mmmhmm.

G: And I enjoyed the fact that I was paying for it myself.

I: Right. Now ah . . . you had . . . How many students did you have at about that time?

G: Oh . . . about seven or eight, nine.

I: Okay. And on the basis of that, then, you would save that money and *you* would get lessons?

G: Mmmhmm. That's right.

I: Were you getting lessons regularly from one person?

G: Most of the time, yes.

I: What were your, what were your plans at that time? What were the expectations that you had at that time? Can you remember, if you can take yourself back to then, what were your expectations?

G: I really don't believe I had any specific thing in mind because finances were not available.

I: Right.

G: My parents were in very moderate circumstances. In other words, we were poor but we didn't know it.

I: Uhmhmm.

G: So my parents were not too definite about the future. Probably be better off to get married, settle down.

I: I see. There was never any clear thought in your mind that music might be the career, the main career, or that sort of thing?

G: I don't believe so. I really don't believe so. I liked to write at that time, although I had no training in that field. But I did like to do writing . . . writing plays and things, just as I'm doing now.

I: Mmhmm.

G: Not big productions. And I did some little shows for various churches in order to raise a little money for some event. And I had no specific . . .

I: You enjoyed doing these things?

G: *I LOVED* doing them!

I: You loved doing them . . .

G: That was my . . .

I: And regardless of whether you'd become a professional at it, that never occurred to you?

G: I didn't believe that I could. I never thought that I was that good.

I: Oh?

G: I knew I . . .

I: In either the writing or the music?

G: That's right. I knew I had a specific talent. You see, I had what was called absolute pitch. I still have it. In other words, I don't know if you're familiar with what absolute pitch is.

I: No.

G: Well, I could be in another room or away from a musical instrument and whatever notes they were playing I new which notes they were playing. I had absolute pitch. I knew what "A" sounded like whether or not it was in the middle of the piano or the bass of the piano or anyplace else.

I: Mmmhmm.

G: Not many people are born with absolute pitch, but I didn't think it was anything remarkable. It was nothing I did to achieve. I had it.

I: Right, inborn?

G: Inborn. It was an inborn thing. I also played before I took any lessons.

I: Mmhmm.

G: I probably played when I was around 3 years old. My mother was frightened, as a matter of fact. She heard someone playing the piano, and I played because I heard things out in the backyard, one of these drum and oompah bands, and that's how I started to play. My parents knew that I had talent, but you see this was a long time ago. This was when I was about 3 or 4 years old, which was 81, 82 years ago. I'm 85 years old, past 85. And in those days we didn't have people who supported the arts. We didn't have people who were knowledgeable about going to somebody to promote . . . Now maybe if the right person had come along and said, "Look, here's a child who has talent, give her some extra lessons." It never happened.

I: And therefore you didn't get any cues or leads from your parents or anyone else that this, this talent, might be an exceptional one that could be promoted?

G: No, no. They were very modest people. My mother sang beautifully. But I mean . . . that's where it ended.

I: Mmhmm. Mmhmm.

G: There was nothing specific in mind. They encouraged me to play.

I: And you enjoyed it. Just for the sake of it?

G: Well, the reason I think I enjoyed it was because many people used to come to our home. As I said, we were in very moderate circumstances, but we had a very happy home life, and we were six children, and I was the youngest of six. They would come to our home, young people and sometimes older people, and in those days you didn't have a television set or a radio to turn on. You didn't run out because restaurants were not the "in" thing at that time. So somebody would say, "Oh Ruth, would you play the piano for us?" Of course, and then somebody would get up and sing. Maybe somebody would tell little funny stories, but the piano was the focus of the whole household, and I was there to play for them.

I: I see. So it was a very important role that you had in a sense . . .

G: That's right.

I: And it was very much, very much in the center of things.

G: That's right.

I: Mmhmm. And it was very much the center of socializing or sociability?

G: That's right. That was our social life.

I: Right. Mmhmm.

G: We didn't have very much outside social life at all. We didn't seem to need it.

I: Mmhmm. And that was part of the enjoyment also, right? The, ahh, it's not simply the playing but the playing in a social atmosphere . . .

G: That's right. It was a happy situation. It was a happy home.

I: Mmhmm.

G: I was very fortunate to grow up in that atmosphere.

I: Good. That makes a lot of sense. So that what you were saying is that you were getting your satisfaction all along with the music, and it wasn't as though, ahh . . . you had any great expectation that somehow you might be able to study with some master?

G: In the back of my mind I probably did, but I never made too much of it (*laughter*).

I: You never made too much of it. Okay. Now, when you were giving the lessons, you were able to take lessons at about age 15. That went on for about how long?

G: Well, that went on for a good many years. Probably almost until I was married.

I: Almost until you were married. Then there's the fact that you had to take over the house, that you had to take over the responsibility for the house . . .

G: That's right.

I: Did that impinge on your lessons?

G: Not really. No, because, ahh, well I may have . . . I don't remember telling you about the time I needed a new piano.

I: No.

G: My husband surprised me. I had seen, and heard, and played on this new Steinway at a store in Albany, and I came home and raved about this beautiful instrument. It had a special case besides being a very fine instrument. I came home and I raved about it, and my husband surprised me with it. They took my Baldwin in trade, and I got this piano. I had it until recently when I moved here, and it was in perfect condition because I kept it in very fine condition. It was hard parting with it. I'll never forget my feelings when it went out the door.

I: Feelings of loss?

G: However, it was only a thing.

I: But lots of memories attached to that.

G: Yes, yes, but you see there's nothing that you can't do without. You just adjust to it, that's all. Not always the easiest thing. What are you going to do? You forget about it.

I: On the other hand, some people claim that there are some things, you know, their most cherished possessions. Do you have a most cherished possession?

G: Yes.

I: And what would that be? (*She shows me a pendant or medal she is wearing on a chain around her neck.*)

G: I never go out without it, and it's a very private thing. Other things are just things.

I: But that's the most cherished . . .

G: This is the most cherished of my possessions. And I say it with no hesitation.

I: Right. Why would you say that is? Why is it there is no hesitation? And that's interesting because you're not alone in that. I think many people have that feeling, there is something they can say without a moment's . . . with very little hesitation . . .

G: It's my most cherished possession because my husband was very special to me. He was my most cherished possession if you can use the word "possession" applying to a human person. I was very proud of what he had accomplished in his life. In the days when he was appointed to West Point there were very few Jewish people in West Point. He was one of four in the whole class of 272, and I really feel that over the years I was very special to have him. He was a very special person to me, having won that battle, at that time. From what I was told, newspapers had a great write-up about it. I never saw the article, but I was told about it—I probably could still get a copy but, however, that's unimportant. But I felt he was so very special.

I: And that is, it really does symbolize an accomplishment in itself.

G: It does because it keeps him very close. There's nobody in the world who could ever take his place. And my children are wonderful children. So devoted, I could never complain. Even my daughter-in-law and son-in-law are so close to me. My daughter-in-law is just like my own daughter, but nothing could ever take his place, much as I love my children and as great as I think they are.

I: You know, when you were in the reminiscence group and were asked what you think about when you think of the past, you would always go back to the graduation dance at West Point. Now, am I right in assuming that the reason that stands out in your mind so much is that it also associated with your husband and the fact that you got to know him better then? And that it was the beginning, in a sense?

G: Yes.

I: Of your relationship.

G: Yes.

I: Now that all makes sense.

G: He was a very unusual person and very athletic. He was an excellent member of track

Mrs. Gold went on to describe how her husband was also an excellent boxer. He had won the lightweight championship at the Military Academy, and the pendant she wore around her neck was actually the medal he was awarded for winning the championship.

She went on to say that this was the high point of her husband's military career. It had special meaning because he was Jewish, and the stereotype prevalent in the military then was that Jewish men were brainy but not very athletic. However, her husband believed he could excel in boxing, and he proved it. She went on to describe what this said about him, about his determination, about overcoming the stigma of being Jewish in an elitist, predominantly white Protestant institution.

She said she wore it constantly, that she would never part with it. It gave her much reassurance and courage. It never failed to evoke many fond memories and many positive associations. This should be contrasted with the comment Mrs. Gold made about the Steinway piano she had to part with: "However, it was only a thing."

Any analysis of a life theme in Ruth Gold's case cannot overlook the significant event of her mother's death. This represented a profound loss and dislocation in her life. It meets all of the criteria of a major psychosocial transition as these have been formulated by C. Murray Parkes (1971) on the basis of his work with loss and bereavement. Parkes has noted the need for a massive change or shift in the person's inner "assumptive world" in order to bring it in line with the drastically changed external world after such a transitional event.

In Ruth Gold's case she had been the youngest child and a talented one, who was obviously doted upon according to her own description. From being a center of attention in the family and the recipient of some adulation as well as nurturance, her role in the family changed profoundly. Not only did she have to cope with the emotional trauma of the loss of her mother, but she had to transform herself into an active provider of sustenance and nurturance rather than being the recipient of it in the family. She tells us how her neighbor helped her to cope instrumentally with these new responsibilities, but she reveals little about the expressive coping she must have engaged in to overcome the emotional impact of her mother's death and her new existential situation.

But cope she did. Furthermore, she did it with little or no evident complaint. There must have been remorse over her mother's death but no apparent question or complaint about what she had to do. Indeed, far from being a "complainer," she made herself into much the opposite—someone who has little use for complainers. One has to read carefully between the lines to find any evidence of negative emotions in response to the emotional stress she must have experienced in the process of that psychosocial transition.

This, then, was her central existential problem: to come to terms with the loss of her mother and the profound shift in family (and life) role it entailed. It should be noted that she does not specifically identify this as her central problem in her narrative. Nor does she attribute the cause to her mother's death, to bad luck, to women's disadvantaged and exploited family position in those days, or to other such factors, since she does not recognize it as a formative, existential problem in her life. She takes it as something that just happened, something important and upsetting but something that had to be made the best of. To use her own characteristic statement to cover all such contingencies—"This is it!" (and, we might add, "You make the most of it"). This credo or philosophy becomes her method of solution to the problem, and it guides her behavior and reactions to all subsequent major events in her life.

There would be a strong tendency at this particular point in American social history to focus on her loss of a potential musical career in order to meet the societal and familial expectations for young women in her situation at that time. That is the reason I went back to explore the meaning and place of music in her life at that time, to be sure that she did not see herself as deprived of a career that would have led to greater individuality and self-identity, if not fame. On the basis of this exploration in the second interview and my reading of the transcript, I cannot say that a thwarted career was the central existential problem in her life.

Mrs. Gold's acceptance of her dramatically altered social role definitely points to hers as an "accepted" life theme. There was no attempt to generalize this personal problem into a more universal one, as Max Korvitz had done, because she did not identify it as an "existential problem" — one of the criteria for a discovered life theme. She probably felt great love and concern for and indebtedness to her father, which might have entered into the direction her life took. There was no evidence of overt pressure from her father for her to do so, as far as we can tell from her narrative. We can only surmise, but one observation about life themes comes to mind here:

> The structure of the life theme is established by a matrix of early experiences, especially by the cognitive coding used in the family. The definition of the problem, its causes, and possible means of solution are facilitated by the patterns of explanation taken for granted in the family, which makes up the person's first and in many ways only coherent "symbolic universe." (Csikszentmihalyi & Beattie, 1979)

The arrival of her husband on the scene enabled her to build upon and play out her accepted familial life theme on into old age. He seemed to epitomize many of the essential things she was looking for. He had the qualities she most admired (i.e., the grit and determination to overcome obstacles and *to do it in style*). This is her very own theme and credo. He overcame obstacles "in style" by succeeding at the exclusive and elitist institution of West Point in the World War I era despite his immigrant Jewish status. Not only that, but he became a champion athlete and a boxer, the last thing expected of a young Jew in that place at that time.

This brings us to the most cherished object as a factor in this analysis. Ruth Gold's identification with her husband's boxing medal is coterminous with him as the most important person in her life. The medal embodies, just as he personally did, the values, affections, loyalties, and most profound meanings in her life. There can be little doubt that this object is very central to both her reminiscence and her self in old age.

THE INTERPRETATION OF THEMES

It is inevitable that any student of thematic elements in life stories must engage in some sort of interpretation in order to tease out those themes. One would expect this in the case of an accepted life theme in which the person has gone along with or taken for granted certain prescribed or socially available roles, behaviors, self-definitions, and so on. However, some interpretation is necessary as well in cases of discovered life themes. Although the central themes are apt to be much more accessible to awareness in discovered life themes, since there is recognition implied in anything "discovered," the themes may not readily be apparent to the person or become explicit in his or her life narrative. It will be recalled that I had to pose questions to Max Korvitz that were quite directly aimed at eliciting his life theme, even though it had been implicit in much of what he was saying.

How much more of a problem is it to detect a life theme if one can only read a transcript or listen to a taped interview or oral history, without being able to explore or probe as an interviewer? Yet most current research in life narratives must rely upon such existing written or spoken "texts." This is why it is necessary to use hermeneutical methods in such research. Hermeneutics is the "science" of interpretation, and the need for such an interpretive approach will become much more evident in the next chapter, which is devoted to life stories in the form of self-narratives. However, in this chapter it is apparent that some interpretation was inevitable in the cases of Max Korvitz and Ruth Gold, even though the interviews were specifically geared toward eliciting life themes.

The idea of discovered versus accepted life themes is a provocative one, and it has apparent heuristic value for the study of lives. There is something that makes intuitive sense about the idea that certain people discover meaning and purpose in the course of their lives to a greater extent than do others. These others appear to live out their lives on more of a day-to-day basis within the more immediately given and institutionalized categories of meaning and purpose. Although this all seems to have a certain validity on the face of it, there are a number of serious questions that have to be raised about the whole idea.

First, what difference does it make whether a person has a discovered or accepted life theme? Such a question only begs another—difference for what? I was able to raise these questions with Professor Csikszentmihalyi, and he was able to respond to them in the light of subsequent research that he, some of his colleagues, and students at the University of Chicago have been doing.[3] He candidly acknowledged that the answers are not clear as yet. There seems to be no evidence that there is a predictable or expected relationship of life themes to mental health or emotional well-being, although there have been no direct studies of this relationship as yet. It is worth noting in this regard that on our two indicators of well-being from the Group Project, The Life Satisfaction Index-A and the Monge Self-Concept Scale, Ruth Gold scored significantly higher than Max Korvitz in all three testing periods of the project. Although Mr. K.' s scores were probably affected by the dissonance he was experiencing, it is highly unlikely that after his life-review experience his scores would be higher or even as high as hers. Yet she had an accepted life theme, and we probably would anticipate higher well-being scores, especially Life Satisfaction, from someone with a discovered life theme. Obviously, it is not that simple, and it is probably not legitimate to equate issues of meaning and purpose with happiness or morale.

Another question is raised about the two types of life theme by the issue of gender in these two cases. It should be recalled that the earlier research by Csikszentmihalyi on life themes was based on the study of men. Max Korvitz and Ruth Gold were both octogenarians and similar in age, but there had to be significant differences in social opportunities and expectations between men and women of their generation. Finding a thematic solution to an existential problem through a career had to be much more open and available to men than to women. Csikszentmihalyi not only acknowledged this but added that the issue for women of the current generation has become even further complicated. He and his colleagues have found that the mothers of many of these women had discovered life themes. They came from immigrant or traditional American families in which the role of women was clear-cut and circumscribed. They had to assert their discovered life themes and identities against these familial and social constraints and expectations in order to carve out careers in business, law, medicine, and other professions. Now their expectations and efforts are geared toward their daughters' pursuing such careers. This presents a dilemma for the daughters, for if they "accept" the career options proposed by their mothers, this would not be consistent with the criteria of the discovered life theme. Some have opted to devote themselves more to their families and the raising of their children than to their careers after obtaining professional education in line with their mothers' expectations. Paradoxically, then, their "discovered" life themes look more like their grandmothers' accepted life themes.

The gender issue complicates the matter even further when we consider the way women define themselves, according to Carol Gilligan and other new feminist thinkers in developmental psychology (Gilligan, 1982; Gilligan, Ward, & Taylor, 1989). The way women define themselves, make their moral choices, and presumably find their life themes and choose careers is in the context of human relationships. According to most prevailing (male-developed) theories of selfhood, men are motivated by an individualistic need to survive and prevail against all odds and all others, if necessary.

Csikszentmihalyi (1989) says that by contrast Gilligan's suggestion that care and responsibility for the well-being of others represents qualities at least as desirable as these other prevailing theories of selfhood, and adds: "This picture of a self that is responsive and dependent on others is a definite improvement." So he also sees need for a critical second look at the concept of the life theme from this expanded gender perspective.

We can certainly see these gender differences played out in lives and life themes of Ruth Gold and Max Korvitz. It is interesting, too, that the related issues of intimacy versus isolation and identity versus identity diffusion from Erik Erikson's developmental theory are played out in their lives as well. It has been said that men have difficulty with the essential Eriksonian task of young adulthood, which is to achieve *intimacy* over isolation; whereas women have problems with the essential task of adolescence, which is achieving ego *identity* over identity confusion (Rubin, 1983; Tamir, 1982). Women's generally more successful resolution of the intimacy task is in line with Gilligan's thinking, whereas men's more successful resolution of the identity task, even at the cost of isolation, is in line with the individualistic, Lone Ranger type of achievement proposed in earlier theories of selfhood. However, in Erikson's epigenetic, stepladder model of development, successful achievement of any developmental task requires resolution of all earlier tasks or steps. Thus, by the time they get to the last task of life, ego integrity versus despair, *both* men and women would generally have difficulty in achieving ego integrity because of failure to resolve the earlier tasks of intimacy and identity, respectively.

The life cycles of Max Korvitz and Ruth Gold did seem to reflect this. Mr. K. revealed in his self-concept and life-satisfaction responses that he felt some isolation and deprivation of intimacy and nurturance in his life. He repeatedly talked about his "lost youth" and lack of a childhood. It is significant that in the course of four interviews the only time he mentioned his wife and children was when he said he had to give up spending sufficient time with them due to his labor organizing and other activist involvements. There was some regret that this was all for naught because his involvements and efforts did not bring about the desired social change. All of the photographs he showed me and discussed had to do with his social activism, even though photographs of his family were all over the living room. His cherished photo in Varna, so prominently displayed in his living room, symbolized his essential identity as well as his life theme.

Ruth Gold's most cherished possession, on the other hand, was something achieved by her husband. However, it strongly symbolized their *relationship* for her, and that more closely represents her life theme than a highly individualized identity.

Does this mean that Max Korvitz and Ruth Gold *both* lacked ego integrity because of failure to resolve earlier developmental tasks? The whole concept of *resolution* is a problematic one in Erikson's model. Again, Vivian Clayton's (1975) conclusion that most individuals seek foreclosure after adolescence and "realistically" opt for compromise rather than complete resolution between conflicting forces at each major life stage and crisis makes sense. Her contention that this ability to compromise is an ego strength that enables people to achieve some degree of integrity has the ring of validity to it. I prefer the word *synthesis* to her word *compromise* because it expresses the dialectical process of opposing forces faced throughout life, which become synthesized in a larger process of integration.

The type of dialectical model proposed by Clayton (1975), Datan (1976), Riegel (1976), and other like-minded gerontologists seems to have much more explanatory power for the findings we obtained in both the life-theme materials of the Individual Reminiscence Survey and the ego-integrity materials of the Integrity Survey. The latter survey will be discussed and illustrated in the next chapter with case materials, but it would be well here to go back to the dialectic model described and depicted in Figure 1 in Chapter 5 for looking at the cases presented in this chapter.

The dialectic between world and self is a powerful one in determining life trajectories and life themes. The effects of significant others, events, and circumstances, which are frequently beyond the control of the individual and often unanticipated, can have profound and lasting effects on lives. This certainly held true in the lives of Max Korvitz and Ruth Gold. In the case of Mr. K., although he had a clear identity, that identity was created in large part by events and forces well beyond his control. First, there were the circumstances he was born into, such as the disadvantaged social, ethnic, and economic position of his family. Then there was the advent of World War I, his conscription, capture, and experiences in the prisoner-of-war camps. He did discover a theme in all of this and dedicated his life to the fulfillment of that ideal. However, the identity that was built on this ideal was at odds with the economic and political realities in the world of his old age. He was frustrated and in a state of dissonance because current external circumstances, particularly the beliefs of most young people, did not validate his identity—if anything, they mocked it.

It is worth noting that Mr. K.'s identity was very much lodged in his Social Me, to use William James's term. His existential problem was not only located in his socioeconomic circumstances, but the fact that his solution to that problem was in the form of social action and solidarity speaks to the social nature of his identity. However, this identity, which was forged in action and coping with the conflicting forces in his life—the first dialectic of Figure 1—had to be integrated with the new reality of the world in his old age. That took more interior "gut-work" involving the I–Me or second dialectic of the self. The dramatic increase in his level of experiencing (EXP scores of 5, 6, and 7) in the third and fourth interviews is reflective of that interior process. Finally, he came to terms with and synthesized this dissonance in his late life through the second, I–Me, dialectic. To use William James's language again, he had to move from the Social Me to the Spiritual Me for a dialogue with the I at the innermost core of the self.

Now, Ruth Gold gave no indication of any such dissonance or inner dialectic. Her whole approach to life, which was to accept things as they came and make the most of them, precluded the need for that sort of dialectic. It is noteworthy that her experiential level in the interviews were generally at EXP Level 3, for she was a lively and fluent narrator of her own story but never went into the more introspective and searching levels (EXP scores of 5 and above). Despite this fact and the fact that she had an accepted rather than a discovered life theme, there was an integrity about her. She did develop a philosophy of life from her experiences, and it seemed to be working very well for her in her old age, judging by her self-concept and life-satisfaction scores.

So we would have to say that the type of life theme does not have a predictable relationship to ego integrity any more than it has to mental health or morale. However, it *does* have a relationship to life stories or self-narratives, as we shall see in the next chapter. This is because of the importance of *agency*, that is, the I, or intentional, agent in the plots and themes of life stories. It is not just that things "happen" to people in life stories; people make things happen as well. As Jerome Bruner (1986) put it, "The matching of 'inner' vision and 'outer' reality is . . . a classic human plight" in the life story. We shall take a much closer look at this matching process in the self-narratives to be presented in the next chapter along with the findings of the Integrity Survey, the third and last in the series on reminiscence.

NOTES

1. All names used here are pseudonyms for purposes of confidentiality.

2. The "I" stands for interviewer and the "K" for Mr. K.

3. I consulted with Dr. Csikszentmihalyi on November 20, 1986, at the University of Chicago, where he was chair of the Department of Behavioral Sciences, about the cases and themes presented in this chapter. For further published work on the life theme since his 1979 article with Beattie, see Csikszentmihalyi and Larson (1984) and Freeman, Csikszentmihalyi, and Larson (1986)

8

Variations on a Theme

The title of this chapter relates directly to the title of the book: *Reminiscence and the self in Old age*. Most reminiscence is a variation on the theme of the self, whether it is in the form of public reminiscing, private reminiscing, or the self-told life story. Julian Jaynes (1976) summed it up as follows:

> Reminiscence is a succession of excerptions (of reality). Each so-called association and consciousness is an excerption, an aspect or image ... excerpted from the experience on the basis of personality and changing situations. In consciousness, we are always seeking our vicarial selves as the main figures in the stories of our lives.

The first phase of the Integrity Survey, conducted in 1989, was intended to look systematically at the different ways in which reminiscence related to ego integrity, specifically the four ego-integrity statuses identified by Walaskay, Whitbourne, and Nehrke (1983–84): integrity achieving, dissonant, despairing, and foreclosed. We used a questionnaire for the first phase of the survey, and it included questions about the forms and functions of reminiscence for the respondents using a typology developed by Michael and Jean Romaniuk (1981). It also included a set of questions that comprised a measure called the Ego Integrity Scale (Boylin, Gordon, & Nehrke, 1976). In addition, the questionnaire included an instrument called the Affect-Balance Scale, which was intended to measure the person's current mood or affect (Bradburn & Caplowitz, 1965) Then there were also some open-ended questions about cherished objects and memorabilia as reminiscentia, which provided some of the findings reported in Chapter 6.

The second phase of the Integrity Survey consisted of tape-recorded interviews with a subsample of the respondents from the questionnaire survey. They were selected on the basis of the patterns of reminiscence, integrity status, and affect measures that emerged from the questionnaire survey. A total of 100 questionnaires was obtained, and from this sample 40 persons were identified and interviewed. The respondents from both phases came from four upstate New York communities, three urban and one suburban, and were paid for completing the questionnaires and for providing the tape-recorded narratives.

VARIATIONS IN REMINISCENCES AND NARRATIVES OF THE SELF

Three patterns of reminiscence merged from the statistical analysis of the questionnaire responses. Two of them had very obvious relationships to the self, although for quite different reasons. The first pattern was what the Romaniuks called "Self-Regard/Image Enhancement," and our findings were essentially the same as what they found in their factor analysis of this cluster of uses of reminiscence. These uses had a positive relationship with affect or mood and included the following reasons or functions: (1) because memories are pleasant, enjoyable, and help to pass the time of day; (2) to teach others by drawing on your past experiences; (3) to inform people about the successes and accomplishments in your life; and (4) because recalling memories lifts your spirits. There were several other uses in this cluster, but they did not show the same significant relationship to affect that these did. It can be seen quite readily that these are self-enhancing and mood-enhancing uses of reminiscence.

The second pattern we found was quite similar to what the Romaniuks called "Existential/Self-Understanding." The critical item in this pattern that distinguished it as related to the respondent's self was the following use of reminiscing: "to arrive at a better understanding of your past life and yourself." Another use in this pattern was "to determine life's meaning," and it was closely related to the self-understanding item. We found a third item in this pattern that was also closely related to self-understanding, but this differed somewhat from the Romaniuk's cluster and will be discussed in more detail shortly.

The third pattern we found was quite similar to a cluster of uses the Romaniuks found that they called "Present Problem Solving." Here again, however, there was one significant difference in the makeup of this pattern as compared to what the Romaniuks found in their cluster. The item that was not in their cluster but was prominent in our pattern was "to solve something in your past that is troubling you." This related closely to two other items that were included in our pattern and their cluster: (1) "to cope with a loss in your life; and (2) to deal with some difficulty you are experiencing." It can be seen that the one thing all three items have in common is *problem solving* but not just problems or difficulties in the present, as identified in their cluster. Consequently, we simply renamed this pattern "Problem-Solving." Some of the people we found exhibiting this pattern of reminiscence were the following: several widows dealing with recent and not-so-recent deaths of their husbands, some people with serious and progressive health problems, one whose spouse was terminally ill, and some who were contending with feelings of loneliness and isolation from living alone. Although there is an implicit relationship to self in this pattern, there is a much more immediate relationship to problems and circumstances.

The second pattern, "Existential/Self-Understanding," was more directly related to self and included one item not found in Romaniuks' cluster with that name. It was reminiscing "to make plans for the future." This related closely to the other two items we found in this pattern: "to arrive at a better understanding of your past life and yourself," and "to determine life's meaning." The Romaniuks felt that "Existential/Self-Understanding" uses comprised life-review reminiscing, and our impression was very much in accord with theirs—when the pattern included future plans rather than past losses. In other words, "making plans for the future" showed a clear empirical fit with the life-review pattern of reminiscing on the basis of our statistical findings from the 100 respondents. This also fits quite well with Robert Butler's definition of the life review as a process of "reintegration of past, present, and future" so that there can be an ultimate acceptance of life experiences as they were actually lived. The idea behind this is that there is a need to review the past, not only to know oneself but also to know how to live in the present and future on the basis of this knowledge of past and self.

There were only 15 people in our sample of 100 who exhibited all three uses in this pattern: (1) self-understanding, (2) future plans, and (3) life's meaning. Within this small group there were two subgroups, one representing the integrity-achieving status and the other the dissonant status. The six in the integrity-achieving subgroup showed more positive affect, and in addition to the life review uses they used reminiscence for pleasure and self-enhancement more than did the other subgroup. The nine dissonants, on the other hand, did not as often find themselves engaging in pleasurable reminiscence but more frequently in the problem-solving types, in addition to the three life-review uses. Consequently, their affect was much less positive than that of the first subgroup.

There were probably some people who had already gone through their life reviews and were no longer engaged in that pattern at the time of the study. They probably engaged most often in the more pleasurable, mood-enhancing types of reminiscence, and they could be classified as in the integrity-achieving status. However, we had no way of knowing just how many of these there were with any statistical accuracy. The numbers would perhaps be in the neighborhood of 25 or 30 at most. This is similar to the findings of Lieberman and Tobin (1983) as well as to Whitbourne and Weinstock's (1986) observation that relatively few individuals seem to meet all of the criteria included in Erikson's concept of ego integrity. These findings also lend further credence to Clayton's (1975) contention that the concept does not fit the majority of elderly persons.

The 40 people selected for the life-narrative interviews represented the four integrity statuses as well as the three patterns of reminiscence. They ranged in age from 61 to 94 and varied widely in social, educational, and vocational background. They ranged from unschooled laborers, tenant farmers, charwomen, and so on to university professors and other professionals. The interviews were all conducted in the same straightforward and relatively simple way, based on Bruner's (1987) approach to obtaining self-told life narratives. It basically consisted of asking people to tell the story of their lives in the context of a one or one-and-a-half-hour interview. The respondents were told that the stories did not have to be neat and well-organized and that we were just interested in "how people see their lives," not in judging them.

We suggested they might begin by telling where and when they were born, a little about their parents and what they were like, then what early home life was like and from there begin to work up to the present. After they had done this, we asked them about the kinds of events they considered crucial in their lives—the circumstances, happenings, crises, or turning points that might have shaped their lives. This latter set of questions was intended to pick up any themes that might not have been included in the preceding narrative.

The themes that emerged from the interviews were characteristically in the form of interpretive comments or self-observations that were repeated throughout the narrative. Their frequency and consistency indicated to us that they did indeed represent themes in the lives of the narrators. While describing life experiences or circumstances, the respondent would add interpretive or evaluative comments about their reactions, behavior, and so on to the events and circumstances described. It was apparent that they were defining themselves or aspects of themselves in relating the experiences, reflecting upon them, and interpreting them. In the narrative process they were formulating or expressing an identity, an identifiable sense of self in the world. They might be talking about a particular past experience in their work life and then might add some interpretive comment like "I always worked hard—all my life—at whatever I did." Such interpretive statements were often restated in various ways throughout the narratives, and they were thematic not only of the experience but of the self.

These were generally related in the form of episodes in the life narrative, as mentioned in Chapter 2 under "Narrative Reminiscence." These have been called "nuclear episodes," which are "the significant life episodes that, in the narrating mind of the individual are reconstructed—to fit into the life story as its most significant scenes (McAdams, 1988). These scenes are most significant because they are reflective of the self in the world (i.e., the person's identity). As Erikson (1959) put it, in order to find an "anchor point" for the discussion of the genetics of identity "it would be well to trace it through significant life episodes of ordinary individuals."

It was noted earlier that relatively few of our respondents fit all of the criteria of the integrity-achieving status, but even those who did told very different stories in terms of significant episodes and their interpretations of them. The overall impression in hearing these narratives and the identities formulated in them, is one of immense variety. It is difficult to know which narratives to select for illustration here because they are so varied and unique to each person that they defy classification. Donald Polkinghorne (1988) has observed that researchers investigating the order of meaning in narratives "cannot simply use the principles of categorization and typology that researchers concerned with the natural realm use." That was certainly our experience with these narratives.

There was, however, an identifiable dimension on which to array, if not classify, self-narratives (i.e., the dimension of experiential depth). Bruner (1987) noted that there are "internal criteria relating to how one felt or what one intended [in telling one's story]. . . . Otherwise, we would not be able to say that certain self-narratives are 'shallow' and others 'deep.' We were able to assess this dimension by use of the Experiencing (EXP) Scale, as will be illustrated shortly.

The dimension of depth also enters into the nature of the identity that is being narrated. Erikson (1982) speaks of "an all too limiting identity lived." What he means by this is that from early childhood on some people readily accept and enact the roles, scripts, and prescribed behaviors in conformity with the expectations of parents, family, and society. There is no evidence, in other words, of serious questioning, of an inner searching, or of outer testing of other options and potentials. As Bruner would put it, there was no matching of inner vision with outer reality; the latter was simply accepted on its own terms.

The method we used to study this dimension in the life stories was to follow the "shape of agency" in the narrative. That is, we followed closely the narrating "I" as protagonist of the life story and tried to discern the extent to which that "I" is portrayed as an active agent in shaping his or her life in terms of an inner vision or intention. Bruner (1987) found Amelia Rorty's characterizations of agents in the historical development of literary forms to be revealing and quite descriptive of what he was finding in his own study of self-narratives. Rorty (1976) proposed that there has been a steady movement toward an empowerment and subjective enrichment of the protagonist agent in the history of Western literary forms, from the early folktales to present-day forms of novels, short stories, and plays. Several of her characterizations seemed particularly descriptive of agency in the self-narratives of our Integrity Survey as well.

Three of her agent types or characterizations that were especially pertinent for our purposes were what she termed "figures," "persons," and "individuals." In folktales *figures* show little or no clear evidence of proactive
agency or empowerment, nor of subjective enrichment by experience. *Persons*, by comparison, are defined by roles in a society that provides them
certain rights in return, roles that allow for some empowerment, active
agency, and subjective enrichment. *Individuals*, on the other hand, have to
resist or transcend society and its constraints and must create or actively
claim their rights. "Individuals" are thus the most proactive and self-creative
of the kinds of agents. As Bruner says, these are "characterizations of the
forms of relationship between an intention-driven actor and the settings in
which he must act to achieve his goals."

These three characterizations will be further delineated and illustrated in
the following sections. They are meant only to be descriptive of the "shape
of agency" in the case illustrations and self-narratives to be presented.
Whether or not they have any relationship to reminiscence patterns, integrity status, level of experiencing, integration of identity, and so on will be
discussed in conjunction with each case illustration and narrative.

NARRATIVE OF "FIGURE"

Figures are agents whose identities are not fully delineated in life or in the
self-narrative. If we look at Bruner's formula "of relationship between an intention-driven actor and the setting in which he must act to achieve his
goals," the first and most obvious thing missing in the self-narrative of a figure is the sense of an "intention-driven actor." Instead, "the setting" (i.e., the
world of significant objects, events, and circumstances) seems to be doing
the driving. Rather than creating it, the figure follows the pattern or plot of
the life narrative as it unfolds. That pattern might have been predetermined
and fatalistically accepted in the mind of the figure, but the important point
is that this pattern is externally orchestrated.

Rorty states that most figures are not identified by their occupation or social roles but from their place in the plot or pattern of their lives and narratives. As she puts it, "A figure is neither found by nor owns experiences," for
figures "watch the unfolding of their lives" following the pattern laid out for
them (Rorty, 1976). This last phrase was highly descriptive of the self-narratives of a number of the respondents in the Integrity Survey. Therefore, it
would be well to present a self-narrative that represents the essential features of a figure as laid out above. The following case illustration represents
the kind of characterization or identity that comes through in the self-narratives of such figures.

Frances J., a 77-year-old woman living with her retired husband, was interviewed in their senior apartment dwelling in a small upstate New York city. She was dressed in a plain house dress, and although of medium build and not frail in physical appearance, she looked her 77 years. She began her self-narrative by describing her grandparents. She described her maternal grandparents as "well-to-do farmers with many, many acres of land down-state." Her paternal grandparents, on the other hand, were "more humble folk." Her grandfather was a clerk on the railroad and "grandma just raised the kids." She claimed to be especially fond of this grandmother. Then she went on to say that her own mother was "just a housewife . . . stayed home and raised the five kids." Her father was a foreman in a cement factory just a few miles outside the city in which she was currently living. Neither she nor her husband had lived outside this area of the state at any time in their lives. She provided the following truncated story of her life:

J: I was the middle one of five kids. We had a lot of fun . . . and we sort of just grew. We were all close together in age, and we would go to school together. It was a mile walk to school, but it was a lot of fun. I sometimes feel sorry for the kids today . . . they have to go to school on buses, even in the first and second grade. We went to that same school all the way through grammar school, and it was a lot of fun to be able to walk and run and play all the way to and back from school. The kids today don't seem to get that. I guess we were just lucky. We lived through the Depression and all that, but Dad was never out of work . . . and we always had a roof over our heads and food to eat. It was a simple life but a good one. Anyway, we went on to high school . . . and then we had to take the bus. So I did that for the next four years.

I: You graduated from high school, then?

J: Yes, I didn't go any further, though. I worked in department stores during the summer in my junior and senior years. Then, when I graduated, I went to work full-time in one of the department stores . . . did that for a couple of years, and then I met my husband. We met at a dance. We both loved dancing. Then we got married. He worked for a milk company, and he stayed with that company until he retired eight years ago. The company moved out of the town we were married in, and he moved with the company. That's why we're here now. Anyway, just before we moved up here we had our one son, and after that I was very sick for months and months . . . and in that time I grew a lot because I had time to think and read a lot, you know?

I: You grew a lot?

J: Yeh. So, then we sort of . . . it's a very quiet life isn't it? I'm trying to think . . . what else? Maybe if I think about it for a minute . . .

I: Sure . . . *(long pause)*

J: I think that when I got so very sick that changed my whole life a lot. I couldn't' have any more children because of it. So I had to do something.

I: You had only the one son?

J: Right. We have only the one son, but we have two grandchildren and they are great . . . we really enjoy them. Anyway, when I was so very sick I had all this time to think, and I began to wonder what I wanted to do. I had my son to take care of but there was lots of time when he was in school. So I thought, "What would I like to do?" Then one of my son's teachers told us that he seemed to have real artistic talent and that it would be good if we could get him some oil paints and other art materials. . . . Well, we did, and it dawned on me that I always liked cutting out pictures and making collages and stuff. So I tried some of his paints . . . and then I was hooked!

I: Hooked?

J: Yeh. I wanted to learn how to paint, so I asked my son's teacher if the school had anything to offer along that line. She told me the local high school was offering an evening beginner's course for the public. So I went . . . and I took other courses later, too.

I: So you really went into painting in a serious way.

J: Sort of. I'm a very plain painter. . . . I like pictures that are very ornate and beautiful, but I don't paint that way. I paint things that are very plain . . . but I enjoy it.

I: Have you ever sold any of your art work?

J: (*Laughs*) Once . . . I sold a painting at an exhibit we had at our senior center . . . and that was nice because they asked me if I could teach an art class at the center. . . . They knew I had taken some art courses in the evening. So I have taught a couple of classes over the past few years, and I really like it.

I: So the painting really did come through for you when you were wondering about what you would do.

J: Oh yeh . . . but that's not all. I always read a lot, so at about that same time I thought I would like to write some poetry, so I joined the writing group at the center. That's been fun, too.

Later in the interview I asked Mrs. J. if there were any critical events or turning points in her life, and she came back again to the time she was sick and had time to think. She repeated that she felt she grew at that time, but she could identify no other turning points. Since her life narrative was so abbreviated, I began to explore some of the responses she had put on her questionnaire about the reminiscing and memorabilia/cherished objects questions. She had checked off that she found herself engaging in reminiscing "fairly often" and gave the following uses or reasons: (1) because memories are pleasant, enjoyable, and help to pass the time of day; (2) to let people know that the past had a lot to offer that cannot be found today; and (3) because recalling memories lifts spirits. I then mentioned that there were a number she had not checked off and asked if she would be willing to go over them again. She readily agreed, and when I mentioned reminiscing "to determine life's meaning" she gave the following response:

J: (*Tittering*) Oh dear, I certainly hope not.

I: So in thinking back over your life, you haven't even wondered, "What does it all mean?"

J: Heavens, no. I mean . . . after all, things are the way they are. . . . Life goes on.

I: On the other hand, would you say you have developed a kind of philosophy of life over the years?

J: No . . . no . . . just sort of took it as it came. You just go along and then hope it works out OK. (*Pause*) Family is very important, though.

I: Yes, You said on your questionnaire that the reasons your cherished objects had such special meaning to you was because "they were always there in the *family*."

J: That's right. Those lovely old dishes and plates (*points to them on the shelves in the dining room*) were my mother's "Sunday best." Those brass candlesticks belonged to Grandma Min, and I was very fond of her. They bring back good memories.

When the interview was over, she seemed almost apologetic and said she felt a little guilty about taking the $20 payment for the interview. She said: "It's a very . . . mundane . . . kind of life. Is that the right word for it? Not really, we had a lot of fun."

There are several ways in which Mrs. J. fits Rorty's characterization of a figure. She did appear to "watch the unfolding" of her life and to follow the pattern that seemed laid out for her. She, like her mother and grandmother, would get married and raise children. She indicated this later in explaining that the reason she could not have any more children was because she had to have a hysterectomy at the time she was so sick. She and her husband had expected to have a larger family, and she had fully expected to be spending most of her young adult years raising children. Dealing with that disappointment and loss, as well as finding something else to do, is apparently what she meant about having "grown a lot" when she had so much time to think and read.

The interesting point is that the solution she came up with was a domestic rather than a career one. She did not choose to go back to work, but she did choose to pursue painting and writing, which would allow her to remain mostly at home. On the other hand, she was characteristically modest about any artistic aspirations or the significance and quality of her work. In fact, the theme that pervades her narrative is that of modest aspiration and accomplishment. She used adjectives such as plain, ordinary, quiet, and mundane in describing her life and herself. Her use of the words *mundane* and *ornate* indicate an above-average vocabulary, and her reading and writing of poetry suggest more than "mundane" interests.

Yet she never articulated any of the motivating factors, intentions, or even feelings about these more creative interests, other than to evaluate them as plain or ordinary. It is noteworthy, also, that she describes her mother as "just a housewife" and says that her maternal grandmother "just raised the kids." That she was very attached to these two women and all they represented in her life were attested to by her cherished objects and the loving way she cared for and spoke about those objects in the interview. To aspire beyond these beloved and respected women, or beyond what society generally prescribed for young women in the rural or small-town America of her childhood, was not in her repertoire or her inner vision as best as we can tell from her self-narrative.

There is no clear sense of an "intention-driven actor" in Mrs. J.'s self-narrative. Even when she is faced with the reality of not having any more children in her life, the alternatives to child rearing that she finally adopted were less intentional or inwardly impelled than they were "recognitions" of some capacities and interests after the fact. As she said, "it dawned on me that I always liked [art work]," and because she enjoyed reading, she would try writing. It was also hard to tell from her EXP level what these alternatives meant to her. Her experiencing level throughout her self-narrative was usually at about EXP Stage 2 in which she related events, ideas, and actions in an interested and fluent manner, with the use of personal pronouns such as *I* and *we*, and at times she would reach EXP Stage 3 in which she would give parenthetical or very limited references to feelings. She never really communicated any sense of what it was like to be her, to know her subjective experiences, associations, and feelings from the language and gestures she used. Even her description of the turning point in her life, the inability to have more children, never reached EXP Stage 4 or even EXP 3, for the most part.

Nevertheless, she was a fairly animated and affable narrator who could laugh or chuckle about things she related. She gave every indication of having good morale in person, and her questionnaire responses showed her affect, or mood, score to be quite positive. She did appear to fit the "foreclosed" integrity status on the basis of the questionnaire and interview findings. She did not exhibit any evidence of a life-review process in her self-narrative or in her pattern of reminiscence. Furthermore, she did not appear to be dissonant or despairing, expressing no regrets or unresolved issues from the past. In her own words, she "just sort of took it [life] as it came," and she gave no indication of efforts (past or present) to resolve any outstanding critical issues in order to achieve a state of ego integrity. There were, however, indications that she had accommodated and accepted a number of things along the way that enabled her to live a "quiet" life with some degree of equilibrium and enjoyment.

NARRATIVE OF A "PERSON"

The idea of roles is central to the concept of "person" in Rorty's scheme. While we may have predetermined or assigned roles in life and in any social structure, 20th-century America has generally provided some opportunity to achieve higher social status or greater personal satisfaction on the basis of role performance or choice of adult roles. Furthermore, rights as well as obligations devolve from roles so that the person is able to enact these rights and is thereby empowered to some extent. There is a sense of active agency in which the person can and does make choices by which he or she can be judged by self and by others. This also means accepting responsibility for decisions made, whether good or bad. Consequently, there can be a sense of regret as well as accomplishment for decisions made and actions taken.

Ethel T., a 67-year-old woman living with her retired husband in a new and attractive condominium apartment, illustrates the development of a person from the defined and constraining roles of childhood to the more empowered and enactive roles of adulthood. She looked younger than her years, trim, and attractively though informally dressed for the interview. She quickly got to the central theme or issue of her life in her self-narrative simply by relating her relationship to her parents, particularly her mother, from childhood on. It was her struggle to become "her own person." Therefore, we can just begin with her narrative from its start.

T: Childhood was very good for me. I remember I had a lot of pleasant memories. I was an only child for seven years, and then my sister came along . . . and it was a good family, basically. Then I had a younger brother, so I was the oldest of three children and basically feeling life was good. My father tended to be a little more lenient than my mother. She was more of the disciplinarian. He died at an early age and I missed him (*Pause*). I still do. He was 57 when he died, so he was really young. I still delight when we talk about him. I have wonderful, wonderful memories of him.

I: How old was he . . . were your parents when you were born?

T: Oh, they were very young. They were still in their twenties.

I: So you were in your thirties when your father died?

T: Yes, I was. I had two children at the time . . . and we all missed him a lot . . . my brother especially. He was only 16 when my father died. That was hard. As I say, my mother was very domineering. There are still a lot of things . . . ah . . . about her. She just passed away. It was just a year ago. Now there are a lot of things about my childhood that I recall. Things she had done, you know. She ruled with an iron hand. . . . It wasn't that I loved her any less, you know. It was just a different kind of love I had for her than I had for my dad. I felt a little more at east with him. I had pleasant memories, and we did a lot of things.

I: Uh hum.

T: We weren't well off, and there were times that things were rough because it was in the middle of the Depression when I was growing up. Nevertheless, it worked out well. I enjoyed high school, and I had good friends. I did say this, though, that when I got married I was going to let my kids have a little more freedom

than my mother allowed us to have . . . and I think I did. She could not . . . right
to the end . . . maybe it was me being the oldest . . . she could not let go of me. I
got married, but I never left home . . . at least not for a long time.

I: Uh-hum.

T: I always felt that it was my duty to take care of my mother. Especially because
my father died so young. My brother and sister were living out of town. So it just
seemed to be my responsibility to do this, to take her in with us. Consequently,
my children grew up around my mother, and they adored her. They really did.
She was hard at times, but still it meant a lot to them to have a grandma here.

I: Was she a lot different with them than she was with you as a child?

T: Oh yes! (*With much expression and emphasis*) Oh indeed. Her father was domineering with her life like she was with me. So it was like a cycle. Only I broke it.
I broke it with my kids and how I raised them.

Mrs. T. then went on to tell how she had met her husband and how they
dated when he was home on leave from the army in World War II. She had
also indicated that her father had lost his butcher store during the Depression, and they had had to give up their home. Her mother had to go to work
"to help make ends meet, and she worked hard, so we never really went
without food or clothing." She then went on to say the following:

T: The one regret that I had is that I wanted to go on to college. I wanted to be a
nurse, but my mother discouraged me. She didn't think it was a good profession.
Neither one of them *ever* wanted me to leave home. In the Forties, during the
war, I took a civil service exam for a job in Washington. A couple of my friends
had done this and went to live there. Well, I passed the exam, and I really
wanted to go . . . and my parents said. "Oh no, no, no." So I said why did you let
me go through all this? They said something like they wanted me to know that I
could pass it but not that I should go there. And that's the way it had to be, but
then I made up my mind . . . if I ever got married, I would let my kids make up
their own minds about what they wanted. I just wasn't given enough credit to
make my own decisions. My kids were going to be able to make their own decisions, and if anything went wrong, they could come to us if they wanted to. I
tried to guide them, not domineer . . . and I think they came out pretty good.

Mrs. T. married her husband one year after the war and felt that it was a
whole new life for her. She felt like a "grown-up" for the first time in her life
even though she had been working and financially self-supporting since she
left high school. The fact that she was living with her parents and what she
called their "overprotective attitude" toward her prevented her from feeling
like an adult. When she got married, her husband treated her like an adult
and an equal. She even went back to work as a secretary to help him go on
to graduate study when their three children were all in school. This made

her feel even more like a competent and contributing adult, and their marriage took on the shape of "a real partnership." It grew that way in terms of all major decisions in their married life and parenting of the children. Consequently, when her widowed mother was no longer physically able to maintain herself alone, Mrs. T. and her husband did not hesitate to take her mother in. Mrs. T. had some qualms about how they would get along together, but she no longer feared that her mother could dominate her in the way she had in childhood. In fact, there was a reversal of roles, whereby she felt more like a parent toward her more dependent mother right up to the time of her mother's death a year prior to the interview.

That latter period with her mother proved to Mrs. T. that she was indeed "her own person." However, she still had some negative and unresolved feelings about her mother. This was evident in the ambivalent way she would juxtapose positive qualifiers to the essentially negative statements she would make about her mother, such as: "She was domineering and overbearing, but I think she felt it was in my best interest," or "She was very strict and demanding, but then, she worked hard for us."

Contrast this to the way in which she spoke of her maternal grandmother: "Such a sweet, gentle lady . . . so different than my mother. I had such wonderful conversations with her. She was born in Russia and came over here when she was about 16, and did she have fascinating things to tell me about what it was like! I reminisce about her a lot. I can still hear her words and feel her warmth. She used to wear a certain powder that I loved, and I can still smell it. She was so good to me. I guess it was because I was the first grandchild."

It is significant that she identified her most cherished objects as several pieces of cut glass that belonged to this grandmother, and she commented: "I always remember these at my grandmother's home as a child. They meant a great deal to them, and now to me, because I loved my grandparents, and these objects keep their meaning alive." She said that these objects would set her to reminiscing about her grandparents, particularly her grandmother, and then she added: "It works like a therapy for me."

Her experiencing level throughout most of the narrative was an EXP 3, with expression of personal interest and reactions as well as some references to feelings and other indicators of affect such as sighing. She reached EXP 4 in talking about her grandmother, with focused voice and expressions of affect along with the vivid sensory associations and subjective experiences illustrated in the above quotation. On the other hand, her experiencing level did not reach an EXP 4 when discussing her mother. There were still underlying resentments that were not being directly expressed but rather fended off with the ambivalent kinds of qualifiers noted earlier.

It would be premature to say that Mrs. T. was in a "foreclosed" integrity status the way Mrs. J. was. Actually, Mrs. T. was somewhat dissonant, as evidenced by some negative responses on her Affect-Balance Scale and the fact that she reported using reminiscence to deal with difficulties she was experiencing as well as to cope with a loss in her life. Hers was actually a mixed reminiscence pattern, showing these problem-solving uses along with more pleasurable, entertaining, and mood-enhancing uses. On the other hand, she was not engaging in a life-review form of reminiscing because she did not engage in reminiscing to determine life's meaning or to plan for the future. She did, however, find herself reminiscing to arrive at a better understanding of herself and her past life.

This latter form of reminiscence is quite consistent with her high motivation to engage in the self-narrative. She was eager to be interviewed and talk about her life when she filled out the Integrity Survey questionnaire. It provided an opportunity to articulate and reinforce the identity she had been attaining as a "person." Rorty (1976) noted that the search for "that core person" is not a matter of mere curiosity because "here the stage is set for identity crises, for wondering who one *really* is, behind the multifold variety of actions and roles."

Mrs. T. had gone a long way in resolving her identity crisis through the advent of her marriage, which she identified as the turning point in her life. She articulated in her narrative her sense of becoming more her own person in the course of her marriage, but the pervasive subjective presence of her mother even in death seemed to hover in the background, ready to erode the sense of security in that identity as "person." There was still a great deal of unfinished business and some regrets.

As narrative, Mrs. T.'s self-told life story is generally cohesive in terms of the plot and theme; that is, the development of an overprotected and dominated daughter into an enabling mother and wife. Still, more reconstructing at a more experiential level would need to occur in the form of a full life review if the major ghosts of the past are to be laid to rest and ego integrity achieved. However, even if that does not come to pass, Mrs. T. has become a "person," which is no small achievement in the context of her life.

NARRATIVE OF AN "INDIVIDUAL"

It is in Rorty's "individual" that we see the most intention-driven actor. Agency in the self-narrative of an individual is that of a very proactive protagonist bent on achieving his or her goals. There is also a strong assertion of a self-created identity throughout the narrative. Rorty (1976) writes that "an individual transcends and resists what is binding and oppressive in society and does so from an original natural position." Whether the source of binding and oppression is from family, community, or society at large the individual *will* combat and transcend it in the creation of a unique identity.

Ralph D. represents such an individual in his self-narrative. He was 70 years of age and living with his wife in their suburban home at the time of the Integrity Survey interview. He was a youthful 70, athletic-looking in his Cornell University sweatshirt, with a short and stocky but powerful build. He introduced himself as "Dr. D.," which was how he was referred to in his last preretirement position as director of research and development in a large, privately endowed training school for youthful offenders. His doctorate was a Ph.D. in criminal justice from a large midwestern university, but this anticipates an important element in his self-told life story. Like Ethel T., the preceding "person," he very quickly got into the central theme of his narrative, as follows:

I: As I mentioned on the phone, I will be asking you here to do the impossible by telling your life story in about a half an hour.

D: OK. I was born in Waterford, New York, August 19, 1919, so I'm going on 70. Family background? I had a brother—13 years older—died last year. A sister ten years older and another sister nine years older. Family background—OK—very authoritarian—mother who was kind of subdued, rather passive-aggressive I guess you'd call it. Father—very authoritarian . . . ah, his idea was that the oldest son receive the birthright. The youngest son—he was very—*insignificant.* Ah . . . I suppose I could say in today's parlance I would be considered "emotionally abused." I can't ever remember my father putting his arm around me or acting like a father. His idea was, during the Depression, putting food on the table. . . . This is where his responsibility ended. Ah . . . *never* took me out. I never had a toy. It's funny, last night, watching the [July Fourth] fireworks, I remembered sitting alone in my yard watching the kid next door shoot his fireworks off. So it was a very unhappy situation, but it made me independent. There wasn't a *gap* with my father . . . ah . . . that maybe some other kinds had. If that's the way he was, then, "This is it," I'd better get resigned to it.

I: Yes. I see.

D: I wasn't supposed to achieve. My older brother was supposed to achieve. He was the one who was supposed to go to college, and I wasn't. So I made up my mind I was going to do something. So in high school I was good—got B pluses, A minus, president of the Student Council—later head of the student newspaper. Well, came 1940 you could sign up for the army if you had intention of going to college, so I joined the army—and, ah . . . as an enlisted man . . . but a year later I got a commission, which was an achievement for me since I didn't have a college education. But I did very well in the army . . . went into combat in North Africa, Italy, France . . . ah, was in a year before Pearl Harbor and was out five years later.

I: Yes. So you saw the whole thing through.

D: Oh yes, I saw a lot of service. So I stayed in the active reserve, and I was recalled to Vietnam for three years. Although I didn't get over there, I was called in for training purposes with the army. I retired . . . I guess four, five years ago as full colonel. I liked the army. I guess I'm one of the few people who did. But to go

back . . . this is a long way around for family background. My father finally recognized me. I recall once having met the pope. There were five of us on leave in
Italy, and we met the pope. When my father found out *that*, his whole attitude
toward me changed. At least here was something he hadn't seen before.

I: Un-hum.

D: Well, it didn't make much difference to me at the time. I didn't really need that,
because at an early age I felt that I really had to become independent . . . ah
umh . . . emotionally independent, which I believe I did. Maybe there was a
blank there (*pause, with pained expression*) . . . I don't know, but I believe I felt
that . . . from me . . . my kids weren't going to be exposed to that same kind of
. . . of . . . *rejection.* So I guess my mother was passive-resistant. I took a lot of
whacks that weren't meant for me, but he would hit and ask questions later.
Very authoritarian. I don't think there was much love there, 'cause I never felt
any from him. So . . . does that give you an idea of what it was like?

I: Yes, it does. What did your father do for a living?

D: He manufactured jewelry, and he was very successful at it. We never wanted for
any food during the Depression.

I: Your going into the army, to go to college, to become an officer . . . was that to
show him, in a sense?

D: Umh . . . I . . . I don't . . think so. (*Long pause*) Let me think. (*Another pause —
then speaking slowly*) There might have been a little of that, but I had a personal
desire to achieve. It wasn't really to show him. It just so happened that I liked
what I was doing. I liked the army, and I was good at it.

I: What branch of the Army?

D: I was in the infantry. I was an enlisted man for a year until I got my commission,
and I had command all the way through. I didn't go to college until *after* I got
out of World War II. Got shot up a couple of times . . . some decorations, that
kind of thing.

Dr. D. went on to relate that he was released from the army in 1946 but
remained in the active reserve. On returning home he met his wife-to-be
and he went to a local college on the GI Bill. They were married in his
sophomore year, and they had their first child, a son, as Dr. D. entered his
senior year. He than took a sales job to augment his GI stipend to support
his family. Then he graduated with a degree in sociology, summa cum laude,
and received a fellowship for doctoral study at Cornell University. He noted
parenthetically that his father was again impressed with him, this time for
going to an Ivy League school. However, after getting a master's degree in
sociology from Cornell he decided to go into the Ph.D. program in criminal
justice in the Midwest.

He could not see himself leading an academic life, and he felt that he
could put his capacity for command to good use in the field of corrections.
By getting a doctorate in the relatively new discipline of criminal justice he
felt he could advance quickly in the field of corrections, juvenile corrections

in particular, which interested him most. Upon receiving his Ph.D. he did in fact take a prestigious position as the first director of a new, large, and progressive state institution for youthful offenders, which was supposed to be something of an experiment in juvenile corrections and had a strong component of community involvement and follow-up of the young offenders. He attempted some new programs for involving the offenders in work, social activities, and living in the local community. There were negative reactions to this from local groups, and he found himself constrained by higher authorities in state government, who were fearful of political repercussions in the local community.

Consequently, he was "kicked upstairs" to become Director of Youth Parole in the state capital. He accepted this because it meant an increase in salary, and he had a wife and three children to support at that time. Since he did not have the latitude he had expected as superintendent of the new juvenile correction setting, he thought he might have more influence at the state level. However, he found the state bureaucracy to be "suffocating" and unreceptive to many of his ideas on programs and policies in youth corrections. Therefore, he took the position of director of research and development at the boys' training school because it offered the opportunity for developing his ideas, if not for being in command. Besides, it brought him and his wife back to where they had grown up, met and married.

He had to admit, however, that he did not mind leaving the research job when he was called back to active service during the Vietnam War. His children were all grown, and his wife was willing to have him go back because he would not be in combat. She joined him when he went to an army camp down south to train recruits. He went back to his job at the boys' training school after three years, but he had already earned an army pension as a full colonel and he was only "serving his time" at the school until he could get an additional smaller pension from there.

He claimed to be very much enjoying his retirement. He did some occasional consulting on research and program planning in juvenile corrections in various parts of the country, but most of all he enjoyed his leisure activities. He was active in an athletic club and worked out several times a week. He and his wife enjoyed a number of cultural activities together, attending a local reading and discussion group as well as plays and musical events. They also enjoyed their grandchildren, since two of their three children were raising their own families in the local area.

As he thought back over his life, Ralph D. claimed that his most vivid memories were about the service. He reported on his questionnaire that he seldom reminisced in conversations with others; but when he was alone, his thoughts usually went back to the past, and that past was usually in the army. He said, "I reminisce about the service all the time." Then after a moment's thought he said, "I'd go back tomorrow if I had the chance—it was when I was most alive. It wasn't just the danger and the excitement, though there was plenty of that. It was that I was good at it and that I was totally in command . . . of myself . . . and of everything else. Give me the job, give me the authority, and I'll get it done."

Then he went on to say that from the time he was a boy of 8 or 9 the army seemed to be the center point of his wishes and fantasies. He said:

> This will sound strange, but I had this consuming passion . . . an obsession to become a captain in the army. Why a captain? I don't know, but it was very definite. The funny thing is that I went beyond that. . . . I became a full colo-nel. . . . Now that I think of it, the other thing I always wanted from the time I was in high school was to go to an Ivy League college, and I did that, too. So I guess I really achieved everything I wanted.

His late-life adjustment did appear to be very good. He had a very high score on the Affect-Balance Scale as well as the Ego Integrity Scale. Unlike Max Korvitz, in Chapter 7, who also had an unhappy childhood, there was no evidence of dissonance in his self-narrative or in his reported uses of reminiscence. He used it to enhance his mood, to lift his spirits, to teach others, to inform others about his past accomplishments, and so on, but he did not use it to deal with present difficulties, solve something from the past, or cope with a loss. Also unlike Max Korvitz, his wife and children fig-ured prominently in the later stages of his narrative. Also, he identified pho-tographs of his wife and children as his most cherished objects.

At the same time, the memorabilia that would tend to set off his reminisc-ing more than any others were decorations and medals from World War II and photos of his old platoons and regiments. He claimed to have a real fondness for those men—not any one in particular, just a strong and . . . warm feeling of attachment and commitment, or camaraderie, with them. "It gives me a very strong sense of being involved in . . . of being part of . . . something very big and important."

He did check off on the questionnaire that he reminisced to arrive at a better understanding of his past life and himself, but he did not do so to plan for the future or to determine life's meaning. When I commented on the latter point in the interview he said, "No, I don't think about life's mean-ing; I guess I'm not a philosopher." In addition to that, one would have to add that he was a "doer" and a man of action. So his pattern of reminiscence does not show the dissonance or existential elements of meaning associated with life review. Nevertheless, he did report reminiscing for better under-standing of the past and himself. There was clear indication in his self-nar-rative that he was in the process of integrating his identity in terms of the past even if it not to resolve issues from the past to achieve ego integrity.

The integration process was going on in the interview itself, where his ex-

periencing level went up to an EXP 4 and even 5 as he spoke about his father's change of attitude about him after hearing about the visit to the pope.
His language and his nonverbal expression as he talked about what that
meant, or did not mean, to him became more groping and inwardly attuned
to what he was experiencing at that moment in the process of thinking
about it. What he came up with was that what he did in his life was not to
show his father but to be what he wanted to be, to achieve his *own* goals.
Above all, he wanted to be in command. If there was any central theme in
his narrative it was the theme of being in command — of being in charge —
responsible but not authoritarian. In that respect he would not be like his
father, but that would be because of who he was, of what his inner vision
and intention was, not because of what his father was.

There can be little doubt that Ralph D.'s narrative is that of an intention-
driven actor, of an "individual" in Rorty's full sense of the term. He did transcend and resist what was "binding and oppressive" (i.e., his father and what
he represented). Furthermore, he did so from "an original natural position,"
from his own inner impulses and vision, not simply from a reactive rebellion
against his father.

IDENTITY AND PROCESS IN THE SELF-NARRATIVE

The kind of integrating process Ralph D. demonstrated in his narrative was
true to some extent of just about every self-narrative in the Integrity Survey.
Regardless of how "deep" or "shallow" the narrative might be, the respondent would usually remark about some new understanding or perspective
concerning an aspect or an element in the lifestory that he or she became
aware of in the process. Sometimes it was a minor element, sometimes a
major one, or sometimes a vague impression from the past that then became more of a certainty in the course of the narrative. This might have explained some of the motivation for participating in the interview. At any rate
this would be consistent with the earlier quotation by Jaynes that "we are
always seeking our vicarial selves as the main figures in the stories of our
lives."

The opportunity to talk about yourself for one or one-and-a-half hours —
and be paid for it — would therefore seem to be a compelling motive. Whatever the reasons, only 2 of the 42 people we had contacted for an interview
declined the invitation. One of them reported that her husband's health had
taken a turn for the worse since she filled out the questionnaire and that
she was too preoccupied with caring for him to be interviewed. The other
person said that she was "just not up to it right now, maybe later." Her responses on the questionnaire to the Affect-Balance Scale indicated that she
was indeed in a depressed mood at the time. The others, however, not only

agreed to be interviewed but seemed to enjoy it. A number of them said half-jokingly that *they* should pay to tell their life stories, rather than vice versa.

The "vicarial selves" that most of the respondents seemed to be seeking were their *identifiable* selves (i.e., their *identities* as the main figures in their lives. Such identities are formulated and reformulated, to a greater or lesser extent, among different individuals over the entire life-span. Thus, we can say this formulation and reformulation of identities is an ongoing process and that to speak of identity as a fait accompli is misleading. Perhaps in late adulthood we can speak of identity as being largely formed, but many, many unformulated or partly formulated aspects of the self remain and provide the material for further review and exploration. Foreclosure, of course, can constrain this process but cannot entirely stifle it. Even Frances J., in the first self-narrative of this chapter, gave some evidence of reflecting upon unformulated or partly formulated aspects of herself and her life in the narrative process. although these were not really articulated in her discourse.

It is worth emphasizing here that 54 of our 100 questionnaire respondents reported that they reminisced to arrive at a better understanding of their past lives and themselves.[1] If over half the respondents freely reminisced for the purpose of self-understanding, it is likely that even more would do so in the structured context of an interview designed to obtain their life stories. That, of course, was the kind of process we were seeing in the interviews, even among those who claimed on the questionnaire that they did not reminisce to arrive at a better understanding of themselves.

A self-narrative is not simply a chronicle of what happened in a person's life; it also has a plot that pulls those happenings together into a meaningful whole. That is emplotment, which is the move from "*What* happened?" to "*Why* did it happen?" This also moves into the area of the *meaning* of life's events for the self. It has been referred to as the process of "turning happenings into meanings," and it appears to be universal in human narratives (Spence, 1987). It is safe to say that humans will endure just about any *what* of living if they understand a *why*. That is, there appears to be a fundamental need to make sense out of their lives.

It is interesting to recall that Ralph D., of the last self-narrative of this chapter, indicated on his questionnaire that he did not reminisce "to determine life's meaning." His response to my inquiry about that was that he was "not a philosopher." When my inquiry was pushed further in our subsequent discussion, he indicated that his understanding of the statement on the questionnaire was that it referred to life *in general*, not to his life in particular. When it was reframed in terms of *his* life, he did indeed acknowledge reminiscing about why (the meanings of) the happenings of his life occurred as they did.

When I asked him during the interview if he had undertaken his military career and his professional education and advancement "to show" his father, I was asking him a "why" question. His answer showed that he had given consideration to this question of meaning, and he later actually acknowledged that he had thought about it many times in the past but had never talked about it before. His answer was no, it was not to show his father. At most that was only a by-product of his "personal desire to achieve." As he said later, he had an image and inner vision, an "obsession" he called it, to become a captain in the army, and he achieved that and more. *That* was why he had done what he had in life. Again, from the point of view of agency, Ralph D. was an intention-driven "individual."

Since this is an experiential study, the self-narrative needs to be looked at as an experience in its own right. It has already been mentioned that most of the respondents enjoyed the experience of telling their life stories and became aware of new and different aspects of their stories and of themselves in the process. The levels of experience as measured by the EXP Scale varied from person to person, as evidenced in just the three self-narratives that were presented in this chapter. It was also evident that some people changed in the process (i.e., the *experience*) of narrating their life stories. At least 6 of the 40 interviewees said so explicitly, and it was apparent in a number more. Those who claimed they changed said the change was mostly in how they *felt* and then in how they looked at certain events or aspects of their lives and themselves.

This phenomenon of change based on an experiencing or reexperiencing of something so long after the fact, whether in free reminiscing or in a self-narrative, requires some explanation. An explanation from cognitive psychology is based on the distinction between the "agent" and the "experiencer" (Aylwin, 1985). The agent is the initiator of feelings. Since most of us are usually in our agent or action mode, especially in our younger years, we frequently do not take the time to assimilate the feelings associated with the enactive events of our lives.

Ralph D. provides an excellent example of this. He demonstrates an "enactive imagery" in which he vigorously enacts his image and intention of achievement in life (Aylwin, 1985). Since he was in this mode throughout his youth and most of his adult years, he was rarely the experiencer. This has not changed, and the balance has shifted in his retirement. While remaining active, which is his wont, he now takes time and uses the increased interiority of his maturity to mine his active past for its rich trove of experience. This is most evident in his reminiscing about his many experiences and associations in the service during World War II. He is now alone in this, of course. Many persons become accomplished experiencers through reminiscence in their old age. It is indeed a creative kind of endeavor or pastime, with some distinctly aesthetic elements to it. It can provide a great deal of enjoyment and satisfaction and can also be the source of much meaning, insight, and wisdom in the later years. This and other creative aspects of reminiscence will be discussed and illustrated in the next chapter.

NOTE

1. By comparison, Romaniuk and Romaniuk (1981) found that a comparable 51% of their elderly respondents reported reminiscing to arrive at a better understanding of their past lives and themselves.

9
The Art of Reminiscence

So far we have looked at reminiscence largely in terms of its usefulness for some other purpose, goal, or objective. Even in considering the simple enjoyment and pleasure it provides we have tended to look at this as a means of enhancing mood and thereby the quality of everyday life among the elderly. In an even more purposeful and serious vein we have looked at reminiscence for coping with losses and stresses, as well as for problem solving in terms of the past and present. Life-review reminiscence has been looked at in the same way, much as Robert Butler intended it, as a means to ego integrity or optimal psychosocial adjustment in late life. Much of the research and writing on reminiscence in gerontological literature has been driven by these practical imperatives. Hovering in the background and permeating that literature have been the issues of positive mood or happiness versus unhappiness or depression and ego integrity versus despair. Consequently, most of the outcome measures or dependent variables of these studies have been scales of happiness, affect, or morale, usually in the form of a life-satisfaction index. I am no exception to this general approach, and in fact, two of the three studies reported here draw upon such measures.

Now it is time to look at a whole different dimension of reminiscence, that is, as an aesthetic and creative experience. Creativity is a process that has its own rewards, which can be quite independent of happiness, mood, and morale, although those desirable states are frequently by-products of it. One gerontologist came to the conclusion on the basis of her research that construction of the life story and reconstruction of one's self in that story are more important to many older persons than happiness and morale (Kaufman, 1986). This conclusion was based on the life-story interviews she conducted with her study sample of 60 elderly persons.

The point here is that just as narrative can be an art form, so narrative reminiscence and the self-narrative, whether oral or written, can be a creative and aesthetic experience for the self and others. Some individuals in the Integrity Survey demonstrated this creativity or artistry very effectively in both their spoken and written reminiscences. Yet some of these individuals had relatively low scores on the Affect-Balance and Ego Integrity scales. We found that for these individuals the creative construction of their life stories and of themselves within those stories was more important to them than their current mood or general state of happiness. The creative narratives, reminiscences, and writings of several of these unknown people will be presented in this chapter along with those of some known creative writers. It will be seen that reminiscence in these more creative forms contains rich, complex, and sometimes contradictory mixtures of feeling, tone, mood, and meaning.

Whether reminiscence is private in the form of thoughts and images or public in the form of group memory-sharing or telling someone your life story, it is an experience in its own right, and as such it has the potential of being a creative activity—an art, if you will. Since this is an experiential study. it may come as no surprise to the reader that the conception of art taken here is essentially the same as that John Dewey (1934) set forth in *Art as Experience*. For him, the function of art is to organize experience more vividly, more coherently, and more meaningfully than life ordinarily allows. Art is experience, therefore, when it is expressed in its most articulate form, when it expresses "the union of sense, mood, impulse, and action characteristic of the live creature."

Dewey (1934) wrote, "An experience has a unity that gives it its name, that meal, that storm, that rupture of friendship," and "the existence of this unity is constituted by a single *quality* that pervades the entire experience in spite of the variation of its constituent parts." If one can capture and express *that* quality that constitutes the unity of an experience, *that* is a piece of art. Thus, the elderly person who can capture and express this with a past experience is engaging in the "art of reminiscence."

It is important to add that for Dewey art could not be a mere escape or pastime any more than it could be a purposeful discipline undertaken only for the sake of its consequences. He was very critical of the tendency in our civilization to separate means and ends. He saw art more as a unitary process that combines means and ends than one with an exclusive focus on product or object. This very much expresses the creative kind of reminiscence that is the subject of this chapter. It is not simply for enjoyment, for problem-solving, or for ego integrity. Yet it can be immensely satisfying in its own right and often in its consequences.

Marcel Proust, perhaps the greatest master of reminiscence, explained in the last volume of his *Remembrance of Things Past* that he was trying to recapture the small, purely personal, and often mistaken impressions that would bring back *an experience* in its entirety. This is certainly reminiscence as an art form, and it is in total accord with Dewey's conception of art as experience. Even if there is a triviality or falseness to the impressions, they can bring back a whole experience, just as the taste of the little cake dipped in lime-blossom tea brought back Proust's whole childhood. Lest we get stuck on the significance, accuracy, or falseness of the impression, look at what a remarkably creative and aesthetic product resulted from Proust's impressions, however trivial the subject matter.

We can paraphrase Dewey and say that art formalizes experience. Thus, to the extent that reminiscence captures and expresses past experience and formalizes it in words, then it is an art form that is available to most older persons for their own creative expression and experience. Andre Maurois (1929) put it this way: "Memory is a great artist. For every man and for every women it makes the recollection of his or her life a work of art and an unfaithful record." Whether the older person chooses to engage in this art or not is another matter, but it is important to note that this is not something that is determined by the past. That is, it is not what happened to the person in the past that determines the artistic and aesthetic quality of the reminiscence. It is not necessary that the person's life had to be unusually colorful or exciting. In fact, we can call most creative reminiscences, in the words of James Joyce, "epiphanies of the ordinary." Most certainly, Proust's tasting of the madeleine was not an extraordinary life event.

The important point of experience is the present, not the past. Our memory of past experience may indeed be flawed, but it is the experiential context of the present that gives to the past its particular flavor, tonality, and meaning (Rosenfield, 1988; Rubin, 1983). There is ample empirical evidence from neurobiology and cognitive psychology about this to begin exploring its implications for the creative and aesthetic aspects of reminiscence. As one writer on the art of autobiography put it: "Why should we not take memory for what it richly is—a function of present consciousness—rather than worrying about what it is not, and cannot be? Of course memory will never give us objective truth about the past. . . . Though, it is powerless in the past, however, memory can and will create a subjective and vastly important truth about the present" (Olney, 1972). Once we have accepted memory and, therefore reminiscence as a function of the present, we can move on to the role of imagination in creative reminiscence.

IMAGINATIVE REMINISCENCE

Ernst Cassirer (1944) once wrote that imagination is "a necessary element of true recollection." In point of fact, the ancient Greeks invented an art of memory, later passed on to Rome and Europe, which involved the "manipulation of images in memory" using actual architectural and spatial contexts as visual backdrops and mnemonic devices for the storage and retrieval of information from the past (Yates, 1966). Although this was a specific art form that used real physical structures as mental props or devices, it was the imaginative, not the physical, aspects of it that made it an art. In defining art, Melvin Rader (1952) noted that "the work of art, which exists only when the imagination is kindled, is therefore not a physical but a phenomenal or imaginary object, possessing qualities that the mind lends to it." He goes on to say that it is "this phenomenal character that makes the work an expression of the artist's mood." We should add here that it is the artist's *present* mood, for this very much colors the imaginative process of recollection in reminiscence.

To illustrate the powerful effect of the present on the imaginative recollection of the past, let us take two brief examples. An elderly woman poring over an old photo album remarks: "I turn more pages: here is a snapshot of myself, looking solemn. Why do I remember only being happy?" Another elderly woman recalls: "My father used to speak with loving yearning about the marvelous rolls served in the local café when he was a medical student in Berlin. My mother confided to me that they were quite ordinary rolls; it was only that he was young and poor and hungry." The father's imaginative recollection of the rolls was certainly colored by his nostalgic mood of the moment, and it stands out when contrasted with the mother's matter-of-fact evaluation of the rolls and their place in the context of her husband's youth.

The latter example brings to mind a saying by Proust: "The only true paradise is the paradise we have lost." The youth of the man who recalled the marvelous rolls could not have been a paradise, given his wife's description of it, but there was at least one thing in his youth that he saw as paradisaical. This, then, brings to mind another author who said that "Proust knew the joy of remembering what we have never really known" (Harper, 1965). Of course, Proust's joy of remembering was not based on what was "really known" in his past. It was based on the ineffable impressions of past experiences rather than their actuality.

Frequently, the experience of reminiscence, especially spontaneous and unsolicited reminiscence, is ineffable. The memory trace or impression has an inexpressible quality that intrigues us and that we would like to share if only we could express it. Proust, of course, was a master at expressing the ineffable in reminiscence, but it is something I have heard elderly persons with no literary pretensions actually do in group reminiscence and life-interview situations. When they do it, of course, they are in an experiencing mode (an EXP level of 4 and above) as they search inwardly for the words that will capture the quality of that past experience.

In this regard it is important to recall the discussion in Chapter 3 about embodied reminiscence. There is indeed an embodied, sensate quality to the ineffable experiences encountered in reminiscence, and it is this sensate quality that we would like to articulate and share with others. As Merleau-Ponty (1968) would say, such sensate experiences are "like life, a treasury ever full of things to say." Such experiences led Bernard Berenson (1963) to say at age 83, "I can't believe it not worth living, for an infinity of ideated sensations remain in memory to be combined and recombined in charming ways." Of course, it takes imagination to combine and recombine these sensations in creative and charming ways.

To do this one has to get in touch with those "structures of imagination and understanding that emerge from our embodied experience" and then express the quality of that experience in words, usually in the figurative language of metaphor (Johnson, 1987). T. S. Eliot (1964) speaks of an "auditory imagination . . . penetrating far below the conscious levels of thought and feeling, invigorating every word; sinking to the most primitive and forgotten, returning to the origin and bringing something back" fusing "the old and obliterated and the trite, the current, and the new and surprising." Such auditory imagination works particularly well in poetry, where it can be most aptly expressed, and we shall see some examples of this in the poetry of some older persons from the Integrity Survey. In one specific case the person could express the poignancy and depth of some past experience *only* in poetry.

Sometimes, however, there are images from the past that cannot be expressed, even in poetry, and they are also inexplicable. About these Eliot (1964) asked: "Why, for all of us out of all that we have heard, seen, felt, in a lifetime do certain images recur, charged with emotions . . . the leap of one fish . . . the scent of one flower . . .?" He felt that "such memories may have symbolic value, but of what we cannot tell, for they come to represent the depths of feeling into which we cannot peer." As far as the art of reminiscence is concerned, it is not necessary to understand the symbolic meaning of such memories, and they can remain unexpressed, to be savored and appreciated as subjective aesthetic experiences in their own right. How often are we taken by surprise and momentarily delighted by such images from the past? The important point is not to dismiss them as inexplicable and therefore valueless, for they can and do provide experiences and intimations beyond much of the humdrum reality of everyday life in old age.

Hobbes (1952) once wrote that "imagination and memory are but one thing, which for diverse considerations hath diverse names." In the preceding discussion we have seen the workings of imagination in the past, in memory, and how we tend to remember the past from the imaginative perspective of the present. Now, consider the following interesting phrase: "remembering the future." There is in this paradoxical phrase the germ of an idea with profound implications for the role of imagination and creativity in reminiscence, identity work, and meaning in old age. The provocative germ in "remembering the future" is the idea of remembering what in the past we imagined the future would be. We all attempt to imagine what the future will be like, even the oldest among us, but rarely do we attempt to remember what we thought or imagined in the past about what we or our futures would be. To do so is a very revealing and significant undertaking.

The central idea in narrative theory—that we are all authors of our own lives—when considered in the light of reminiscence and the past, means that you must consider that the person was author of his or her own life in the past, imagining what he or she expected, wanted, or chose to become in the future. The task and the final value of your personal life-narrative, then, is to appropriate your own history—and, moral philosophers might add, take responsibility for it (Nozick, 1989). One of the best ways to facilitate a creative life review or self-narrative with older persons is to ask them to recall what they imagined they and their futures would be like at various points in the past—in childhood, adolescence, early adulthood and so on.

Robert Grudin (1982), in his book *Time and the Art of Living*, made the following observation:

> At certain moments in life, prompted by the excitement of some major event, we look ahead in time and think quite simply, "I shall remember this forever." And this awareness in itself seems to change the present experience, to enhance it like some object being lit suddenly from a new side. These are among the very few times that we have direct and honest contact with our future selves. Otherwise we are largely, and in a sense unnecessarily, exiled from our own future.

He goes on to say, in effect, that our failure to remember the future condemns us to a constricted present. Further, we tend to plan for the future in terms of "specific and disembodied" goals rather than for future developments of identity or states of mind. Grudin (1982) observes that because of this:

> We often look back at our own past with some alienation, even disbelief, as though someone else had lived it. The failure to look at things from the future side, and the subsequent lack of temporal coherence, are part of what I mean when I say we are trapped in time. Our freedom lies in an art which is easier to describe than to practice: the willing extension of self into the future.

His point about temporal coherence takes on particular relevance for the life review, which should enable us to integrate past, present, and future in old age. What is needed is to rekindle the creative capacity to recall or recreate what we had imagined and intended in the past for our future. This can provide powerful validation of identity and continuity of the self in old age. Reminiscence in this sense is "a commemoration, a ritual, recall of our lives to the images in the background . . . by remembering, we give a kind of commemorative legend, a founding image to our present lives" (Hillman, 1983).

SELF-CREATIVITY IN REMINISCENCE

When we consider the role of reminiscence in relation to formulation and reformulation of identity and the self in old age, we are moving into the autobiographical realm, and autobiography is certainly a literary art form. To reminisce (i.e. to think *and* talk about past experiences) in the context of a life-narrative interview is really an oral form of autobiography, and there is no question that this was more of art for some of our respondents in the Integrity Survey than for others.

One of the greatest autobiographers, Montaigne, said: "The whole duty of man lies in the making of the self according to its own natural laws and necessities" (1957). For May Sarton (1980), an aging writer recovering from the debilitating effects of a major stroke, the activity of creating the self was a "sacred duty." This became for her a moral imperative by virtue of the fact that the stroke was a profound threat to her identity as a writer, to her capacity to think, to imagine, and to express herself in words. For many older persons such threats to one's life and identity turn their thoughts of the past, their reminiscences, to the question of who they have been, to provide some continuity of self in the light of what they might become. Such crises and disruptive life events have led to depression, hopelessness, and despair, but sometimes they lead to creative insights and reformulations of identity and meaning in the lives of some older persons. Reformulations of self in the face of such crises and calamities is almost a matter of necessity for survival and continuity (Parkes, 1971).

But this chapter is about the art of reminiscence, and as we said at the start, art is not something that has to be driven by necessity, to cope with or overcome some problem. Also, it should probably not be something that is considered a duty but should be something more rewarding in itself. One writer on creativity in old age has observed that in autobiography "the self has the pleasure of reconstituting, recreating in artistic (because selective and consciously chosen) terms the image and the myth of the self" (Cuisa, 1973) Jerome Bruner (1960) speaks of the life story as the making of myths. He says that the "mythologically instructed community provides its members with a library of scripts" against which the person may judge his or her own "internal drama." He goes on to say that it is important to discover the personal myth that animates a person's life. There has been a recent upsurge of interest in the subject of personal mythology in the fields of counseling and psychotherapy, which has led to specific practice methodologies for discovering and, if necessary, altering personal myths that animate peoples' lives (Feinstein & Krippner, 1988; Keen & Valley-Fox, 1973).

Without recourse to myths or scripts, a number of clinical practitioners have been aware of the need to guide the people they are counseling into a creative mode and imaginative frame of mind when working on identity issues. I have already mentioned that I will ask older persons to recall from the past what they imagined they would become in the future. This can be done by evoking or asking for images from the past or just a narrative description of it, and of course this can be and is done as well with younger persons receiving such counseling. One practitioner encourages the person who is formulating or reformulating an identity to think about himself or herself as a story writer — "a biographer of self" (McAdams, 1988).

Our experience with the oral autobiographies in the self-narrative interviews of the Integrity Survey certainly indicated that most older people are not only willing but delighted to tell their own life stories. Their ready acceptance of the offer and the nature of their participation in the actual process attest to that. Of course, it is hard to know whether this represented a creative effort at self-understanding and reformulation, or simply the pleasure of talking about oneself and enhancing self-image. Sometimes it was even a mixture of the two, usually with the person starting out in the image-enhancement mode but after a while encountering and reflecting upon certain questions about the self in relation to various aspects of the past. It should be recalled in this regard that 54 out of 100 respondents to our questionnaire reported reminiscing for the purpose of arriving at a better understanding of their past lives and themselves.

Regardless of the magnitude of occurrence, a number of the respondents were truly in an experiential and reconstructive mode, tapping their memories and imaginations in a creative manner as evidenced by EXP levels of 4 and above as they encountered and expressed previously unarticulated aspects of the self. To be party to and witness to such a process as an interviewer is itself something of an aesthetic experience, so for the respondents it must have been an artistic one. Edward Casey (1989) has expressed this experience well from the phenomenological perspective: "I find myself able to connect temporally diverse aspects of myself and put them into meaningful communication with each other. Even more importantly, I can consolidate the self I have been and shape of self I am coming to be."

Casey equates this capacity for self-creativity with freedom. He expresses this "freedom to be oneself" as follows:

> I am free in establishing my ongoing and future personal identity by means of my own remembering. This remembering determines (in Lacan's formula) "what I shall have been for what I am in the process of becoming." What I shall have been, my eventual identity, is very much a function of what I shall remember myself to have been. And what I now remember myself to have been is by no means a fixed affair. It is once more a matter of freedom, specifically the freedom to decide which features of my previous life to honor or reject, celebrate or revile, in the future. This freedom is expressly evaluative; it is a freedom realized through assessing my own past as a prologue for my own

future—an assessment carried out on the basis I am maintaining in the present. (Casey, 1989)

It is important to emphasize Casey's observation that present remembrance of what one's self had been is no fixed affair. This obviously has profound implications for self-identity in old age. As he put it so well, "It is an inescapable fact about human existence that we are made of our memories: *we are what we remember ourselves to be*" (Casey, 1989).

CREATIONS OF MEANING IN REMINISCENCE

All of the foregoing adds up to an ongoing future for the self, even in very old age. The broader and more comprehensive perception of self, which draws upon what was only implicit in the past as one ages, always allows for future self-creativity. Paul Ricoeur (1977) refers to this creative capacity as "predicative assimilation," which is the synthetic activity of bringing together the old and the new in a work of productive imagining. This capacity works not only for the self but for life in general.

The late George Kelly, who developed personal construct theory, is reported to have said: "Life is a way of using the *present* to link the future with the past in some original fashion" (quoted in Epting, 1984). Kelly, a psychologist, said this long before narrative theory made any impact on psychology, and he was talking about life rather than the life-narrative, but it expresses the creative potentiality (the originality) that is inherent in the self-told life story. The creative potential of the life story is actualized by turning the *happenings* of the past into *meanings* for the present and future, to paraphrase Donald Spence (1987).

For a life story to have meaning it needs a plot. This is because "to plot is to move from asking the question *and then what happened?* to the question *why did it happen?*" (Hillman, 1983). Plots in this sense are our theories, or the ways we put together the vagaries and intentions of human nature so that we can understand the *why*, between the sequence of events in a story. This *why* is essentially a question of causality. Now, some persons might propose certain causes and determining circumstances in their life stories that are entirely external to the self. Their narrative language will reflect this because they will more or less depict themselves as objects in a sequence of events. Regardless of the "truth value" of the narrative and the external factors, this is not *creative* narrative because there is no agent or intentional actor who links past dreams, wishes, and purposes with the present in any meaningful way. In short, the narrative gives no sense of the subjective reality of the objective events.

Before events or happenings can be turned into meaning, they have to become experiences. This means moving from outer to inner in order to experience inwardly the outer reality. This is a dialectic of inner and outer that may transpire at the time of the event, sometimes after it, or perhaps never. Anthony Storr (1988) has put this phenomenon well:

> There are good biological reasons for accepting the fact that man is so constituted that he possesses an inner world of the imagination which is different from, though connected to, the world of external reality. It is the discrepancy between the two worlds which motivates creative imagination. People who realize their creative potential are constantly bridging the gap between inner and outer. They invest the external world with meaning because they disown neither the world's objectivity nor their own subjectivity.

Using Storr's formulation, turning events into meanings is very much a dialectical process, and it is a necessary one to reconcile the actuality of events with the inner images and motivations of the actor so as to explain the *why,* of the happenings. This is the sort of dialectic that goes on when older persons reminisce to understand themselves and their pasts, and it can be seen as quite consistent with the purpose of the life review as proposed by Butler. They need to know better what their own motivations were, some of which they were not even conscious of at the time, in the significant events of their lives. Of course, psychodynamic theories such as Freud's go far in giving answers to the *why* question, and older persons are becoming increasingly aware and more conversant with such psychodynamic explanations. Consequently, the plots (i.e., theories) in their life stories are going to contain more such psychological causal explanations as time goes on.

There are different plots or ways of turning events into meanings in the life narrative that do not draw upon the same kind of psychological determinism as Freud's. The why of happenings can be answered in Freud's theory only in terms of time sequences, in terms of what happened first and what happened after that. This is developmental in a linear time sequence because current behavior is determined by *earlier* childhood events and dynamics.

There is another kind of "inner causality," which asks *what for?* instead of *why?* It has to do with teleological and characterological questions. It asks, for example, "What types of myths or archetypes are at work in the life story, and toward what ends?" These are the kinds of questions Jung asked, for he believed that we have to look at the intentionality of the characters and where they are heading because character and intentionality have the primary influence upon the shape of the life stories. As one Jungian analyst and writer on narrative put it, each character "carries his own plot with him, writing his story, both backwards and forwards as he individuates" (Hillman, 1983).

This way of approaching the life narrative has certain advantages. It not only addresses the *why* question from an inner perspective, it also offers a teleological perspective on the *what for* question. It does this by addressing the question of what in the actor's character and intentionality provides clues to final cause or ultimate ends and purpose in his or her life. The clues are apt to be found in a personal myth or directive image of what one is, was, or is yet to become. Consequently, this approach to narrative makes objective Ricoeur's (1977) concept of predicative assimilation. It is also consistent with Bruner's criteria for a fully developed self-narrative, particularly the intention-driven agent and the element of personal mythology.

This approach also incorporates the dialectic of the inner world of imagination with the world of external reality, which Storr sees as necessary for the creation of meaning. In this approach the dialectic has to be worked out in a way that not only accepts and invests the external world with meaning but needs to be in essential concordance with the inner vision or directive image in order to be a creative synthesis. Otherwise, the dissonance between outer reality and inner vision continues or is largely bypassed in foreclosure.

There is a temporal dimensions to this dialectic as well, since much of the outer reality of an elderly person's life lies in the past. This involves reconciling aspects of reality from the past with the personal myth or directive image retained by the older person in the present. This, then, would be a process of going back and forth between past and present, with the present giving meaning to the past, just as the past can give meaning to the present (and future). Thus, there would be a continued fitting and fine-tuning of past with present, with implications for the future. This iterative process can be an ongoing one, like a perpetual hermeneutic circle of interpretation of a life, one that is always available to the creative and imaginative older person. This fine-tuning can at times be exquisite, a thoroughly satisfying and aesthetic experience when the pieces of past, present, future, imagination, and reality fit harmoniously into the larger tapestry of a person's life. Thus, meaning is both created and experienced with a consummate kind of artistry.

There was one woman in the Integrity Survey who expressed this aesthetic experience and process quite directly. She said:

> I can reminisce . . . go back and forth from then to now, and I always seem to come up with something new . . . something a little different from a new angle. Things seem to fit together a little different . . . and it always gives me satisfaction . . . even if I think about bad memories, because now they fit. I see where they fit . . . but they didn't before. It's like . . . they *had* to be that way

... for the whole thing to make sense. Does that make sense? Or does it sound crazy?

Rosa V. often interrupted her life narrative with the statement "This is going to sound crazy to you," as she would express some of the spontaneous memories and associations that punctuated her discourse. Although her self-narrative moved generally in a past-to-present path, there would be frequent interjections of content and images from either more remote or more recent events and experiences to connect with and amplify the past experience she was currently describing. Her self-narrative rather clearly illustrated the dialectic and hermeneutic nature of the process in this regard.

Mrs. V. was an Italian war bride who came to the United States in 1945 with her soldier-husband after having directly experienced the chaos and near-starvation of many Italian civilians who were caught up in the battles raging between the retreating Germans and advancing Allies. She had many vivid and painful memories of that period that would intrude on her self-narrative, but she nevertheless was able to weave them into her narrative as events that provided object lessons or some other meaning for her life in general.

She was small in stature, barely over five feet tall, but she had a sinewy strength and energy that would be characteristic of a person 15 years younger than her 69 years. Her face, on the other hand, looked more her age, with a few deep wrinkles marking a dark olive complexion surrounded by light, almost white, gray hair. She was vivacious and animated throughout the entire one-and-a-half-hour interview and seemed to relish the whole experience.

Mrs. V. still spoke with a rather thick Italian accent and sometimes her syntax was more Italian than American, but at times she exhibited a surprisingly advanced vocabulary. She attributed this to the fact that she was an avid reader and always had been, as we shall see. Since some of her descriptions were so vivid and her narrative so lively, the beginning of it is presented verbatim below so as to give a flavor of it.

V: My mother's father was a sculptor, an artist—taught art for 29 years at the University of Lucca. You know Lucca? It is a beautiful medieval city, with towers, walls, narrow cobblestone streets—very romantic.

My father came from the mountains north of Padua. He was in the Italian army during the First World War, and he was stationed near Lucca, where he met my mother. They got married, and he tried to find work in Lucca, but all he could get was menial jobs, very menial. Things were not good in Italy after the war—no jobs, no future. So my father took my mother and me—I was four years old—to Brazil, to a town—Jacobina—where we lived for about six years.

I loved it in Brazil. I really play over there—wild! With all those kids—black, white, every color . . . and, oh . . . it was beautiful—the fruit, the sun—it would shine all the time . . . but after my brother was born, after five years in Brazil, my parents got homesick, and we went back to Lucca. I still remember the day we got back. We hired a horse and coach at the train station at four o'clock in the afternoon. The sky was dark, and it was starting to rain . . . and I was so upset! I didn't like it—Italy—over in Brazil it was beautiful . . . blue skies, sun, and children that play all the time! Well, we went to my grandmother's house, and the street looked so dismal because the sky was so gray. I remember going down to the basement in my grandmother's house, and I leaned against the door—I can still feel it and hear it—the rain began to fall outside, and I started to cry. I was in misery, but then—somewhere inside the house—someone started to play the song "Valencia" on the victrola. You know the song "Valencia"? (*Starts to sing it*) We used to play it all the time in Brazil . . . and that was it! That song lifted my spirits—as a child—and I started to feel better.

The vividness of that meaning, the rich contextual description of it and her rendering of her own subjective state of mind was done in words and gestures that were highly evocative of mood and meaning for me as a listener. Obviously, Brazil was a shining image in her narrative. She kept tacking back and forth between her description of experiences in Italy at a later time and the Brazil of her memory and imagination at an earlier time. She went on as follows:

V: I had a hard time to adjust . . . to Italy. I spoke mostly Portuguese, and I was very dark with my tan from Brazil, so the kids in school called me "the nigger." So I had a hard time adjusting to the Italian kids because they . . . because I was black. I was not white like them. And then, after my tan started to fade, I started to fit in with the other kids. This I remember to this day.

I: You remember that part—with the other kids—especially?

V: Oh yes! This I remember because it was—how you say?—a small trauma . . . you, you never . . . I never forget. But, you know, when I play that song "Valencia," I feel better . . . even now.

As those excerpts show, it was possible to know what it was like to be Rosa V. throughout her narrative, even as a young girl. Her level of experiencing would alternate between EXP 3 and EXP 4 in her narrative discourse. When it was at EXP 3, it consisted of vivid descriptions of events, persons, settings, and circumstances, and then it would change to EXP 4 as she described the effects of those external factors on her inner subjective state of feelings and thoughts.

She went on to describe better times after her return to Italy. Her father got a good job, and she, her parents, and her brother lived as an extended family in the home of her widowed maternal grandmother and her uncle. This uncle had been wounded in World War I and had lost his left eye and part of his left arm. The sight in his right eye was also impaired, which was a major blow to him because he had been a talented painter with a bright future before he was drafted into the army in the closing months of World War I. However, he became a sculptor like his father because could see well enough for that and because he could *feel* his work with his good right hand.

Rosa spent a great deal of time with him in her childhood, and he had a formative influence on her life. He taught her all about art, and because he could no longer read, he had her read from good literature, usually classics. She remembered reading from Dante's *Inferno* and *Paradiso*. She remarked that she had to read a lot to him on rainy days when there was not enough light for sculpting—and it rained a lot in Lucca, she said. She very much wanted to become an artist, a painter as her uncle had been before he was wounded. However, by the time she had finished the equivalent of high school in Italy, economic conditions were so bad that her family could not afford to send her to the art school at the University of Lucca where her grandfather had taught.

The best that could be done by the family under the circumstances was to send her to a school that was the equivalent of a two-year community college in the United States, to study pattern design. This would train her to design patterns for clothing, furnishings, and so on. She described the school and the training as "no big deal—it was *cheap*. It was run by the Fascists." While she was attending that school, her uncle died, and after that she simply gave up on the idea of becoming a painter—"I put down my brush, and I never picked it up again, never." Still, she claimed she was glad to get the degree or certificate when she finished that school because it was "something in my hands."

By then World War II was well under way, and northern Italy was being bombed regularly by British and American planes. There were no jobs for textile pattern designers, so she took a three-month crash course in typing and got a job in the office of wealthy industrialist. She said, "I was a bad typist and I hated the job, but the pay was good." However, the bombing was very heavy in the industrial area in which she worked. She said there was much confusion and chaos and suffering there, and it was something she would never forget. She gave some vivid descriptions of charred bodies from the bombings, of Germans dragging Italian men out of their homes and shooting them in front of their wives and children or sending them to concentration camps.

By September 1944, many were starving in Italy. There was no heat, no electricity, no running water, and she had become emaciated because of severe food shortages. That was when she met her husband. He was an American MP stationed down the street from her home, and she would pass by him each day on her way to work. He became attracted to her, but she did not know why. She said: "I was very, very skinny and white—but he said, 'I like that little girl with the long black hair over her shoulders.'" So he had a fellow soldier who could speak Italian introduce him to her. She didn't take the introduction very seriously and promptly forgot about it. However, he came to call on her one day, and her father was shocked when he answered the door only to be confronted by an American military policeman. He did not want the young man around, and since she did not remember him, he was summarily told to leave and not return. However, he was persistent and "kept coming around," so a year later (October 1945) they were married.

Mrs. V. went on to say that she had a very good married life with him. He was a "quiet man, kind and gentle" and a good father to their two daughters. He worked for the post office in his hometown in upstate New York, where he returned with his war bride after his discharge. He was retired from the postal service when he died of leukemia about 15 months prior to my interview with Mrs. V. She said, "He died fast from it, but he suffered for fourteen days and—I don't even want to think about it—so now I'm a widow."

She reported being very distraught over his death and not knowing what to do. Both of her daughters were married and "living their own lives," so she decided to go back to Italy, where her brother was urging her to return. Her parents had died ten years earlier, but she had gone back to Italy for visits just about every year to see her brother, his family, and the many old friends she still had there. So she went back about six months after her husband's death, stayed for about four months, and then suddenly returned to the United States. She described the experience as follows:

V: I didn't like it. I don't know why, but I said to myself, "Rosa, you have to cut the cord." I realized that after my parents died there was nothing there for me anymore. Even though I went back there for visits after they died, Lucca seemed less and less like home. But my brother was so insistent—"Rosa, this is your home. Your roots are here, you belong here." And after Ted [her husband] died, I was lost for awhile. I didn't know who I was or where I belonged, but when I got over there I realized I belong here.

Everybody—my brother, all my friends—told me "Rosa, don't go. Stay, this is your home," and they tried to keep me there every way. They even called me "renegade" when I said I wouldn't stay, but I had to come back here. Now I know this is it. This is my country—I missed the environment, I missed the American people, who I like a lot. The greenery here—it's lovely—I missed it. Over there all the old green places are gone, they're filled with ugly apartments—and cars and trucks. Everything is so crowded—too many people.

There's a feeling about being back here . . . (*long pause*). It's hard to say . . . open, warm, welcoming? Anyway (*excitedly*) I came back, called my daughters right away and said, "I'm back! Really back." So this is it, for good, and no doubt about it.

It was apparent that her husband's death represented a major psychosocial transition in her life. It was not only a major life crisis due to his loss, but it precipitated an actual identity crisis as to who she was (Italian or American) and where she belonged. Beneath the issue of nationality were more pervasive questions of belonging, attachment, and individuation—to cut the cord of her childhood attachment to her parents in Italy and to embrace the newer attachments and commitments of her adulthood in America where she still had children and grandchildren who represented the future.

Later in the interview she identified her husband's death and her experiences following that as the major turning point in her life. She said that after his retirement they would go out driving along the country roads, looking for antiques. She enjoyed the rides in the country with him and the looking, but they were beginning to accumulate a lot of "things." She was beginning to be bothered by this and also by the many hours he would spend on his stamp collection. She said that he was very attached to his stamps and she would try to pry him away so they could do something together. She became acutely aware after his death of how much of their precious time after retirement had been "spent on things." She described this as follows:

V: I used to say, "Ted, stop with those stamps. Hour after hour you spend on them. Let's do something—talk or go somewhere." But he couldn't stop. He'd say, "No, not now. Maybe later." Then we might go out looking at antiques—collecting, always collecting things, like his stamps.

I wish I understood then what I know now. I love things, but I don't get attached. I just enjoy that they are there. I love simple things I see and touch every day—flowers, greenery, a piece of furniture—but I don't have to own them. Like antiques—I gave them all away to my daughters and friends. The beauty of things is enough for me now. It took my husband's death to see that— that what we had as man and wife was more precious than the "things" we had.

I: So your husband's death . . . and what happened after it . . . really *was* a major turning point in your life—changed your ideas about "things."

V: Oh yes! And more than that. You know, this is going to sound crazy—or bad, but I say it anyway. When he died, I cry a lot—sometimes I say, "Ted, why did you leave me alone? I took care of you, fixed special meals for you when you were sick—whatever you wanted whenever you wanted it." Then after awhile that changed. I say, "Now you are gone—I guess God wanted you. Now I'm free. I eat when I want to eat, cook what I want to cook, if I want to go for a walk . . . I can go wherever I want to go—even Italy—whenever I want."

I never feel lonely now. I like my company—(*chuckles*) the holy trinity—me, myself, and I. You know I think solitude is freedom, too. I'm more free now. I miss him, don't get me wrong, but I'm different now—I can be alone and enjoy it. I was never like that before in my life . . . never.

Later in the interview, after she told her life story up to the present, I asked her some questions about her earlier responses to certain items from the Ego Integrity Scale on the survey questionnaire. I asked her if she would expand upon her response to the statement "I would not change my life if I lived it over," a statement she completely agreed with. She said:

V: Oh, definitely. I would not change it. I didn't have a dull life—a very exciting one. Even now, when I'm old, it's not dull. I love my life—nobody else has had a life just exactly like it. There were so many things . . . (*excitedly*) When we went swimming in the creek when we were young! When we rode down the hills on our bikes!

I *do* reminisce—even the war—four horrible years. Even those I don't want to forget. It was all part of the whole thing—of life.

I: Yet you did indicate on the questionnaire that you had some regrets.

V: Of course. Who doesn't? I remember when I found out I couldn't go to art school. I started to cry, and I remember one of my teachers, Mrs. N——. She was an old lady—she put her hand on my shoulder and said: "The first illusion . . . the first sorrow of your life." I still remember that. I think that it was one of the biggest disappointments of my life. If I had fulfilled that—to create, to paint—it would have been marvelous (*long pause*), but I found something else. If I tell you, I know you will think I'm crazy.

I: I'm sure not.

V: I'm a kind of fatalistic person. Since I was a child I had a special love for the American flag. I remember in Lucca there was the Italo-American Bank, and on holidays they would put out two flags—the Italian of red, white, and green and the American of red, white, and blue. I remember as a kid going to school I wanted to reach up and touch that American flag, and I said, "It's mine. It's mine." The other kids made fun of me, and we'd fight with the umbrellas, because it was raining—and they'd say you're stupid, this is your flag, the Italian. So, I was . . . what? . . . 8, 9 years old. . . . How could I know that would be my flag?

I: So it was almost like a premonition?

V: Like a premonition, yes—and I dreamed it. I saw myself coming here in a boat. It was in 1939 just before the war. It wasn't a dream, I *saw* it. So I believe its something like . . . a destiny. Maybe not, but I believe it, and none of that can be changed. That's the way it was supposed to be—no other way.

It is remarkable that this last statement is almost a perfect a paraphrase of Erik Erikson's observation that in order to achieve ego integrity a person has to accept his or her one and only life as something that had to be and that would not permit any substitutions. In fact, her high score on the Ego Integrity Scale, plus her pattern of reminiscence and her Affect-Balance Score, indicated that she was in the integrity-achieving status on the basis of those measures. In person, she certainly gave the impression of someone with ego integrity.

She also gave the impression of an individuated person in terms of Jung's concept of individuation. She showed a well-developed and rounded personality with respect to her capacities for feeling, thinking, sensing, and intuition. She also showed a capacity for solitude as well as relatedness, after working through her husband's death. There is another aspect of her life that has Jungian overtones. It is the belief in her personal destiny to become an American and her description of herself as a "fatalistic person." This sounds like Jung's theory of synchronicity, in which seemingly unrelated events (such as the American-flag incident of her childhood and the dream of coming to America on a boat) become meaningful in terms of later developments and from a life-span perspective. The theory of synchronicity or "meaningful coincidence" has been described as follows: "The coming together by apparent change of factors that are not causally linked but that nevertheless show themselves to be meaningfully related is at the very heart of the process by which the purpose of the individual's life unfolds and becomes his 'fate' " (Progoff, 1973).

Whether or not this represents a "true" personal teleos or purpose in her life, it is a clear and integrated outcome of her creative and imaginative self-narrative. The temporal dialectic of that narrative, in which she moved back and forth from past to present, with its spontaneity, vividness, and expressiveness certainly qualify Rosa V. as an "artist of reminiscence." She never realized the dream of becoming a painter, and she listed per primary occupation as "seamstress" (which she became after raising her daughters) on the Integrity Survey questionnaire, but she realized her dream of artistry in the living and telling of her life story.

WRITTEN REMINISCENCE

There has been no consideration of written reminiscence up to this point, primarily because none of the research reported on so far has drawn upon it. However, it cannot be overlooked, because to do so would be to exclude the rich realm of creative reminiscence available in the form of written autobiographies, diaries, and journals. Paul Ricouer (1984) contends that written language has much greater potential for the creation of meaning and much more "hermeneutic potential" for the interpretation of meaning than does spoken language. This is so, he claims, because writing serves to "fix" or objectify discourse for further interpretive understanding. Edward Casey (1989), in his phenomenological study of remembering, takes Ricouer's position in discussing "auto-reminiscing" (i.e., reminiscing to oneself). He says, "When I reminisce *to* myself, I am treating myself as a reminiscential partner — as an other who listens to himself" and "writing may even be its [auto-reminiscing's] optimal mode of realization" because it can "stabilize an author's understanding of his or her life." However, there is apt to be some ambivalence about this form of reminiscing because, although it makes an understanding available to the author himself or herself, it is also available to others. Since auto-reminiscing is apt to be intensely intimate and personal, there may be considerable reluctance to engage in it in written form.

One person who has made this form of reminiscing available to people in a nonthreatening and creative form is Ira Progoff (1975), with his method of "intensive journal process." As a gerontological practitioner I have found his method to be most helpful for a number of older persons with whom I have worked. It is particularly helpful for older people who are living alone and do not have the opportunity for dialogue and oral reminiscence with others. Many homebound elderly fit this category and could benefit from the intensive journal method.

It is therefore an autogenic and self-help method but of far greater depth and substance than the usual more modish and slick self-help approaches. Consequently, I have referred a number of elderly persons who could afford it to go to one of the many two-day workshops held in various places throughout the country. For those who cannot afford or are physically unable to attend the workshop, I have recommended Progoff's inexpensive paperback book, *At a Journal Workshop*. It is comprehensive, clearly described, and illustrated with examples other people's journal work. Other gerontological practitioners have also found it helpful in their work. One has used it in cases where obsessive reminiscing about a specific past situation will not yield to life-review therapy. She finds "Progoff's technique of relating to a [problematic] piece of the past as if to a 'person' with a process and life history of its own, can provide a route to its inner workings" (Lo-Gerfo, 1980–81).

Actually, the intensive journal method goes well beyond therapy. It provides a way for the person to engage in a process of ongoing creation of self and meaning—to answer *who*, (identity), *what then* (history), *why* (causality), and *what for* (teleological) questions. It does this through an organized system of entries in a journal (looseleaf notebook) divided into 12 sections, or logs. Each section taps a different dimension of the person's life. The following abbreviated description should give a sense of the content and flow of the process.

It begins with a written entry describing the inner and outer events of the most recent period in the person's life. Then the person/author is asked to relax with eyes closed and to let imagery, impression, feelings, and symbols form in the mind. This use of "twilight imagery" (i.e., in the twilight zone between a sleeping and waking state) is a very effective experiential tool that gets below the person's prestructured and habitual cognitive sets and gives the person an interior perspective on his or her life. These images, feelings, and impressions are recorded in writing without concern for logic, grammar, completeness, or any other constraining formalities of public writing. It is highly personal and internal.

The third section, called "Steppingstones," is intended to give a sense of continuity to the person's life by asking for about a dozen key events or milestones in the person's life. Then the author is asked to select one of those events or milestones in which a choice was made. It asks the author to reminisce by writing, "It was a time when . . ." and then go on to record recollections and impressions that might sort out unresolved issues. After making entries in these first four sections, the author takes the thoughts and insights that have arisen and makes entries in one of the other appropriate sections.

The remaining sections include the following: Life History Log (to collect past experiences without interpretation or judgment), Daily Log (to think back over the past 24 hours to record moods, concerns, and thoughts), Dream Log (to record dreams without analysis or interpretation), Dialogue with Persons (after picking a person—living or dead—of inner personal importance and listing *their* life stepping-stones, to record whatever emerges from inside with the statement, "As I consider your life I feel . . ."), Dialogue with Works (after picking a personally important activity and listing the stepping-stones in its life, to record thoughts and feelings about it and letting it respond as in a dialogue), Dialogue with the Body (after listing some remembrances of personal bodily experiences throughout life—sensuality, illness, food, drug use, etc.—to let the body speak back and to record the dialogue), Inner Wisdom Dialogue (to imagine a dialogue with a person considered to be wise—teacher, parent, writer, etc.—about something of important personal concern and to record the discussion), and the Open Moment (to briefly record a vision, hope, prayer, or plan for the next moment in life to help the person focus on where he or she is going).

It can be seen that Progoff's method encompasses all of the major points made in the preceding sections on self-creativity and the creation of meaning, and then some. In the "Open Moment" it looks to the future and enables the person to integrate past, present, and future into a meaningful whole, a being-in-becoming consonant with Butler's definition of a successful life review. It is dialectical in the temporal and spatial dimensions of the person's life as well as dialogical and dialectical in the interpersonal and intrapersonal relationship dimensions. It provides for a fitting together (synthesis) of the outer contents and events of the person's life with the person's internal imagery and intentionality in a genuine experiential process, and it even incorporates embodied reminiscence. Progoff believes that achievement of such a synthesis or integration is a creative act. I would heartily agree and would call such a synthesis an "artistic achievement" in Dewey's sense of art as experience.

In fact, the major focus of Progoff's work has been to help people evoke creativity in their lives. The key to doing this, he says, is the technique of "journal feedback," the interplay between the journal sections that enables people to break through a repetitious cycle to gain insight. This is an effective self-hermeneutic device because it avoids a *repetitious* iterative circle of interpretation in arriving at meaning. However, Progoff eschews intellectual self-analysis and interpretation in favor of an experiential grasp of meaning on the person's part. Further, the writing in the journal is for ongoing exploration, not something that is supposed to end in a definitive interpretation of a life. However, the process is undoubtedly an aesthetic and creative one. With the intensive journal method, in the words of Anaïs Nin, (1975) "all the elements we attribute to the poet, the artist, become available to everyone."

The oral self-narrative of Rosa V., the "artist of reminiscence," seemed to recapitulate in an uncanny way the elements contained in the intensive journal method. There were elements of internal dialogue with self and others, key events or stepping-stones, and the use of imagery and dreams, along with the basic life history. She was unschooled in the method and never attended a workshop, but she seemed to have an intuitive grasp of the essence of the process. This speaks to the fact, it seems to me, that Progoff is tapping a profound and universal experiential dimension of the lived life with his method.

The point was made earlier that the journal method is particularly helpful to older persons living alone. This is especially pertinent for older women, who outlive their spouses in much greater numbers than men. Although Rosa V. did not go through the formal intensive journal process, she went through an analogous life-review process, and she came out of it with an appreciation, an actual cherishing, of solitude. This reminds me of a 75-year-old widow at a Progoff workshop in New York City who read aloud the following entry in the last, "Open Moment," section of her journal: "I wonder what I will be like when I'm 90. Will I be terrible to live with because I like being alone so much?"

The likelihood is, of course, that the capacity for solitude will enhance rather than detract from the capacity for relationship with others. One woman, a creative writer, who showed this dual capacity was May Sarton (1977), who said in her later years, "Solitude grows richer for me each year." She recorded the following observations about it: "We are one, the house and I, and I am happy to be alone—time to think, time to be . . . ," and "I am here [in the house] for the first time in weeks to take up my 'real life' again at last. . . . When I am alone the flowers are really seen; I can pay attention to them. They are felt presences" (Berman, 1989).

With Sarton's highly expressive description of the flowers it is time to move to the poetry of reminiscence. It is in that form that the ineffable sensate dimensions of reminiscence are most aptly expressed, for it speaks, in a few words, volumes about the experienced past that cannot be said in lengthy life narratives.

THE POETRY OF REMINISCENCE

A number of the ideas about reminiscence covered so far in this book have been expressed by poets in a much briefer and more telling way. For example, the idea that reminiscence about the past can be an artistic experience and accomplishment as well as an opening upon new experiences from the past has been expressed by William Carlos Williams (1938) in his poem "The Descent," in which he writes of memory as "a kind of accomplishment and a sort of renewal":

> The descent beckons
>   as the ascent beckoned
>   Memory is a kind
> of accomplishment
>   a sort of renewal
>   even
> an invitation, since the spaces it opens are new places
>   inhabited by hordes
>   heretofore unrealized
> of new kinds —
>   since their movements
>   are towards new objectives
> (even though formerly they were abandoned).

The idea that reminiscence and the self are inseparable in old age has been expressed by Robert Penn Warren (1985), who believes that poetry is "a kind of unconscious autobiography," when he says: "Almost everybody, of course, has been a subject of self-scrutiny, and I have spent hours speculating why things have fallen out as they have. As the breath of four-score blows hotter on the back of the neck, a man must ponder whatever logic he can find in those swift-footed years." Malcolm Cowley expressed the same octogenarian sentiment about the swiftness of the years of one's life when reminiscing about the past. In his book *The View from 80* (1980), he captures this sentiment, together with Williams's image of the descent, in writing about himself in the following poem, "The Red Wagon":

For his birthday they gave him a red express
    wagon
with a driver's high seat and a handle that
    steered
His mother pulled him around the yard.
"Giddyap," he said, but she laughed and went
    off
to wash the breakfast dishes

"I want to ride too," his sister said,
and he pulled her to the edge of a hill.
"Now, sister, go home and wait for me,
but first give a push to the wagon."

He climbed again to the high seat,
this time grasping the handle-that-steered.
The red wagon rolled slowly down the slope,
then faster as it passed the schoolhouse
and faster as it passed the store,
the road still dropping away.
Oh, it was fun.
But would it ever stop?
Would the road always go downhill?

The red wagon rolled faster.
Now it was in strange country.
It passed a white house he must have dreamed about
deep woods he had never seen,
a graveyard where, something told him his sister was buried

Far below
the sun was sinking into a broad plain.

The red wagon rolled faster.
Now he was clutching the seat, not even trying to steer.
Sweat clouded his heavy spectacles.
His white hair streamed in the wind.

Cowley certainly illustrates poetry's capacity to telescope the past. Yet poetry also has the capacity to catch and hold a vivid image or memory from the past, to expand it within the present, and even to project it into the future as a memory of the present. This capacity is evident, of course, in the hands of an accomplished writer like Cowley, but what about poetry's capacity in the hands of "ordinary" elderly persons wishing to express the ineffable in their reminiscences in that form?

We had the good fortune to have included in the Integrity Survey several members of a writers' group in one of the survey sites, a senior service center that offered a writing workshop under the tutelage of a volunteer teacher of creative writing from the faculty of a local college. It was one of the most successful and highly regarded programs in that center, and its elderly participants could not say enough about what it had meant to them in their later years.[1]

There was, of course, great variability in the writing skills of these participants because a number of them never finished grammar school, and almost all had no prior experience in writing poetry. I would like now to present some of their poems, without regard to technical or aesthetic merit, to illustrate how the writers used poetry to express what they had not been able to express in the straight narrative of their life-history interviews.

One of the recurrent themes that showed up in the reminiscences and self-narratives of the Integrity Survey was the increased reverence for nature, its seasons, its beauty, its moods, and above all its various forms of renewal. This high regard for the elemental and often simple forms seemed to show up most frequently in the symbol of the flower. This is expressed in all of its directness and simplicity in the following poem, entitled "Age," by an 82-year-old woman in the writer's group:

> Age, I keep one step ahead
> But I'm showing —
> Not much I can do.
> My steps are slowing.
> Where did my vim and vigor go?
> I'd like to know.
> Ah well, I will not fret —
> There's life in the old girl yet.
> I think I'll go plant a tulip

The next poem, "Full Moon," by a 77-year-old woman from the group depicts a pervasive quality of shifting mood in the workings of nature. It also illustrates the complex interrelationship of present to past and future by projecting a present mood into the future as an anticipated remembrance of the present.

I long
for the January Thaw —
and yet,
when it takes the North,
I'll know,
for all of my jubilance,
I've lost
this bitter daybreak's drama
of a thin gunmetal sky
imprisoning a while
for me
a far and frozen moon.

The following poem not only identifies the pervasive theme of nature in its title, it intimates the importance of the writers' group for this person. It also introduces another theme we found among a number of participants in the Integrity Survey, the idea of an unexpressed but knowing person within the self.

Nature

Inside me is another person —
I want to let her out.
She knows more than I do
But has never had a chance.
Please help her out.

Memory of a large aquarium filled
with a school of minnows
swimming in unison of silver flashing
in the light. Surreal

I walked to Poetry Class today
At last I found the Senior Citizens
meeting place.
I'd looked so often but it eluded me before.
Today I had the number

The author of the above poem was a member of the original writers' group, but she died at age 80 just before the Integrity Survey began. So she was not a participant in the study. However, the following poem was written about her by a participant and a fellow member of the writers' group who was particularly fond of her. It is entitled "In Memoriam," and it illustrates one of the most important poetic forms of reminiscence, the memorial remembrance or commemoration, in this instance of a much beloved person.

The script goes blank
and sound cannot give voice
                        to phrase.
But memories still frame
                        for me her smile.
untouched, surrounded
                        roundly reminded
                        of her infinite power.
Doomsday has now embraced
                        unspoken lines—
                        lines uttered by
                        a solitary kiss that
                                corners my heart.
That passing time is finally *said*.
Goodbye, my sweet. Brave Alice,
          loving friend and ever loved.
We know
Salvation will find us together
                        once again
but even until then, a wasteland
                        finds this wanderer buoyed
by memories
          of grace
                        in you.

The theme of an unexpressed self in the earlier poem, "Nature," became abundantly clear in a number of the self-narratives in which the narrators could express the depth of feeling or degree of insight they actually had about themselves, their loved ones, and critical happenings in their lives. One of the most dramatic instances of this was with a 76-year-old man from the writers' group who had lived a life of poverty, dislocation, and marginal employment for lack of an education he so desperately wanted. He had completed only the sixth grade, and as a teenager during the Depression he had to ride the rails, hopping freight cars from town to town and job to job, spending time in transit labor camps and occasionally in jails. He had developed in the course of these life experiences a rather tough, factual, no-nonsense way of talking. yet it was apparent from the descriptive facts and details from his many travels that he had developed a deep and abiding love of nature. He was the oldest member of a local hiking group just so that he could make regular excursions on foot into nature preserves, woods, mountains, and streams. Rather than talk about this love of nature he showed me the following poem:

Spring

There's a wren in my throat
And it calls and sings
And my heart's a white flutter
Of mocking birds' wings

What struck me about this poem was not just the prominence of nature's creatures, the birds, but their metaphorical placement in his body. It was as though he wished they could express through his throat what he was feeling in his heart. This impression became even stronger as he told about his recently deceased mother. She had led an extremely hard life of poverty, hard work, and abuse from several men with whom she had lived. Through all of this she had tried to nurture and provide for him and his younger brother and sister to the extent she could. When talking about her, tears came to the edge of his eyes, and he broke off his narrative to show me this poem:

Soon

An old woman is living
slowly, slowly—
Breath after difficult breath—
I watch and life seems a little.
Too lowly to win the favor of death
Death is too mighty, too proud—
He has suns to darken.
How should death pause to still
An old woman's tired heart?
Yet hearken! (and yet)
His step is on the sill

Through a number of the self-narratives the image or figure of the mother was very prominent. Perhaps a good way to end this section on the poetry of reminiscence is to present a poem with the figure of a mother. The following poem by A. Mary Robinson (1980) does this, and it treats of the moods created by nature's diurnal changes and how these change in the course of a life. Finally, a telling testimonial of the value of reminiscence in old age is captured in her expression "memories more exquisite than hope."

Twilight

When I was young the twilight seemed too long.
How often on the western window-seat
    I leaned my book against the misty pane
    And spelled the last enchanting lines again,
The while my mother hummed an ancient song,
Or sighed a little and said: "The hour is sweet!"
When I, rebellious, clamored for the light.

But now I love the soft approach of night,
    And now with folded hands I sit and dream
    While all too fleet the hours of twilight seem;
And thus I know that I am growing old.

O granaries of Age! O manifold
And royal harvest of the common years!
There are in all thy treasure-house no ways
But lead by soft descent and gradual slope
To memories more exquisite than hope.
Thine is the iris born of olden tears,
And thrice more happy are the happy days
That live divinely in the lingering rays.

NOTE

1. The members of this writers' group were most willing to share their writings. As a group, they had a keen interest in the reminiscence and self-narrative aspects of the Integrity Survey because they saw these as central elements in their current involvement and interest in creative writing.

10
Private Endings

This book began with the observation that it represents a journey of exploration in greater and greater depth of the phenomenon of reminiscence in old age. The origins of the exploration process were in the public application and demonstration of the efficacy of group reminiscence for elderly persons who were still living in the community and outside of institutions. Some of the intriguing findings from the Group Project led to the Individual Reminiscence Survey and an in-depth exploration of what the experience of reminiscence was like for the Group Project participants as individuals. We had clearly moved from the public to the private realm of reminiscence in the Individual Survey. Then, in the third and last study, the Integrity Survey, we not only asked questions about the public and private uses of reminiscence among community elderly but also asked them to reminisce at length about themselves and to tell their life stories in the form of audiotaped self-narratives.

Now, in a sense, we come to the most private aspect of this whole experiential study, and that is for me as author to sort through and attempt to integrate the more salient findings that have emerged in the study process. The writing itself has been an experiential process, a very subjective and private one, in which certain findings have emerged as salient in ways that were unanticipated in the beginning. Since it has been such a subjective process, I cannot lay claim to even-handed objectivity in the following discussion of salient findings and their implications. If anything, I have become something of a partisan of, if not an advocate for, the value of reminiscence in the course of the three studies and the writing of the book. Consequently, the findings that I see as salient are apt to reflect the bias of my own changed perspective at this time.

Perhaps the best policy at this point is to acknowledge this and then indicate what others have found and said about the same or related phenomena, so that this does not become a purely private exercise. With that in mind, we can turn now to those salient findings and see what their implications are when compared and combined with the findings of other gerontological investigators. As will be seen, the implications of a number of these findings go well beyond the phenomenon and experience of reminiscence into broader concerns about the experience of aging and being old in our society.

FINDINGS AND IMPLICATIONS

There is very little doubt about the value of group reminiscence for community elderly. Its value for institutionalized elderly persons had been pretty well established prior to the Group Project, but it was not clear whether group reminiscence among community elderly could *prevent* premature or unnecessary institutionalization. The self-initiated and reconstituted groups of the elderly persons in three of our four study settings demonstrated the efficacy of group reminiscence for the development of self-support groups and networks that could prevent some unnecessary institutionalization of isolated or unattached elderly persons.

Groups are widely used for all sorts of programs and activities in senior service centers and congregate senior housing settings across America, so it would not be difficult to implement more groups for memory-sharing and reminiscence in those community settings. It would be advantageous to use the life-span (early childhood to old age) format of life-review groups because it offers the opportunity for self-integration and for dealing with possible unresolved issues from the past. In this regard it would be important to have practitioners available to undertake life-review therapy or counseling with individuals who request it and are in need of it, just as we did in the Group Project. Groups, therefore, provide an excellent opportunity for assessment or diagnosis of the need for life-review therapy. Apropos of assessment, Gendlin's experiencing construct in its operative form of the Experiencing (EXP) Scale became a surprisingly effective assessment device in indicating which persons were beginning to grapple with life-review issues requiring some resolution. It can be used quite unobtrusively by practitioners who have learned and incorporated its rationale and respective stages into their thinking. It has also sensitized me to the more subtle changes and opportunities for movement in individual therapy, so it has clear implications for that area of practice as well as in work with groups.

Another finding with immediate practice implications was the active (not simply reactive) interest of the participants in the Integrity Survey in telling their life stories in the self-narrative interviews. A number of those who had filled out the reminiscence questionnaire expressed disappointment at not being selected for the interview subsample. It has been said that everyone has a story to tell, and all that is lacking is the permission and a person to tell it to. Not only was there active interest in telling the story, but there was evidence of positive change in the telling, such as greater insight, clarified self-concept, increased self-esteem, and enhanced morale. Of course evidence of these positive changes is based more on direct observations and impressions then on controlled or quantified research methods, but they did appear to be by-products of an integrative process carried on through the narrative.

This suggests that the self-narrative has certain therapeutic value. This has, of course, been recognized by a number of people from various schools of thought. Some psychoanalysts have proposed that the analyst's role should be that of a collaborator in a narrative and as an interpreter and editor of a living text (Schafer, 1978; Spence, 1987). A psychologist, Donald Polkinghorne (1988), has observed that since humans use narrative structure to organize the events of their lives and to provide a scheme for their own self-identity, it has direct implications for the practice of psychotherapy and personal change. He notes that the goals of narrative practice might vary, for example, to make the latent narrative manifest, to help construct a unifying narrative, or to reconstruct a more coherent and workable interpretation of past events and future projects than the person's current narrative will allow. In any case, it behooves us as practitioners to understand the nature of narrative in order to apply it appropriately. It is important to understand that past events cannot be changed, but the narrative used to connect them can be. A self-narrative that overlooks or denies events in a person's life in order for it to be more pleasant or consistent runs counter to a commitment to truth in therapy. However, it is important to keep in mind that we are talking about narrative truth rather than historical truth. That is, rather than detailed descriptions of actual past events, the therapist has to work with the person's narrative constructions of those events. Then, when the new story of reconstructed narrative is completed, it must have the power of conviction for both the person telling it and the practitioner hearing it.

Here again, the experiencing construct and EXP Scale has something to offer. It can sensitize the practitioner to the levels of lived experience expressed in the narrative, and it can help to distinguish more intellectualized and rationalized versions of past experience from lived (i.e. experienced) ones. It can also help to indicate when and how the person might have access to new experiencing and integration in the narrative process.

The value of narrative for self-integration raises the issue of self-integration versus ego integrity, which was touched upon at the end of Chapter 5. It will be recalled that several studies, including the Integrity Survey, found that more elderly people seem to fit the foreclosed status than the integrity-achieving status. This, in turn, raises a question about the use of life review to achieve ego integrity and how it compares with the self-narrative to achieve greater self-integration. Butler's concept of the life review is an extremely valuable one, but there is a major difficulty with it when its primary purpose is seen as *resolution* of past issues in order to achieve ego integrity. I agree with Vivian Clayton that the possibility of resolving earlier developmental issues around basic trust versus mistrust, autonomy versus shame and doubt, initiative versus guilt, and the other weighty issues, all the way through generativity versus stagnation in middle-age is quite unlikely for most people (Clayton, 1975). However, there is reason to believe that the issue of identity versus identity confusion has probably been the central one in Erikson's thinking about the entire life cycle (Erikson, 1959, 1982). It is, of course, the one that deals most centrally with the self at all life stages from adolescence on.

There was no question in the Integrity Survey that the issue of identity was a central feature of the reminiscences and self-narratives of the participants. It will be recalled that over half of the respondents indicated that they used reminiscence for the purpose of achieving greater understanding of themselves and their lives. Even among those who could be identified as foreclosed rather than integrity-achieving, there was evidence of what has been called the "autobiographical impulse," the desire to tell their personal life story. If this kind of impulse or desire is what Butler meant by the universal nature of the life review among the elderly, then the Integrity Survey tended to corroborate his view. In this respect the self-narrative and the life review (without the goal of resolution) are both aimed at the same outcome—greater self-integration and a clearer sense of identity.

This process of self-integration and a greater centering in the self has been observed by other investigators. Based on their in-depth study of a sample of American men, Daniel Levinson and his colleagues (1978) came to the conclusion that this process is part of a developmental task that usually leads to what they called a "distinctive and fulfilling season" in the lives of men from about 60 to 85. They describe it as follows:

> A primary developmental task of late adulthood is to find a new balance of involvement with society and with the self. A man in this era is experiencing more fully the process of dying and he should have the possibility of choosing more freely his mode of living. Without losing his love of humanity, of his own tribe and of his self, he can form a broader perspective and recognize more profoundly our human contradictions, creativity and destructiveness. Greater wisdom regarding the external world can be gained only through a stronger centering in the self. This does not mean that a man becomes more selfish or vain. Just the opposite. It means that he becomes less interested in obtaining the rewards offered by society and more interested in utilizing his own inner resources. The voices within the self become, as it were, more audible and more worthy of attention. He continues to be actively engaged with the voices and realities of the external world, but he seeks a new balance in which the self has greater primacy.

Based on my own practice and research experience, I would say that this season also occurs in the lives of women. Although it might be somewhat different in form because of social and cultural factors related to gender, it is experientially the same. I have had the opportunity to compare this impression personally with Levinson, and it is in agreement with the findings from his subsequent study of women (Sherman, 1987a). What comes from the "stronger centering of the self" for men and women alike in that season of their lives is a blurring of the distinction between work and play so that the two can co-mingle in a creative way. As Levinson put it, the person can devote himself or herself "in a serious-playful way to the interests that flow most directly from the depths of the self" and can "enjoy the creative possibilities of this season." There is a shift from primarily *doing* (work qua work) to a state of *being*, with a more natural flow of work-play on the basis of emergent interest according to the context of time, place, and mood.

American society is not very well organized for this kind of shift in the lives of its older citizens. There is a pervasive and powerful emphasis upon production and consumption of goods and services that requires an ethos of *doing* and *having*. This is expressed in the functionalistic ethic, mentioned previously in Chapter 5, by which people are evaluated by self and others according to their functional value in such a society. This has led to the so-called activity theory of aging, whereby the elderly person should remain as active and functional as possible for as long as possible. According to this theory, it would be normative for them to function as actively as middle-aged people well into old age, presumably until they become totally exhausted or drop dead. There is no apparent room in this theory for a natural progression of changes in the human body and mind.

It reflects a value orientation that the anthropologists Kluckhohn and Strodtbeck (1961) identified as the "doing" orientation in their cross-cultural studies. They described this orientation as follows:

> Its most distinctive feature is a demand for the kind of activity which results in accomplishments that are measurable by standards conceived to be external to the individual. That aspect of self-judgment or judgment of others which relates to the nature of activity is based mainly upon a measurable accomplishment achieved by acting upon persons, things, or situations. What does the individual do? What can he or will he accomplish? There are almost always the primary questions in the American's appraisal of persons. "Getting things done" and "let's *do* something about it" are stock American phrases.

Many older Americans do indeed live by this ethos, driven by its external imperatives. On the other hand, there are many who retire but come back to selectively take part-time work that can be carried out on the basis of their creative energies and interests rather than the extrinsic rewards of increased wages, status, or authority. Then there are those who *choose* to continue working full-time, but it is an authentic internal choice because their work *is* their play, and it expresses their creativity. Too frequently, however, work is used by older persons to fend off feelings of worthlessness based upon the functionalistic ethic. There is a strong emphasis on doing, making, and planning for consumption and enjoyment in the future within this orientation, which is fine for younger persons. The elderly, however, factually have much less of a future for which to plan.

There is evidence that the better psychological adjustment in old age is associated with a present-time orientation, and gerontologists have noted that there is a "presentness," a great interest in the immediate experiences of the moment among those who seem to age successfully (Buhler, 1968). Kluckhohn and Strodtbeck identified this as a "being" orientation, which is atypical of North Americans and more typical of Central and South Americans. Yet anthropologists and psychiatrists alike have found better emotional adjustment among the elderly with a being orientation and a greater incidence of mental illness among older persons in the United States who have more of a doing value orientation (Clark & Anderson, 1967; Weinberg, 1975). Frequently, there is a compulsive and mindless kind of activity that has been described as the defense of "busyness' to defend against depression and feelings of emptiness in the old age (Butler & Lewis, 1983). This mindlessness is precisely the opposite of the kind of mindfulness of the elderly person who is actively tuned into the experience of the present moment, a person in the "being mode."

REMINISCENCE AND BEING IN OLD AGE

It has been noted a number of times in preceding parts of this book that reminiscence, particularly the more embodied and highly experiencing kind of reminiscence, is very much a function of the present. Present context, mood, physical and emotional state very much set the tone for reminiscence. Thus, the more experiential forms of reminiscence are definitely in the being mode. The older person who can allow himself or herself to freely and imaginatively engage in reminiscence can experience the "is-ness" of the present moment from traces of the past. Erich Fromm (1981) described reminiscence in the being mode as follows:

> One can experience a situation of the past with the same freshness as if it occurred in the here and now; that is, one can re-create the past, bring it to life (resurrect the dead, symbolically speaking). To the extent that one does so, the past ceases to be the past; it *is* the here and now.

In order to engage in this more active and creative reconstructing of the past, the person has to be centered in the self; for if the person is more tuned in to the distractions and rewards of the external world, such reminiscence cannot take place. Older persons who are more centered have the capacity to simply enjoy their being of the moment, including images of the past and future. Those who are centered and in the being mode appear to be doubly blessed when it comes to the experiential quality of late life. One such person who was so blessed was Michel de Montaigne, who in his essay "On Experience" (1952) described it as follows: "It is an absolute perfection and virtually divine to know how to enjoy our being rightfully. We seek other conditions because we do not understand the use of our own and go outside of ourselves because we do not know what it is like inside."

This calls for a more contemplative and less doing frame of mind, and, in fact, Erikson felt that it was necessary for the older person to develop that frame of mind more fully. Interestingly, although Erikson was highly sensitive to the fit between individual and society for other age groups, he did not have much to say about the apparent mismatch between this contemplative side of older adults and the predominant doing orientation of the larger society. This prompted Robert Bellah (1976) to write, "If Erik Erikson found that the mature personality expresses itself in both action and contemplation, then we might ask whether a culture that exclusively emphasizes action (or contemplation either, for that matter) can be a very healthy environment for human growth."

It was noted in Chapter 5 that David Gutmann (1977) had found in his cross-cultural studies a shift from "active" to "passive mastery" occurring among the elderly in very different societies and cultures. Unfortunately, his term "passive" has a pejorative connotation in our action-oriented and doing society. However, Erich Fromm (1981) has remarked that activity and passivity can have two very different meanings: "Alienated activity in the sense of mere busyness, is actually 'passivity,' in the sense of productivity; while passivity, in terms of nonbusyness, may be nonalienated activity." Of course, he is talking about creative (nonalienated) productivity in this quote. Fromm goes on to say that Aristotle did not share our present concepts of activity and passivity because the highest form of praxis (i.e., of activity) — even above political activity — for him was the *contemplative life* devoted to the search for truth.

Reminiscence in its more experiential forms is a highly contemplative activity even if it is not necessarily devoted to the search for truth. Thus, the observed increase in reminiscence in old age would appear to be consistent with the move toward passive mastery and a more contemplative life. Gutmann also remarked on the increase among the elderly of an interest in the sacred and the elemental, particularly through ritual. There does indeed seem to be a return to the elemental in old age, and it is often expressed through ritual, for as Susanne Langer (1957) put it, "Ritual is the most primitive reflection of serious thought, a slow deposit, as it were, of people's imaginative insight into life."

One writer on the stages of life describes this whole process very effectively in its temporal and mundane form in old age with reference to his grandfather:

> [T]ime in old age becomes the "moving image of eternity." In this aspect time is expressed by repetition, cyclical movement, the drawn circle, ritual. Ritual sanctifies life by expressing the eternal within it, and this sanctification is the responsibility of old age. My grandfather's found daily attentions to three possessions—his pipe, his pen, and his pocketknife—invested hastening time with the touch of eternal, as did his meticulous daily gardening. . . . Amidst changes in the family pattern these things endured, conferring substance and weight. (Norton, 1976)

The love of gardening, of flowers, and of the nature generally among the elderly was remarked upon in the last chapter. With some elderly there is almost a spiritual aura to it. For example, in discussions with the writers' group this was expressed as a return to the earth—a "being in and with nature"—and there was a piety about it. This was the kind of piety Santayana (1955) described as "man's reverent attachment to the sources of his being and the steadying of his life by that attachment."

During the Group Project we became aware of a number of elderly participants—usually the most elderly, those well into their eighties—who appeared to be quite contented and at peace with themselves. They talked little and tended to participate less frequently in memory-sharing but would nod their heads in apparent recognition and understanding of what the other group participants were saying about their own past experiences. They enjoyed being there and said so on their evaluation forms when the project ended, but we had the impression they would enjoy being elsewhere as well, either alone or with others.

They appeared quite similar to the group of elderly people found in the Chicago study, referred to earlier in his book, reported by Lieberman and Tobin in *The Experience of Old Age*. Those investigators found their group to be in their eighties and nineties and to be rated high in mental health. The people in their group also had a high degree of life satisfaction, and although they evaluated their lives positively, it was with only "moderate affective intensity." They were in fact much more contemplative than emotive. Lieberman and Tobin speculated that they had earlier (in their sixties and seventies) engaged in an active life review and achieved some degree of resolution and "an attitude of serenity in regard to transitory emotional states." We obtained the same results for our group on their life satisfaction and self-concept measures.

We attempted to find out whether these same kinds of individuals in our project had gone through an earlier life review by asking about this in the in-depth interviews of the Individual Reminiscence Survey. They did indeed report having gone through an earlier period of every active reminiscing, with much more affective intensity, and it did have all of the earmarks of the life-review process. There was no clear indication that they were aware of *resolving* major developmental issues and crises in the Eriksonian sense, but they were aware of feeling more reconciled within themselves and enjoying their current lives as a result. They reported becoming more philosophical and less emotional, as well. There was no question that they were in a more contemplative "being" mode of existence. They personified in their demeanor and their relatively few words the fruits of the last stage of life as described by David Norton (1976):

> As the gift of old age to life itself, the substantialization of the human world expresses the definitive virtue of life's fourth stage, namely the profound generosity that is the expression of its mode of being. As inertia is generosity with respect to action, and silence is generosity with respect to speech, so death is generosity with respect to existence. Old age is the stage of *Gelassenhait*, or universal "letting be."

REMINISCENCE AND BECOMING IN OLD AGE

Reminiscence is of course about the past, but the point has been made repeatedly in this study that it also has implications for the future. To the extent that we are reconstructing our pasts and ourselves through reminiscence in the life review we are "becoming" someone in the process—someone who is a little different from the one we took for granted in the past or perhaps a very different person from one we ever imagined in the past.

For Socrates the quest of life was to "know thyself," but this was not just for the sake of self-knowledge. The idea was to consciously seek and live out the identity and destiny that was contained in the self-to-be-known. His imperative to know thyself is frequently joined with Pindar's well-known injunction to "become who you are." In our youth, especially in the identity crises of adolescence, we attempt to learn who we are, and thereafter we attempt to live out the life pattern or destiny that we think is most expressive of our inner selves. Of course, as noted earlier, many people do not seriously examine themselves or their lives. They may accept a moratorium at adolescence and live out a "foreclosed" life pattern that is largely externally determined, whether by family, clan, society, or culture.

The reality probably is that most of us do not live a fully examined life. In fact, we find out that important roads we took and important decisions made were *not* made on the basis of a planful or conscious examination of ourselves, our values, or our lives. This does not necessarily mean the roads or decisions were taken because they were externally determined and not part of our own intentionality. As a matter of fact, they might have been taken because of a personal intentionality, a will, or an internal direction of which we were not consciously aware.

When we think of intention and will, we tend to think of it in terms of the commonsense notion of willpower, which presses toward some specific objective. Willpower is very conscious and goal-directed, for example, to lose weight, stop smoking, to learn to drive, to earn a degree of diploma, etc. In this type of utilitarian willing the person is consciously saying, in effect, "I will do this in order to achieve that." However, this is only one type of will, as was noted by Leslie Farber in his book, *The Ways of the Will* (1966). Based on his psychiatric practice and research at the William Allanson White Institute, Farber came to the conclusion that there is another type of will that is not experienced consciously as an *act* of the will but can only be inferred after an *event*. Although this type of will provides directionality and movement to a person's life, it is not immediately available for scrutiny. He concluded that many if not most of the important choices people make in life are not consciously experienced as choices but become known only (if ever) after the fact.

Along with quite a few other practitioners, I agree with Farber on this point. I have had a number of older persons tell me that they did not become aware until after retirement of a number of key choices they had enacted or lived out in their lives that they had not been aware of deciding upon beforehand. These sometimes came to awareness out of the reminiscences of the life-review process. It is as though they did not know the selves they were when they made those decisions, but now they are embarked upon a kind of self-discovery in the life-review process of old age. This is certainly a form of becoming, of becoming aware of who you are, have been, and will continue to be to some extent into the future.

There is a great deal of undifferentiated experience that people live out in their lives that has not been thought about or expressed in language. That is why the opportunity for a self-narrative can add so much to the life-review process and to a greater understanding of self in old age. Such a narrative allows the speaker to draw out from his or her undifferentiated experience a new meaning and to fix it in a statement, in words. Thus, language can be an important resource for the elderly in drawing out the unexamined and unmined experiences of their lives and in seeking personal metaphors that can highlight and make coherent their lives and their selves.

In this respect written reminiscences and self-narratives are particularly valuable, and that is why Progoff's intensive journal method is so effective. It helps people fix experience, without regard to grammar or spelling, in visible words that can be read, reexperienced, and thought about further. It is no accident, by the way, that the journal method has a section for writing about roads taken and not taken in life. By recalling these and writing them out the person can become aware of decisions that were made in that tacit nonconscious way of the will identified by Farber.

Given the many undifferentiated experiences and myriad circumstances of each of our lives, the possibility of any two life stories being the same is quite remote. It has been said that what all persons have in common is their uniqueness. This is extremely important to keep in mind when it comes to the elderly, for they tend to be stereotyped by others as looking alike, thinking alike, and acting alike. Therefore, the more opportunities we can give them to express and experience their uniqueness in group and individual reminiscence or self-narratives, the better. In so doing we are not attempting to make them distinct and *separate* from their fellows, for in reality it is their uniqueness that they can share and have in common. The universal, then, lies at the heart of uniqueness, and this can be experienced by them in a communal way.

We can talk about three kinds of selves: the public, the private, and the unknown. The first is known to others as well as to the self; the second is known to the self but not to others; and the third is not known to the self or to others. We have talked mostly about the first two and just touched on the third in the preceding discussion of unconscious intentions or will. Now, that third self is accessible to awareness, as was indicated earlier with regard to the elderly persons who became aware of the past unconscious life decisions in their reminiscing. To use the language of the self given in Chapter 5, we can say that the dialectical relationship of the I and the Me is always available for the older person to gain new awareness and understandings of the self in the past and present. This experiential inner dialogue can provide for fresh insights, new integrations, and new perspectives in late life, when there is greater reflectiveness, interiority of personality, and (one hopes) greater time to engage in it. Thus, the various deconstructions, reconstructions, and integrations of the self that can come out of this process can be seen as forms of being in becoming.

In the final analysis, however, there is one brute fact that intrudes on any consideration of becoming in late life, and that is death. Surely, this has to put a damper on any sense of becoming, does it not? After all, when compared with other periods of life, the fact that stands out about old age is that there is no period following it. This fact undoubtedly does put a damper on any sense of becoming for many older people. Yet, paradoxically, it has just the opposite effect on others. Facing the fact of death has often led to a radical change in perspective about life and self among the elderly over the course of history. This is what led Saint Augustine to say, "It is only in the fact of death that man's self is born."

How can this be? In answering, it should be recalled that when Robert Butler (1980–81) proposed his theory of the life review, he said that the review process is initiated by the recognition in old age of the imminence of one's personal death. It would not be stretching a point to say that a self can be born in the life-review process while facing the fact of death. Much of the prior material in this book was presented to describe and illustrate the kinds of constructions and reconstructions of self older people engage in during the life-review process. However, the self that is born in such reconstructions is one of identity rather than eternity. That is, it is not an immortal self, and as Ernest Becker (1973) so powerfully demonstrated in *The Denial of Death*, we are all concerned with our own immortality.

The elderly are no exception to this; in fact they are even more concerned about the issue of immortality by virtue of their heightened awareness of the imminence of death. This fact led Robert J. Lifton (1979) to see the life review not only as a means to ego identity and integrity but as a search for "symbolic immortality." Older persons search for immortality through the symbolisms of "living on" in their children, their children's children, their groups and organizations, their works and their religions—usually in the form of a hereafter. However, on the basis of his psychiatric studies of the survivors and effects of nuclear annihilation in Hiroshima and genocide in the Holocaust of World War II, he thinks these long-standing institutional modes of symbolic immortality are not as viable as they once were for most of us.

He does not see the search as hopeless, but it does call for an "intimacy with death" by looking at it squarely and imaginatively in all of its dimensions. If it is denied or if there is no attempt at intimacy with it, the result is a kind of psychic numbing that allows one to go through the motions of preparing for death but not to experience its full existential reality. This would explain the finding of Whitbourne and Weinstock (1986) that the "foreclosed" elderly they studied were able to go through the mechanics of making arrangements for their funerals, burials, and leaving their worldly possessions to their loved ones. Lifton would probably see this as a rather rote institutionalized form of dealing with death and attempting to "live on," but he would see it as lacking real experiential substance.

However, for those elderly who are willing to confront it fully, death enhances imagination, and this enables them to deal with it as a formative or constitutive symbol which Lifton believes can become an element of creativity and renewal:

> Death then symbolizes the human capacity to confront in some way the most fearful aspects of experience and emerge with deepened sensibility and extended vitality and reach. This is what Heinrich Boll had in mind when he said, "The artist carries death in him like a good priest his breviary." Maintaining a psychic place for death, that is, enhances that which is most human, the imagination. (Lifton, 1976)

The use of imagination in Lifton's scheme would include images from the past that can be arranged in new forms and constellations in the life-review process. The reworking of these images in the face of death would lead to an "inner psychological reordering," or what he calls an "experiential transcendence," which he describes as a feeling of oneness in which past, present, and future, as well as self, others, and universe, are merged. However, this level of experience can be reached only by "genuine inner contact leading to confrontation, reordering, and renewal" in the "formative zone of the psyche" (Lifton, 1976). Lifton calls this zone the person's road to the self, the road to the 'center' of his being." There, in that formative zone "the vision of death gives life," and that is a "becoming."

PERSONAL REFLECTIONS

Lifton's language is highly figurative, almost poetic, and it is appealing in terms of the conceptions of the self and experiencing set forth in the earlier chapters. However, what he wrote did not become real for me until I could actually associate it with a real person, someone whose experiences fit his descriptions. I will give an example of one such person shortly, but I would first like to explain something about this section on "personal reflections." Not only is it personal in the sense that it represents my subjective reflections on the salient findings of this study, as noted in the beginning of this chapter, it also reflects my personal reactions to what I learned from the people I was presumably "studying."

What I discovered in the course of the Integrity Survey is that I was actually learning a great deal personally from the elderly respondents in a very direct experiential way. I found myself checking my own aging experiences with theirs as they described them. I became aware that I was engaging in a kind of dialogic process of learning directly from them rather than from their responses on a questionnaire or to structured questions in an interview. There was that, too, but that was planned for and anticipated. That was not the same as the direct knowledge I gained from the accumulated experience and wisdom of the elderly participants in our face-to-face contacts. With this in mind, I would like to turn now to a participant from whom I learned a great deal and who personified Lifton's views on the confrontation with and experiential transcendence of death.

Grace Worth was a member of the senior center writing group described in the preceding chapter. She was a soft-spoken woman of 67 who had been widowed for eight years at the time she was interviewed in the Integrity Survey. Although tall and statuesque, with an attractive strawberry blond complexion, there was a frailty in her physical appearance. This was explained by the fact that she had a serious heart condition, having suffered a cardiac arrest a year earlier, which necessitated implantation of a pace-maker. There was also a pervasive theme of sudden illness and premature deaths in her life story. Her experience with death began early, when she was pronounced dead of diphtheria at age 3 but somehow had begun breathing again and had pulled through. She was the youngest of six children, seven years younger than her youngest brother. She described her childhood as "a very, very good one," and she had very warm memories of the time when the whole family was together in the large old house in the Vermont countryside from as far back as she could remember.

Despite closeness and happiness of the family there was a great deal of serious illness. Her mother and father died when she was a senior in high school. As the youngest child in the large family she was the only one to finish high school, and they had all looked forward to her graduation. However, her mother and father died three months apart, just a few months before her graduation. All but one of her brothers and sisters had died when they were in their forties. The last one, her youngest brother, had died just three months before the survey interview.

She was acutely aware of the discontinuity of the generations in her family, and her biggest regret was that her parents never lived to see her own children "because they dearly loved children." She had four children of her own, but her oldest daughter died at age 38, on the day of her parents' 40th anniversary. Mrs. Worth's husband then died one month later. All of these losses were devastating to her, but the death of her last remaining sibling three months before shook her to her very foundations. She said she lost all sense of security and continuity because he was the last link to her childhood. She described what she went through, and it clearly represented a major psychosocial transition and life review that had all the earmarks of the "inner psychological reordering" and "experiential transcendence" described by Lifton.

Her imagery and reminiscences were vivid. For example, she could recall frequently sitting in her mother's lap in an old rocking chair, and she could not only visualize her mother but could distinctly recall the fresh scent her mother always had. She would invariably associate that scent with her mother in the fond and reassuring recollections she had of her childhood.

Such imagery was very much a part of the transitional period after her youngest brother's death, and in the process she began connecting the images of her own childhood (parents and siblings) with images of her own children and grandchildren. Her love of the countryside was also very prominent in that imagery, and as a result she now found herself taking her grandchildren at every opportunity into the countryside to point out the joys and beauty of nature to them. After describing this she went on to say the following: "You know, material things, possessions, don't matter to me; I've seen so much transience of things—and people. I find the greatest satisfactions in the simple everyday experiences—like seeing the moon through the trees . . . the sunrise . . . snow on the meadow . . . a creek in the woods . . ."

This reminded her of being by a trout stream with one of her grandchildren on a recent trip to Vermont. She enthusiastically described the setting and the profound pleasure of being there with her granddaughter. It was so memorable that she had the impulse to write a piece of poetry about the setting when they got back. She did so and then gave it to her granddaughter as a remembrance of their communion with one another and with nature. She said this was the kind of legacy she would like to pass on to the future in her grandchildren—that is the same reverent love of nature and of being a part of nature. Given her heart and her family history, she was acutely aware of her own personal transience and of how precious, therefore, the present is in all of its natural simplicity and directness. She expressed this in a poem entitled "Thanksgiving," which she composed as a member of the writers' group:

Chill, sounds, and smells of autumn
Mine as I walked along
A quiet, peaceful country road
And heard a blue jay's song.

A hen hawk hovered overhead,
More silent than the day.
He searched the wide fields closely
Then soared off on his way.

I thought, why can't the whole world know
Such beauties as I see?
I wish that everyone would own
These shinings in simplicity.

Take moments as *you* walk along
To see the riches yours to see
And count Thanksgiving every day.
Its cornucopia, free.

INTIMATIONS

It has been said that "the past is like the body of time and the future like its soul" (Grudin, 1982). This metaphor is quite appropriate in considering that reminiscence, when fully engaged in, is embodied. The way in which it is experienced and the language in which it is expressed arise from and are embedded in the mortal human body. What then happens to reminiscence and to the quality and meaning of existence (soul) as that body declines in old age? It is necessary to trace out the full implications of this because the concept of embodiment has been so central to this experiential study of reminiscence. This will be difficult to do without my having fully experienced the process firsthand, so the best that can be done is to try to glimpse the intimations within oneself, one's own body, and the intimations provided by others.

It will be recalled that the rather contented and contemplative older persons we found in the Group Project and that Lieberman and Tobin found in their Chicago study engaged in less reminiscing after the life review, although they generally enjoyed it when they did so. What they were saying, in essence, when we interviewed them afterward was that after the life review they found less need to hold onto the past as a distinct entity, as a possession. Past and present seemed to merge, so in a sense the past was somehow immersed in the present and lost as a distinct entity. There was no expression of regret about this but an acceptance of it as a rather natural occurrence that they felt no need to explain. There was also a different quality and purpose to the reminiscence in which they did engage, although our elderly respondents did not fully articulate this.

Carl Jung (1961) did articulate this in his old age, since as a psychiatrist he was more attuned to such inner exploration and explication. He said the following:

> With increasing age, contemplation, and reflection, the inner images naturally play an even greater part in man's life. . . . In old age one begins to let memories unroll before the mind's eye and, musing, to recognize oneself in the inner and outer images of the past. This is like a preparation for an existence in the hereafter, just as in Plato's view, philosophy is a preparation for death.

Although Jung has at times been criticized as having too spiritual a view of human psychology, he remained thoroughly convinced of the biological basis and grounding of human existence in nature. The curve of life conforms to the law of nature, with the acme at middle age and a gradual descent thereafter into and through old age. Within the body's wisdom there is a knowledge of dying, although the conscious mind might deny it or attempt to avoid it by various stratagems. Jung (1959) described the natural life cycle as follows:

> Life is an energy process. Like every energy process, it is in principle irreversible and is therefore unequivocally directed towards a goal. That goal is a state of rest. In the long run everything that happens is, as it were, nothing more than the initial disturbance of a perpetual state of rest which forever attempts to reestablish itself. Life is teleology par excellence; it is the intrinsic striving towards a goal, and the living organism is a system of directed aims which

seek to fulfill themselves. The end of every process is its goal. All energy flow is like a runner who strives with the greatest effort and the utmost expenditure of strength to reach his goal. Youthful longing for the world and for life, for the attainment of high hopes and distant goals, is life's obvious teleological urge which at once changes into fear of life, neurotic resistances, depressions and phobias if at some point it remains caught in the past, or shrinks from risks without which the unseen goal cannot be achieved. With the attainment of maturity and at the zenith of biological existence, life's drive towards a goal in no wise halts. With the same intensity and irresistibility with which it strove upward before middle age, life now descends; for the goal lies no longer on the summit, but in the valley where the ascent began. The curve of life is like the parabola of a projectile which, disturbed from its initial state of rest, rises and then returns to a state of repose.

Jung (1959) felt that it "is just as neurotic in old age not to focus upon the goal of death as it is in youth to repress fantasies which have to do with the future." Thus, he would appreciate the healthy, nonneurotic and natural sentiment expressed by the elderly Landor (1980) when he wrote:

I warmed both hands before the fire of life,
It sinks, and I am ready to depart.

He would also agree with Allan Watts who said, "The secret of life is knowing when to stop" (quoted in Furlong, 1986). Although both Landor and Watts expressed these sentiments when in their seventies, they displayed the same capacity for "letting go" and for not hanging onto the past or life as a hoarded possession, much like the contented 80 and 90-year-olds described earlier.

To return to the earlier question of what happens to reminiscence in relation to soul as the body declines in old age, it can be said that those who cannot confront their mortality and the images of death will attempt to hoard the past in the form of retentive (rather than creative) reminiscence and will not be able to truly live in the present. Jung (1959) expressed it in this way:

Natural life is the nourishing soil of the soul. Anyone who fails to go along with life remains suspended, stiff and rigid in mid-air. That is why so many people get wooden in old age; they look back and cling to the past with a secret fear of death in their hearts. They withdraw from the life process, at least psychologically, and consequently remain fixed like nostalgic pillars of salt, with vivid recollections of youth but no living relation to the present.

Just as there is less need to hold onto the past as a possession, there is less need to hold onto things and material objects as possessions among the more integrated and reconciled elderly. It will be recalled that Rosa V. in

Chapter 9 spoke about the antiques she and her husband had collected as "just things" and that Grace Worth in this chapter expressed a similar indifference to material things, yet these two women were both among the highest in ego integrity, as determined by testing and interview, that we found in the Integrity Survey. They personified the "being" mode of existence that Erich Fromm (1981) contrasted with the "having" mode and that he described as follows: "In the having mode of my existence my relationship to the world is one of possessing and owning, one in which I want to make everybody and everything, including myself, my property." On the other hand, the being mode is equated with "the concept of *process, activity, and movement as an element in being* . . . the idea that being implies change, i.e., that being is *becoming.*" Thus, one mode (being) views life as a process, while the other (having) views life as a concrete substance, something that can be possessed. It seems clear that older persons who view life as a process are better equipped to handle the inevitable losses of things, the self, and life itself than are those who view life as a concrete entity to be possessed.

Fromm claimed that the thinking of Master Eckhart represented one of the clearest positions against the having mode. The essence of Eckhart's concept of nonattachment or "no-thingness" was the idea that the person who wants nothing is the person who is not greedy for anything—things, self, or life. From this perspective and from the view of a natural life descent, the need for reminiscence to retain a distinct sense of self or identity decreases in very late life at a time when one needs to let go of that possessive sense of self or ego in order to die at peace within the larger scheme of life and eternity. This would seem to be the "natural" and only position to take, given the embodied concept of reminiscence and self adopted in this study.

William James (1969) seemed to hold with the concept of nonattachment when he wrote, "Everything added to the Self is a burden as well as a pride" and when he quoted Eckhart on the "still desert" of the Godhead, "where never was seen difference, neither Father, Son, nor Holy Ghost, where there is no one at home, yet where the spark of the soul is more at peace." James was quite concerned about the acquisitive nature of the Material Me and the possessive attachments of the Social Me, and he saw, therefore, that these would have to be "let go" in that order, leaving the remaining Spiritual Me to become the "Thou" to the "I" in the final dialogue of life.

Mead, along with James, saw the I as the growing edge of the self-as-object, of the Me. He also saw it as the spontaneous center of creativity, of insights, and of intentionality. The intentionality of the I is indeed mysterious, but it does exhibit itself objectively in cerebral functioning as Penfield Wilder (1975) found in his research on the human brain. Additionally, Mead saw the I as timeless—as pure experiencing—and it would seem that this timeless I is expressed in "pure being," as this has been described by various authors to be quoted shortly. Erikson (1982) speaks of the I "as a center of awareness in a universe of communicable experience, a center so numinous that it amounts to a sense of being alive and, more, of being the vital condition of existence." Given the natural arc of life, it would seem that in the earlier years of life, when the I is energized by a dynamic élan vital, it expresses our intentionality in spontaneity and action; whereas in old age it becomes more and more of a pure consciousness and being.

Experientially, what appears to be happening is a natural blurring with advanced age of the self–object dichotomy that marks our state of mind during most of our waking hours and lives. In our younger years it is only at peak moments—religious, creative, orgasmic—that we briefly lose that dichotomous state of mind in the form of a true experiential transcendence, but in late life that state of mind becomes more accessible in a less frantic and more contemplative way (Ornstein, 1986).

When we are younger, the physical immediacy of the present in its concrete availability tends to blind us to its spiritual qualities. Even many elderly persons, because of the methodical, object-oriented kind of thinking required in our technological society, foreclose on that potential for a different kind of consciousness in late life. Tillich (1959a) has written that the concentration of peoples' activities upon methodical investigation and technical transformation of their world, including themselves, has led to a loss of "the dimension of depth" in their encounter with reality so that "reality has lost its inner transcendence or, in another metaphor, its transparency for the eternal." He expands upon this idea further:

> People who are never aware of this dimension lose the possibility of resting in the present. As the letter to the Hebrews describes it, they never enter into the divine rest. They are held by the past and cannot separate themselves from it, or they escape towards the future unable to rest in the present. They have not entered the eternal rest which stops the flux of time and gives us the blessing of the present. Perhaps this is the most conspicuous characteristic of our period, especially in the Western world and particularly, in this country. It lacks the courage to accept "presence" because it has lost the dimension of the eternal. (Tillich, 1959b)

Tillich holds that this capacity for "presence" enables us to experience the "eternal now" that suddenly transforms and transcends the flux of time. Mircea Eliade (1959) had called this the "continuous present," which he equates with mythical time as well as with eternity and says that this continuous present is not only apprehended as the here-and-now but also is inseparable from the past and future.

It is in a state of being rather than doing or having that one can experience the eternal now, and the wisdom of being has been expressed in different ways in very different cultures. Eckhart expressed it in the statement

"People should not consider so much what they are to *do* as what they *are*."
Lao-Tse went even further and said, "The Way to do is to be," which is a
credo for all of life, not just old age. In any case, the being mode provides us
with the opportunity to dwell in the present and behold the spirit and inner
transcendence of its reality. It is such experiences that led Gabriel Marcel
(1960) to write at length of the "mystery of being."

CONCLUSIONS

Much of the preceding section had to do with intimations or speculations
about what happens to reminiscence, the self, and consciousness or existence in very late life. yet we are concerned here primarily with the relationship between reminiscence and the self in that part of old age when identity and the self are very central to the person's life. As has been shown
repeatedly in this book, reminiscence has very important functions for the
self throughout most of old age, from about 60 to approximately 85, depending upon organic factors in the aging process.

There is a need here to follow through on the implications of the experiential approach to reminiscence and the self so as to come to some conclusions about the relationship between these central topics of the book.
Again, much of this section is going to be in the nature of personal observations, which have been private up until now, since they were germinating at
an experiential level in the course of this study and have not yet been explicated by me.

Early in the book I mentioned the long relationship in human history between reminiscence and the self going all the way back to Socrates and his
imperative to "know thyself." This could be done only through reminiscence
or the method of discourse known as *anamnesis*. Throughout this whole
study in the back of my mind was a question about Socrates' statement to
the effect that the unexamined life is not worth living. At various points and
in various ways this question has been touched upon in the preceding chapters. However, at this point it has to be confronted head on. Earlier it was
reported, for example, that over half of the respondents in the Integrity Survey claimed that they reminisced in order to come to a better understanding of themselves and their lives. But does this represent an "examined
life"?

Perhaps the best way to approach this whole question is to go back to the
ancient Greek idea, or concept, or *eudaimonia*, which is "the condition of
living in harmony with one's daimon or innate potentiality, 'living in truth to
oneself' " (Norton, 1976). According to this concept every person is both his
empirical actuality and his ideal possibility, or daimon, and it is each person's responsibility to discover the daimon within the self and then to live in

accordance with it. Since the conditions of existence are incompatible with perfection or with becoming the idea (daimon), each person's unique daimon can be approached only in varying degrees of self-actualization. The progressive explication of the daimon in the person's empirical actuality constitutes what the Greeks called the person's "destiny." Heraclitus said, "Man's character is his daimon," and his responsibility was to recognize his daimon, to embrace it, and to embody it as much as humanly possible in himself and his works.

This is, of course, a very modern idea as well. "Self-actualization" is much talked and written about today. Gandhi spoke of *moksha*, or "self-realization," and Jung described his concept of individuation as "becoming what I am by being what I was intended to be." Thus, we can speak of a unique telos, or destiny, for every person, but whether it is recognized or realized by the person is another question. Much of the current writing about using mythology for self-actualization, based heavily on the impressive and significant work of Joseph Campbell, is in effect attempting to help the person to link the self with a myth that expresses the daimon, or ideal, for that person. It is important, however, to distinguish this type of mythologizing from the type that was mentioned earlier in relation to very elderly persons who create myths about themselves and their pasts in order to preserve some sense of self in the face of organic deterioration of mental as well as physical functioning. Such mythologizing tends to be too extreme and grandiose to have any basis in reality and represents a desperate last-ditch effort to retain some identifiable sense of self.

Erikson (1982) warned, "We must acknowledge in old age a retrospective mythologizing that can amount to a pseudointegration as a defense against lurking despair." Apropos of Erikson, his statement that to achieve ego integrity it is necessary to accept one's one and only life cycle as something that "had to be and that would not permit any substitutions" could be related to the eudaimonic idea that each person has a unique life to live based upon the self one was intended to be. Thus, Erikson's statement would not mean fatalistic acceptance that life could not be any other way but that the person recognizes and accepts his or her unique destiny. Those who did not attempt to realize or become themselves would then be in despair in recognizing that they did not become that unique self and that there was too little time left to do so. Erikson (1982) did speak, after all, of "identity potentials bypassed" and of "an all too limiting identity lived."

Such a limiting identity would be the result of accepting readily available or socially prescribed roles or scripts without serious self-examination or concern about authentic self-actualization. This has been called "bad faith" by existentialist writers like Jean-Paul Sartre. One writer described "bad faith" as "resulting from collusion with others about who one is and thus living as a *me* that has lost touch with and suppressed its *I*" (Aylwin, 1985). In his early writings, Sartre (1966) did view the I as, in effect, a pure consciousness from which the individual was utterly free to make choices that were totally autonomous of the socially constructed and attuned Me. However, toward the end of his life—when working on his biographical study of Flaubert—Sartre (1964) said, "Flaubert was free to be Flaubert but not free to be someone else." Thus, in his old age Sartre tempered his initial position of radical existential freedom to one that incorporates *eudaimonia*, or destiny.

I cannot accept the term "bad faith" in the sense Sartre originally meant it when considering the lives of the elderly persons I have studied. The conditions and contingencies of their lives were often such that it is next to impossible to see the absolute freedom to choose that he originally posited. Natanson (1970) used the term "bad faith" to refer to a "freezing of the past" in some elderly persons that allows no flexibility for choice or action in the future. This sort of elderly person would engage in a great deal of retentive reminiscence in which only the past offered any good or valuable options for choice, so it is either impossible or fruitless to choose and to act in the present or future. This is not an uncommon problem among the elderly, but it seems extreme to call even this "bad faith."

Natanson views the I as the seat of intentionality and the source of "authentic" decision making, so the person who has succumbed to the prevailing roles and stereotypes in forming an identity would be seen as "inauthentic" or lacking an authentic self. This term, too, I have difficulty with because it is too categorical and too judgmental. It suggests a dichotomy of authentic or inauthentic and nothing in between. It seems more acceptable to me to speak of a realized self rather than an authentic self, for it allows for degrees of self-realization, which seems more reflective of the realities of human existence.

The term "truth" can also be problematic, as noted earlier in distinguishing between narrative and historical truth. It seems to me that narrative truth has to be based on "truths of self," which Socrates saw as those based on one's daimon. To speak a truth that belongs to someone else is to speak an untruth, and a narrative should hew to those truths that are unique to one's self, to one's daimon. As Norton (1976) states, "Living one's own truth constitutes integrity, the consummate virtue." If character is our daimon, as Heraclitus claimed, then we are in a position to assess whether a person's self-narrative is "true to character," and indeed many of the narratives I have heard *are* true to character, but some are not.

Given the many contingencies and chance happenings that can occur in a person's life, it is important to distinguish destiny from fate. It might be someone's destiny to become a superb concert pianist, but it might be his or her fate to have that career denied because of accident, illness, or some other circumstances. Destiny may reside in the self as a potentiality, but it can be realized only in the outer world. Thus, the dialectic of self–world is crucial in living out one's one and only life cycle.

Often a person's destiny is lived out within the confines and contingencies of a life that does not seem to offer many options for self-realization, yet somehow the person does realize a great deal of self-potential by virtue of an inner vision and application. This kind of self-realization was exemplified by Ralph D., who was presented under "Narrative of an Individual" in Chapter 8. Despite the overt rejection and discouragement of his father, he embraced and lived out his own vision, or *daimon*, to become an army officer and to command men—and to do it exceptionally well. There were others whose self-narratives showed that they had an awareness of living out a unique destiny. To one extent or another this was true of many, if not most, of the elderly persons interviewed in the Integrity Survey because self-realization is a matter of degree, after all. The recognition and reconstruction of that self in the course of reminiscence and the self-narrative were among the most satisfying features of their lives in old age.

Thus, there is the creative pleasure and fascination of re-creating the story of one's destiny and one's self through reminiscence, which we can look forward to in old age. There is also a possibility of a change of consciousness to a more accepting and contemplative state of being. In that state memories can take on a richness never experienced before in life. Robert Ornstein (1986) reports that the vividness and freshness of perception attributed to childhood is actually more often a reconstruction based on later adult associative capacities interacting with a *memory* of the more direct sensory contact of the child. He uses the following passage by Wordsworth to illustrate his point:

> There was a time when meadow, grove, and stream,
> The earth, and every common sight,
> To me did seem
> Apparelled in celestial light,
> The glory and the freshness of a dream.

Ornstein explains that the experience depicted in the poem is probably not within the psychological scope of any child. Instead, the experience gains its richness from adult memories and now functions subject to a different mode of consciousness. This mode of consciousness was available to many of the older persons described in this book. So in addition to the central role it can play in the maintenance, enhancement, and re-creation of the self in old age, reminiscence offers the riches of such memories. Those of us who are already old enough to partake of these riches can attest to them, and those of us who are not yet old can look forward to the treasures they hold.

The mode of consciousness that provides these riches is the mode of being. This is not easily achieved. For most of us it takes a lifetime, and for some others it is never achieved. Its achievement requires a philosophical attitude — contemplative and meditative — not a formal philosophical system or religious creed, although these might help. It is what Erikson (1982) calls the *"philo-sophical"* style of old age, and "in maintaining some order and meaning in the dis-integration of the body and mind, it can also advocate a durable hope in wisdom." Indeed, it does appear that older persons with this more philosophical and contemplative attitude generally show better mental health and life satisfaction, as noted earlier.

Now, there is a view of philosophy that is commensurate with the wisdom of old age posited by Erikson. It has been stated as follows: "The function of philosophy in human life is to help man remember. *It has no other task.* And anything that calls itself a philosophy which does not serve this function is simply not philosophy" (Needleman, 1984). But to remember what? To remember the profound division we all experience from the beginning of our lives between our wish for being and our psychosocial needs. The being we wish for is that state of "presence" or living in the "eternal now" of which Tillich spoke. However, our need to contend with the inner and outer pressures of daily existence preempt this wish for being, particularly in the earlier part of the life cycle. Jacob Needleman (1984), a contemporary American philosopher, has said that it is absolutely essential for man that "he remember this truth about himself. If he does not, he will be absorbed by the external forces of nature and society. He will be 'lived' by the emotions, opinions, obligations, terrors, programs, and conflicts that comprise the day-to-day life of every human being."

Nevertheless, we do get absorbed in this way, even in old age, and "we think of memory only as recall because the experience of deep memory has vanished from our lives" (Needleman, 1984). Therefore, it is necessary to go back to the deep remembering and reminiscence that Socrates practiced with his method of *anamnesis*. His kind of remembering "begins from just this condition of internal division along the ontologically fundamental lines of human nature: on the one hand the primal, original impulse toward being; and on the other hand, the numerous psychological functions and faculties that are designed to deal with the material world around us" (Needleman, 1984). The dialectic between these initially antithetical lines of human nature is not apt to be resolved until old age, when the balance is finally tipped toward being. Only then can we truly remember. "And if one asks, "What, then is remembered?" the answer can only be: my Self" (Needleman, 1984).

Appendix A
The Experiencing Scale

EXP Stage	Content	Treatment
1	External events; refusal to participate	Impersonal, detached
2	External events; behavioral or intellectual self-description	Interest, personal, self-participation
3	Personal reactions to external events; limited self-descriptions; behavioral descriptions of feelings	Reactive, emotionally involved
4	Descriptions of feelings and personal experiences	Self-descriptive, associative
5	Problems or propositions about feeings and personal experiences	Exploratory, elaborative, hypothetical
6	Synthesis of readily accessible feelings and experiences to resolve personally significant issues.	Feelings vividly expressed, integrative, conclusive, or affirmative
7	Full, easy presentation of experiencing; all elements confidently integrated	Expansive, illuminating, confident, buoyant

Appendix B
Focusing: Short Form

1. Clear a Space

- How are you? What's between you and feeling fine?
- Don't answer: let what comes in your body do the answering.
- Don't go into anything.
- Greet each concern that comes. Put each aside for awhile, next to you.
- Except for that, are you fine?

2. Felt Sense

- Pick one problem to focus on.
- Don't go into the problem. What do you sense in your body when you recall the whole of that problem?
- Sense all of that, the sense of the whole thing, the murky discomfort or the unclear body sense of it

3. Get a Handle

- What is the quality of the felt sense?
- What one word, phrase, or image comes out of this felt sense?
- What quality word would fit it best?

4. Resonate

- Go back and forth between words (or images) and the felt sense. Is that right?
- If they match, have the sensation of matching several times.
- If the felt sense changes, follow it with your attention.

5. Ask

- "What is it, about the whole problem, that makes me so . . .?"
- "What is the worst part of it?" "What does it need?"

6. Receive

- Welcome what came. Be glad it spoke. It is only one step on this problem, not the last.
- Now that you know where it is, you can leave it and come back to it later.
- Protect it from critical voices that interrupt.
- Stay with it awhile.

Does your body want another round of focusing, or is this a good stopping place?

References

Arendt, H., *The Human Condition* (Chicago: University of Chicago Press, 1958), 137.

Arieti, S. *Creativity: The Magic Synthesis* (New York: Basic Books, 1976).

Atwood, M. *Cat's Eye* (New York: Doubleday, 1989).

Austin, J. L., *How to Do Things with Words* (Oxford: Clarendon Press, 1962).

Aylwin, S. *Structure in Thought and Feeling* (London: Methuen and Co., 1985).

Bandura, A. "Self-Efficacy: Towards a Unifying Theory of Behavioral Change," *Psychological Review*, 84(1977), 191–215.

Becker, E. *The Denial of Death*, (New York: The Free Press, 1973).

Bellah, R. N. "The Active Life and the Contemplative Life," *Daedalus*, 105(1976), 71–72.

Bengtson, V. L. *The Social Psychology of Aging* (Indianapolis: Bobbs-Merrill, 1973).

Bengtson, V. L., M. N. Reedy, and C. Gordon. "Aging and Self-Conceptions: Personality Processes and Social Contexts." In *Handbook of the Psychology of Aging*, J. E. Birren and K. W. Schaie, Eds. (New York: Van Nostrand Reinhold, 1985), 544–615.

Berenson, B. *Sunset and Twilight* (New York: Harcourt, Brace, & World, 1963).

Berger, P. L., and T. Luckmann. *The Social Construction of Reality* (Garden City, NY: Doubleday, 1966)

Berman, H. J. "May Sarton's Journals: Attachment and Separateness in Late Life." In *Research on Adulthood and Aging*, L. E. Thomas, Ed. (Albany: State University of New York Press, 1989), 19.

Birren, J. E. *The Psychology of Aging* (Englewood Cliffs, NJ: Prentice Hall, 1964).

Boylin, W., S. K. Gordon, and M. F. Nehrke. "Reminiscence and Ego Integrity in Institutionalized Elderly Males," *The Gerontologist*, 16(1976), 118–124.

Bradburn, N. M., and D. Caplowitz. *Reports on Happiness* (Chicago: Aldin, 1965).

Brewer, W. F. "What Is Autobiographical Memory?" In *Autobiographical Memory*, D. C. Rubin, Ed. (Cambridge: Cambridge University Press, 1986), 27.

Bruner, J. S. "Myth and Identity." In *Myth and Mythmaking*, H. A. Murray, Ed. (New York: George Braziller, 1960), 281.

Bruner, J. S. "On Cognitive Growth." In J. S. Bruner, R. R. Oliver, et al., Eds. *Studies in Cognitive Growth* (New York: Wiley, 1966), 1–29.

Bruner, J. S. *Actual Minds, Possible Worlds*. (Cambridge, MA: Harvard University Press, 1986).

Bruner, J. S. "Life as Narrative," *Social Research*, 54(1987), 11–32.

Bugelski, B. R. "Words and Things and Images," *American Psychologist*, 25(1970), 1002–1012.

Buhler, C. "The Course of Human Life as a Psychological Problem," *Human Development*, 11(1968), 184–200.

Butler, J. M., and G. H. Haigh. "Changes in the Relation between Self-Concepts and Ideal Concepts Consequent upon Client-Centered Counseling." In *Psychotherapy and Personality Change*, C. R. Rogers and R. F. Dymond, Eds. (Chicago: University of Chicago Press, 1954), 55–75.

Butler, R. N. "The Life Review: An Interpretation of Reminiscence in the Aged," *Psychiatry*, 26(1963), 65–75.

Butler, R. N. "The Life Review: An Unrecognized Bonanza," *Journal of Aging and Human Development*, 12(1980–81), 35–38.

Butler, R. N., and M. Lewis. *Aging and Mental Health: Positive Psychosocial Approaches* (St. Louis: C. V. Mosby, 1983).

Cairns, D. "An Approach to Husserlian Phenomenology." In *Phenomenology and Existentialism*, R. M. Zaner and D. Ihde, Eds. (New York: G. P. Putnam's Sons, 1973), 32.

Cameron, P. "The Generation Gap: Time Orientation," *The Gerontologist*, 12(1972), 117–119.

Casey, E. S. *Remembering: A Phenomenological Study* (Bloomington: Indiana University Press, 1989).

Cassirer, E. *Essay on Man*, (New York: Doubleday Anchor, 1944), 52.

Castelnuovo-Tedesco, P. "Reminiscence and Nostalgia: The Pleasure and Pain of Remembering." In *The Course of Life: Psychoanalytic Contributions Toward Understanding Personality Development*, Vol. 3, S. Greenspan and G. Pollock, Eds. (Washington, DC: U.S. Department of Health and Human Services, 1980), 115–127.

Chown, S. M. "Age and the Rigidities," *Journal of Gerontology*, 16(1961), 353–362.

Clark, M., and G. Anderson. *Culture and Aging* (Springfield, IL: Charles C. Thomas, 1967).

Clayton, V. "Erikson's Theory of Human Development as It Applies to the Aged: Wisdom as Contradictive Cognition," *Human Development*, 18(1975), 119–128.

Cooley, C. H. *Human Nature and the Social Order* (New York: Charles Scribner's 1902).

Corsa, H. S. "Psychoanalytic Concepts of Creativity and Aging: The Fate of Creativity in Mid-Years and Old Age," *Journal of Geriatric Psychiatry*, 6(1973), 173.

Costa, R. T., and R. R. McCrae. "Age Differences in Personality Structure: A Cluster Analysis Approach," *Journal of Gerontology*, 31(1976), 564–570.

Coulter, J. *The Social Construction of Mind: Studies in Ethnomethodology and Linguistic Philosophy* (Totowa, NJ: Rowman and Littlefield, 1979), 109.

Cowley, M. *The View from 80* (New York: Viking Press, 1980), 6–7.

Csikszentmihalyi, M. "Mapping the Moral Domain," *New York Times* Book Review, 28 May 1989, 6.

Csikszentmihalyi, M., & O. Beattie. "Life Themes: A Theoretical and Empirical Exploration of Their Origins and Effects," *Journal of Humanistic Psychology*, 19(1979), 45–63.

Csikszentmihalyi, M., and R. Larson. *Being Adolescent* (New York: Basic Books, 1984).

Csikszentmihalyi, M., & E. Rochberg-Halton. *The Meaning of Things: Domestic Symbols and the Self* (Cambridge: Cambridge University Press, 1981).

Datan, N. "Male and Female: The Search for Synthesis." In *Dialectic: A Humanistic Rationale for Behavior and Development*, J. F. Rychlak, Ed. (Basel: S. Karger, 1976), 44–52.

de Beauvoir, S. *The Coming of Age* (New York: Warner Paperback Library, 1973), 699.

Denzin, N. K. *Interpretive Interactionism* (Newbury Park, CA: Sage Publications, 1989), 144.

Dewey, J. *Art as Experience* (New York: G. P. Putnam's Sons, 1934).

Edie, J. M. *Speaking and Meaning: The Phenomenology of Language* (Bloomington: Indiana University Press, 1976), 160.

Edie, J. M. *William James and Phenomenology* (Bloomington: Indiana University Press, 1978).

Edwards, N., & L. Klemmack. "Correlates of Life Satisfaction: A Re-examination," *Journal of Gerontology*, 28(1973), 497–502.

Eliade, M. *Cosmos and History: The Myth of the Eternal Return* (New York: Torchbooks, 1959).

Eliot, T. S. *The Use of Poetry and the Use of Criticism* (London: Faber & Faber, 1964), 118–119.

Epting, F. R. *Personal Construct Counseling and Psychotherapy* (Chichester, England: John Wiley & Sons, 1984), 15.

Erikson, E. H. "Identity and the Life Cycle: Selected Papers," *Psychological Issues*, 1(1959), 5–165.

Erikson, E. H. *Childhood and Society*, 2nd ed. (New York: Norton, 1963).

Erikson, E. H. *Identity: Youth and Crisis* (New York: W. W. Norton, 1968)

Erikson, E. H. "Dr. Borg's Life Cycle," *Daedalus*, 105(1976), 23.

Erikson, E. H. "The Galilean Sayings and the Sense of 'I,'" *Yale Review*, 70(1981), 321–362.

Erikson, E. H. *The Life Cycle Completed* (New York: W. W. Norton, 1982), 87.

Erlich, A. B. "The Life Review and the Elderly: A Study in Self-Concept, Recognition, and Re-cognition" (Ph.D. diss., California School of Professional Psychology, Los Angeles, 1979).

Farber, L. H. *The Ways of the Will* (New York: Basic Books, 1966).

Feinstein, D,. and S. Krippner. *Personal Mythology: The Psychology of Your Evolving Self* (Los Angeles: Jeremy D. Tarcher, 1988).

Flew, A. *A Dictionary of Philosophy* (New York: St. Martin's Press, 1979), 284.

Freeman, M., M. Csikszentmihalyi, and R. Larson. "Adolescence and Its Recollection: Toward an Interpretive Model of Development," *Merrill-Palmer Quarterly*, 32(1986), 167–185.

Friedman, I. "Phenomenal, Ideal, and Projected Conceptions of Self," *Journal of Abnormal and Social Psychology*, 51(1955), 611–615.

Fromm, E. *To Have or To Be?* (New York: Bantam Books, 1981), 128.

Furlong, M. *Zen Effects: The Life of Alan Watts* (Boston: Houghton Mifflin, 1986).

Geertz, C. *The Interpretation of Cultures* (New York: Basic Books, 1973), 140.

Gendlin, E. T. *Experiencing and the Creation of Meaning* (New York: Free Press, 1962).

Gendlin, E. T. "Experiential Psychotherapy." In *Current Psychotherapies*, F. Corsini, Ed. (Itasco, IL: F. E. Peacock, 1974).

Gendlin, E. T. *Focusing*, 2nd ed. (New York: Bantam Books, 1981).

Gendlin, E. T. "Experiential Phenomenology," In *Phenomenology and the Social Sciences*, M. Natanson, Ed. (Evanston, IL: Northwestern University Press, 1973).

Gendlin, E. T., J. Beebe, J. Cassens, M. H. Klein, and M. Oberlander. "Focusing Ability in Psychotherapy, Personality, and Creativity." In *Research in Psychotherapy*, Vol. 3, J. Shlein, Ed. (Washington, DC: American Psychological Association, 1967).

Gendlin, E. T., and T. M. Tomlinson. "The Process Conception and Its Measurement." In *The Therapeutic Relationship and Its Impact*, C. Rogers, Ed. (Madison: University of Wisconsin Press, 1967).

Gergen, K. J., and M. M. Gergen. "Narratives of the Self." In *Studies in Social Identity*, T. R. Sarbin and K. E. Scheibe, Eds. (New York: Praeger, 1983).

Giambra, L. "Daydreaming about the Past: The Time Setting of Spontaneous Thought Intrusions," *The Gerontologist*, 17(1977), 35–38.

Gilbert, A. N., and Charles J. Wysocki. "Smell Survey Results," *National Geographic*, 172(1987), 523.

Gilligan, C. *In a Different Voice: Psychological Theory and Women's Development* (Cambridge, MA: Harvard University Press, 1982).

Gilligan, C., J. V. Ward, and J. M. Taylor, Eds. *A Contribution of Women's Thinking to Psychological Theory and Education* (Cambridge, MA: Harvard University Press, 1989).

Giorgi, A. *Psychology as a Human Science: A Phenomenologically Based Approach* (New York: Harper and Row, 1970).

Goffman, E. *The Presentation of Self in Everyday Life* (New York: Doubleday, 1959).

Goldstein, H. *Creative Change: A Cognitive Humanistic Approach to Social Work Practice* (New York: Tavistock, 1984), 45.

Gordon, C., and K. J. Gergen, Eds. *The Self in Social Interaction: Classic and Contemporary Perspectives* (New York: Wiley, 1968).

Grudin, R. *Time and the Art of Living* (New York: Ticknor & Fields, 1982).

Guidano, V. F., and G. Liotti. *Cognitive Processes and Emotional Disorders* (New York: Guilford Press, 1983).

Gutmann, D. "The Cross-Cultural Perspective: Notes toward a Comparative Psychology of Aging." In *Handbook of the Psychology of Aging*. J. E. Birren and K. W. Schaie, Eds. (New York: Van Nostrand Reinhold, 1977).

Harper, R. *The Seventh Solitude* (Baltimore: Johns Hopkins Press, 1965).

Havighurst, R. J., and R. Glasser. "An Exploratory Study of Reminiscence," *Journal of Gerontology*, 17(1972), 245–253.

Hillman, J. *Healing Fiction*, (Barrytown, NY: Station Hill Press, 1983).

Hobbes, T. *Leviathan* (1651). In *The Great Books*, N. Fuller, Ed. (Chicago: University of Chicago Press, 1952).

Ingersoll, B. and A. Silverman. "Comparative Group Psychotherapy for the Aged," *The Gerontologist*, 18(1978), 201–206.

James, W. "The Consciousness of Self." In *The Principles of Psychology*, Vol. 1 (New York: Henry Holt & Co., 1890), 291–401.

James, W. *Essays in Radical Empiricism* (New York: Longmans, Green, 1940).

James, W. *Psychology: The Briefer Course* (New York: Harper and Brothers, 1961), 41.

James, W. *The Varieties of Religious Experience* (Toronto: Collier Books, 1969), 327.

James, W. "The Experience of Activity." In *The Essential Writings*, Bruce Wilshire, Ed. (New York: Harper Torchbook, 1971), 211n.

Jaynes, J. *The Origin of Consciousness in the Breakdown of the Bicameral Mind* (Toronto: University of Toronto Press, 1976).

Johnson, M. *The Body in the Mind: The Bodily Basis of Meaning, Imagination, and Reason* (Chicago: University of Chicago Press, 1987).

Jung, C. G. "The Soul and Death." In *The Meaning of Death*. H. Feifel, Ed. (New York: McGraw-Hill, 1959), 4–5.

Jung, C. G. *Memories, Dreams, Reflections* (New York: Random House, 1961), 320.

Jung, C. G. "The Stages of Life." In *The Portable Jung*, J. Campbell, Ed. (New York: Viking Press, 1971).

Kaufman, S. R. *The Ageless Self: Sources of Meaning in Late Life* (Madison: University of Wisconsin Press, 1986), 162–163.

Keen, S., and A. Valley-Fox. *Your Mythic Journey: Finding Meaning in Your Life through Writing and Storytelling* (Los Angeles: Jeremy P. Tarcher, 1973).

Kiesler, D. J. "Patient Experiencing Level and Successful Outcome in Individual Therapy of Schizophrenics and Psychoneurotics," *Journal of Consulting and Clinical Psychology*, 37(1971), 370–385.

Klein, M. H., P. L. Mathieu, D. P. Kiesler, and E. T. Gendlin. *The Experiencing Scale Manual* (Madison: University of Wisconsin Press, 1970).

Klein, M. H., P. Mathieu-Coughlan, and D. J. Kiesler. "The Experiencing Scales" In *The Therapeutic Process: A Research Handbook*, L. S. Greenberg and W. M. Pinsof, Eds. (New York: Guilford Press, 1986).

Kluckhohn, F. R. and F. L. Strodtbeck. *Variations in Value Orientations* (Evanston, IL: Row Peterson, 1961).

Kuypers, J. A., and V. L. Bengtson. "Competence and Social Breakdown: A Social-Psychological View of Aging," *Human Development*, 16(1972), 37–49.

Kvale, S. "Dialectics and Research on Memory." In *Life-Span Developmental Psychology: Dialectical Perspective on Experimental Research*, N. Datan and H. Reese, Eds. (New York: Academic Press, 1977), 165–189.

Lakoff, G., and M. Johnson. *Metaphors We Live By* (Chicago: University of Chicago Press, 1980), 5.

Landor, W. S. "On His Seventy-Fifth Birthday." In *Middle Age, Old age*, L. G. Lyell, Ed. (New York: Harcourt Brace Jovanovich, 1980), 217.

Langer, S. K. *Philosophy in a New Key*, 3rd ed. (Cambridge: Harvard University Press, 1957), 145.

Lesser, J., L. W. Lazarus, R. Frankel, and S. Havasy. "Reminiscence Group Therapy with Psychotic Geriatric Inpatients," *The Gerontologist*, 21(1981), 291–296.

Leuba, C. "Images as Conditioned Sensations," *Journal of Experimental Psychology*, 26(1940), 345–351.

Levinson, D. J., N. Darrow, E. B. Klein, M. H. Levinson, and B. McKee. *The Seasons of a Man's Life* (New York: Alfred A. Knopf, 1978).

Lewis, C. "Reminiscing and Self-Concept in Old Age," *Journal of Gerontology*, 26(1971), 240–243.

Lewis, M., and R. N. Butler. "Life Review Therapy: Putting Memories to Work in Individual and Group Psychotherapy," *Geriatrics*, 29(1974), 165–169, 172–173.

Lieberman, M. A., and S. S. Tobin. *The Experience of Old Age* (New York: Basic Books, 1983).

Lifton, R. J. *The Life of the Self* (New York: Basic Books, 1976).

Linn, M., and K. Hunter. "Perception of Age in the Elderly," *Journal of Gerontology*, 34(1979), 46–52.

Liton, J., and S. C. Olstein. "Therapeutic Aspects of Reminiscence," *Social Casework*, 50(1969), 263–368.

Lo Gerfo, M. "Three Ways of Reminiscence in Theory and Practice," *Journal of Aging and Human Development*, 12(1980–81), 39–48.

Lowenthal, M. F., and C. Haven. "Interaction and Adaptation: Intimacy as a Critical Variable," *American Sociological Review*, 33(1968), 20–30.

McAdams, D. P. *Power, Intimacy, and the Life Story: Personological Inquiries into Identity* (New York: Guilford Press, 1988).

McCrae, R. R., and R. T. Costa. "Age Personality, and the Spontaneous Self-Concept," *Journal of Gerontology*, 43(1988), S177–185.

McMahon, A. W., and P. J. Rhudick. "Reminiscence: Adaptational Significance in the Aged," *Archives of General Psychiatry*, 10(1964), 292–298.

Maas, H., and J. Kuypers. *From 30 to 70* (San Francisco: Jossey-Bass, 1974).

Mahler, M. *Separation-Individuation* (New York: Jason Aronson, 1979).

Maier, S. F., and M. E. Seligman. "Learned Helplessness: Theory and Evidence," *Journal of Experimental Psychology: General*, 105(1976), 3–46.

Marcel, G. *The Mystery of Being* (Chicago: Henry Regnery Co., 1960).

Marcia, J. "Development and Validation of Ego Identity Status," *Journal of Personality and Social Psychology*, 3(1966), 551–558.

Matheiu-Coughlan, P., and M. H. Klein. "Experiential Psychotherapy: Key Events in Client-Therapist Interaction." In *Patterns of Change: Intensive Analysis of Psychotherapy Process*, L. N. Rice and L. S. Greenberg, Eds. (New York: Guilford Press, 1984), 213–248.

Maurois, A. *Aspects of Biography* (New York: D. Appleton & Co., 1929), 157–158.

Mays, W., and S. C. Brown, Eds. *Linguistic Analysis and Phenomenology* (Lewisburg, PA: Bucknell University Press, 1972).

Meacham, J. A. "The Development of Memory Abilities in the Individual and Society," *Human Development*, 15(1972), 205–228.

Meacham, J. W. "Continuing the Dialogue: Dialectics and Remembering," *Human Development*, 19(1976), 306.

Mead, G. H. *The Philosophy of the Present* (Chicago: Open Court, 1932), 2.

Mead, G. H. *Mind, Self, and Society from the Standpoint of a Social Behaviorist* (Chicago: University of Chicago Press, 1934), 154.

Mead, G. H. "The 'I' and the 'Me.'" In *On Social Psychology*, A. Straus, Ed. (Chicago: University of Chicago Press, 1964), 229.

Merleau-Ponty, M. *Phenomenology of Perception* (New York: Humanities, 1962), ix.

Merleau-Ponty, M. *The Structure of Behavior*, A. L. Fisher, Trans. (Boston: Beacon Press, 1963), 186.

Merleau-Ponty, M. *The Primacy of Perception* (Evanston, IL: Northwestern University press, 1964a).

Merleau-Ponty, M. *Signs* (Evanston, IL: Northwestern University Press, 1964b), 119.

Merleau-Ponty, M. *The Visible and the Invisible* (Evanston, IL: Northwestern University Press, 1968).

Mishler, E. G. "The Analysis of Interview-Narratives." In *Narrative Psychology: The Storied Nature of Human Conduct*, T. R. Sarbin, Ed. (New York: Praeger, 1986), 235.

Monge, R. H. "Structure of the Self-Concept from Adolescence through Old Age," *Experimental Aging Research*, 1(1975), 281–291.

Montaigne, M. de. "Of Experiences." In *Essays III*, reprinted in *The Great Books* (Chicago: University of Chicago Press, 1952), 514–543.

Montaigne, M. de. *The Complete Works of Montaigne*, Donald Frame, Trans. (Stanford, CA: Stanford University Press, 1957).

Myerhoff, B. G. *Number Our Days* (New York: E. P. Dutton, 1979).

Myerhoff, B. G., and V. Tufte. "Life History as Integrations: An Essay on an Experiential Model," *The Gerontologist* (1975), 541–543.

Nabokov, V. *Speak Memory: An Autobiography Revisited* (New York: Wideview/Perigee Books of Putnam, 1966), 20–21.

Natanson, M. *The Journeying Self: A Study in Philosophy and Social Role* (Reading, MA: Addison-Wesley, 1970).

Natanson, M., Ed. *Phenomenology and the Social Sciences* (Evanston, IL: Northwestern University Press, 1973).

Needleman, J. *The Heart of Philosophy* (New York: Bantam Books, 1984).

Neugarten, B. L. "Continuities and Discontinuities of Psychological Issues into Adult Life," *Human Development*, 12(1969), 121–130.

Neugarten, B. L. "The Future and the Young-Old," *The Gerontologist*, 15(1975), 4–9.

Neugarten, B. L., R. J. Havighurst, and S. S. Tobin. "Personality and Patterns of Aging." In *Middle Age and Aging*, B. L. Neugarten, Ed. (Chicago: University of Chicago Press, 1968), 177.

Nin, A. Book review of *At a Journal Workshop* in the *Los Angeles Times* book section, October 19, 1975.

Norton, D. L. *Personal Destinies: A Philosophy of Ethical Individualism* (Princeton, NJ: Princeton University Press, 1976), 208.

Nozick, R. *The Examined Life: Philosophical Meditations* (New York: Simon and Schuster, 1989).

Older Americans Act of 1965, Amendment, P. L. 92–258, Section 710(a).

Olney, J. *Metaphors of Self: The Meaning of Autobiography* (Princeton, NJ: Princeton University Press, 1972), 264.

Ornstein, R. *The Psychology of Consciousness*, 2nd rev. ed. (New York: Penguin Books, 1986), 132.

Ortega y Gasset, J. *Man and Crisis* (New York: Norton, 1958).

Parkes, C. M. "Psychosocial Transitions," *Social Science and Medicine*, 5(1971), 101–115.

Penfield, W. "The Brain's Record of Auditory and Visual Experience—Final Summary," *Brain*, 86(1963), 595–696.

Perky, C. W. "An Experimental Study of Imagination." *American Journal of Psychology*, 21(1910), 422–452.

Phillips, B. "A Role Theory Approach to Adjustment in Old Age," *American Sociological Review*, 22(1957), 212–217.

Polanyi, M. *The Tacit Dimension* (Garden City, NY: Doubleday, 1966).

Polkinghorne, D. E. *Narrative Knowing and the Human Sciences* (Albany: State University of New York Press, 1988), 1.

Progoff, I. *Jung, Synchronicity, and Human Destiny* (New York: Julian Press, 1973), 64.

Progoff, I. *At a Journal Workshop* (New York: Dialogue House Library, 1975).

Rader, M. *A Modern Book of Esthetics: An Anthology* (New York: Henry Holt & Co., 1952), xi–xii.

Reichard, S., F. Livson, and P. G. Peterson. *Aging and Personality* (New York: Wiley, 1962).

Revere, V., and S. S. Tobin. "Myth and Reality: The Older Person's Relationship to His Past," *Journal of Aging and Human Development*, 12(1980–81), 15–26.

Ricoeur, P. *Rule of Metaphor: Multidisciplinary Studies of the Creation of Meaning in Language* (Toronto: University of Toronto Press, 1977).

Ricoeur, P. *Time and Narrative*, Vol. 1. (Chicago: University of Chicago Press, 1984).

Riegel, K. F. "Dialectical Operations of Cognitive Development." In *Contributions to Human Development*, Vol. 2, J. F. Rychlak, Ed. (Basel: S. Karger, 1976), 60–71.

Robinson, A. M. "Twilight." In *Middle Age, Old Age: Short Stories, Poems, Plays and Essays on Aging*, Ruth Granetz Lyell, Ed. (New York: Harcourt Brace Jovanovich, 1980), 218.

Rogers, C. R. "A Process Conception of Psychotherapy," *American Psychologist*, 13(1958), 142–149.

Rogers, C. R. *A Way of Being* (Boston: Houghton-Mifflin, 1980).

Romaniuk, M., and J. G. Romaniuk. "Looking Back: An Analysis of Reminiscence Functions and Triggers," *Experimental Aging Research*, 7(1981), 477–481.

Rorty, A. Q. "A Literary Postscript: Characters Persons, Selves, Individuals." In *The Identity of Persons*, A. O. Rorty, Ed. (Berkeley: University of California Press, 1976).

Rosenberg, M. *Conceiving the Self* (New York: Basic Books, 1979).

Rosenfield, I. *The Invention of Memory: A New View of the Brain* (New York: Basic Books, 1988), 79–80.

Rosow, I. *Socialization to Old Age* (Berkeley: University of California Press, 1973).

Rubin, L. *Intimate Strangers: Men and Women Together* (New York: Harper and Row, 1983).

Santayana, G. *The Life of Reason* (New York: Charles Scribner's Sons, 1955), 258.

Sarbin, T. R., Ed. *Narrative Psychology: The Storied Nature of Human Conduct* (New York: Praeger, 1986).

Sarton, M. *The House by the Sea: A Journal* (New York: Norton, 1977), 61.

Sarton, M. *Recovering: A Journal* (New York: Norton, 1980), 134.

Sartre, J.-P. *The Words* (New York: Braziller, 1964).

Sartre, J.-P. *Being and Nothingness* (New York: Washington Square Press, 1966).

Schachtel, E. *Metamorphosis: On the Development of Affect, Perception, Attention, and Memory* (New York: Basic Books, 1959).

Schafer, R. *Language and Insight* (New Haven, CT: Yale University Press, 1978).

Schaie, K. W., and G. Labouvie-Vief. "Generational Versus Ontogenetic Components of Change in Adult Cognitive Behavior: A Fourteen-Year Cross-Sectional Study," *Developmental Psychology*, 34(1974), 146–158.

Scheibe, K. E. "Memory, Identity, History and the Understanding of Dementia." In *Research on Adulthood and Aging: The Human Science* Approach, L. E. Thomas, Ed. (Albany: State University of New York Press, 1989), 147.

Seligman, M. E. *Helplessness: On Depression, Development, and Death* (San Francisco: Freeman, 1975).

Sheehy, G. *Pathfinders* (New York: Morrow, 1981).

Shcikh, A. A., and N. C. Panagioutou. "Use of Mental Imagery in Psychotherapy: A Critical Review," *Perceptual and Motor Skills*, 41(1975), 557.

Sherman, E. *Counseling the Aging: An Integrative Approach* (New York: Free Press, 1981).

Sherman, E. *Working with Older Persons: Cognitive and Phenomenological Methods* (Boston: Kluwer-Nijhoff, 1984).

Sherman, E. "Social Reconstruction Variables and the Morale of the Aged," *Journal of Aging and Human Development*, 20(1985a), 133–144.

Sherman, E. "A Phenomenological Approach to Reminiscence and Life Review," *Clinical Gerontologist*, 3(1985b), 3–16.

Sherman, E. *Using Reminiscence to Enhance Social Supports among the Elderly* (Washington, DC: AARP Andrus Foundation, 1985c).

Sherman, E. *Meaning in Mid-Life Transitions* (Albany: State University of New York Press, 1987a).

Sherman, E. "Reminiscence Groups for Community Elderly," *The Gerontologist*, 27(1987b), 569–572.

Sherman, E., and E. Newman. "The Meaning of Cherished Personal Possessions for the Elderly," *Journal of Aging and Human Development*, 8(1977–78), 181–192.

Singer, J. L. "Imagery and Affect Psychotherapy: Elaborating Private Scripts and Generating Contents." In *The Potential of Fantasy and Imagination*, A. A. Sheikh and J. T. Shaffer, Eds. (New York: Brandon House, 1979), 36.

Singer, J. L., and K. S. Pope. "The Use of Imagery and Fantasy Techniques in Psychotherapy." In *The Power of Human Imagination*, J. L. Singer and K. S. Pope, Eds. (New York: Plenum, 1978).

Spence, D. P. *Narrative Truth and Historical Truth: Meaning and Interpretation in Psychoanalysis* (New York: W. W. Norton, 1982).

Spence, D. P. "Turning Happenings into Meanings: The Central Role of the Self." In

The Book of the Self: Person, Pretext, Process, P. Young-Eisendrath and J. Hall, Eds. (New York: New York University Press, 1987).

Spielberger, C. P., R. L. Gorsuch, and R. E. Lushene. *STAI Manual for the State-Trait Anxiety Inventory* (Palo Alto, CA: Consulting Psychologists Press, 1970).

Sorabji, R. *Aristotle on Memory* (London: Duckworth, 1972).

Storr, A. *Solitude: A Return to the Self* (New York: Free Press, 1988).

Tamir, L. "Men at Middle Age: Developmental Transitions." In *Middle Age and Late Life Transitions,* F. M. Berardo, Ed. (Beverly Hills, CA: Sage Publications, 1982).

Tillich, P. *Theology of Culture* (London: Oxford University Press, 1959a), 43.

Tillich, P. "The Eternal Now." In *The Meaning of Death,* H. Zeifel, Ed. (New York: McGraw-Hill, 1959b).

Tiryakian, E. A. "The Existential Self and the Person." In *The Self in Social Interaction,* C. Gordon and K. J. Gergen, Eds. (New York: Wiley, 1968).

Tobin, S. S. "Preservation of the Self in Old Age," *Social Casework,* 69(1988), 550–555.

Tobin, S. S., and E. Etigson. "Effect of Stress on Earliest Memory," *Archives of General Psychiatry,* 19(1968), 435–444.

Tun, P. A. "Age of Differences in Processing Expository and Narrative Text," *Journal of Gerontology.* 44(1989), 9–15.

Vizinczey, S. *An Innocent Millionaire* (Boston: The Atlantic Monthly Press, 1983), 321.

Wacker, R. "The Good Die Younger," *Science,* 6(1985), 67.

Walaskay, M., S. K. Whitbourne, and M. F. Nehrke. "Construction and Validation of an Ego Integrity Status Interview," *Journal of Aging and Human Development,* 18(1983–84), 61–72.

Warren, R. P. "Poetry Is a Kind of Unconscious Autobiography," *New York Times Book Review,* 12 May 1985, 9–10.

Weinberg, J. "Psychopathology." In *Modern Perspectives in the Psychiatry of Old Age,* J. G. Howells, Ed. (New York: Brunner/Mazel, 1975).

Whitbourne, S. K. *The Me I Know: A Study of Adult Identity* (New York: Springer-Verlag, 1986).

Whitbourne, S. K., and C. S. Weinstock. *Adult Development,* 2nd ed. (New York: Praeger, 1986).

Whitehead, A. N. *Symbolism: Its Meaning and Effect* (New York: Capricorn Books, 1959), 4.

Wilber, K. *Eye to Eye: The Quest for the New Paradigm* (New York: Anchor Books, 1973), 78.

Wilder, P. *The Mystery of Mind* (Princeton, NJ: Princeton University Press, 1975).

Williams, W. C. *The Collected Earlier Poems of William Carlos Williams* (New York: New Directions, 1938).

Winnicott, D. W. *Playing and Reality* (New York: Basic Books, 1971).

Wittgenstein, L. *Philosophical Investigations* (Oxford: Basil Blackwell, 1953).

Wrong, D. "The Oversocialized Conception of Man in Modern Sociology," *American Sociological Review,* 6(1961), 183–193.

Yates, F. A. *The Art of Memory* (Chicago: University of Chicago Press, 1966).

Young-Eisendrath, P., and J. A. Hall. "Ways of Speaking of Self." In *Book of the Self: Person, Pretext, Process*, P. Young-Eisendrath and J. Hall, Eds. (New York University Press, 1987), 442.

Zarit, S. H. *Aging and Mental Disorders: Psychological Approaches to Assessment and Treatment* (New York: Free Press, 1980).

Zung, W. "A Self-Rating Depression Scale," *Archives of General Psychiatry*, 12(1965), 63–70.

Index

Index